Pennsbury Forever

MEMORIES OF ALUMNI, TEACHERS & COACHES

Edited by
TERRY L. NAU

Pennsbury Forever:
Memories of Alumni, Teachers & Coaches

Copyright © 2022 Terry L. Nau

Produced and printed by Stillwater River Publications. All rights reserved. Written and produced in the United States of America. This book may not be reproduced or sold in any form without the expressed, written permission of the author(s) and publisher.

Visit our website at
www.StillwaterPress.com
for more information.

First Stillwater River Publications Edition

ISBN: 978-1-958217-13-9

Library of Congress Control Number: 2022907619

1 2 3 4 5 6 7 8 9 10

Edited by Terry L. Nau
Front cover photo by Kevin Lendo, class of 1966.
Cover & interior book design by Matthew St. Jean.
Published by Stillwater River Publications,
Pawtucket, RI, USA.

Publisher's Cataloging-In-Publication Data
(Prepared by The Donohue Group, Inc.)

Names: Nau, Terry L., editor.
Title: Pennsbury forever : memories of alumni, teachers & coaches / edited by Terry Nau.
Description: First Stillwater River Publications edition. | Pawtucket, RI, USA : Stillwater River Publications, [2022]
Identifiers: ISBN 9781958217139
Subjects: LCSH: Pennsbury High School--History. | Pennsbury High School--Anecdotes. | High schools--Pennsylvania--Fairless Hills--History. | LCGFT: Anecdotes.
Classification: LCC LD7501.F149 P46 2022 | DDC 373.74821--dc23

The views and opinions expressed
in this book are solely those of the author(s)
and do not necessarily reflect the views
and opinions of the publisher.

This book is dedicated to the teachers and school administrators at Pennsbury High—past and present—who have impacted so many lives during their careers.

Contents

Prologue .... *vii*

PART 1: The Educators
1. 'Mr. Henry' Lived a Very Full Life 1
2. Bill Katz Went from Student to Principal! 5
3. A Lifetime Spent In and Around Pennsbury 19
4. Phys Ed Dept. Stocked With Legends 24
5. A Story of Ed and Diane 29
6. 'City Kid' Takes a Chance on the Suburbs 33
7. A Principal's Memories of Sept. 11, 2001 37

PART 2: Life Stories as Told by Alumni
8. Of Super-Heroes and Second Chances ... 43
9. Looking Back After All These Years 51
10. From South Philly to Levittown's 'Land of Oz' 57
11. A Most Challenging Year at Pennsbury High School 65
12. Pennsbury Is a Piece of Home For Me .. 70
13. Cherishing Memories of My Youth 76
14. My Life's Journey From Philadelphia to France 82
15. On the Road Again With Liza and Friends 89
16. Salley Family Bleeds Black and Orange!.. 98
17. Levittown Life Had Room For Fun 103
18. Eight Brown Siblings Graduated From Pennsbury 109
19. Do We Make Our Own Breaks in Life? 111
20. Greenwood Sisters Loved Scouting 116
21. A Girl Just Has to Have Fun in Life!... 121
22. Moments to Remember… 126
23. Rob McBryar Learned Lessons on the Mat 132
24. The Draft Shadowed Our Lives 137

PART 3: Extracurricular Activities
25. Musical Memories Never Fade 143
26. 'Forgotten' Era in Pennsbury Sports History 150
27. Football Program Grew Into Pennsylvania Power 154
28. We Are the Falcons… 163
29. What Coach Jimmy 'D' Meant to Me 167
30. Chuck Kane's Message Was All-Inclusive 172
31. Falcons' Basketball Program Always Competitive 174
32. Soccer Is a Life-Long Passion 182
33. Coach Kopack Combined Sports and Art 189
34. Falcons Still Building Program Legacy 194
35. Making Memories Is the Key 203

Epilogue *207*

PROLOGUE

What Binds Us?

By Terry Nau, Class of 1965

This book did not start out as a tribute to Pennsbury High. Far from it. Some of my Pennsbury friends missed out on contributing to our 2021 book *Glory Days* and asked if there would be a sequel. What? More stories about growing up in Lower Bucks County? I had to see something more original than that. And so I waited, just as I did with *Glory Days*, waited to see what my friends came up with. They did not disappoint.

I should mention up front that not all of the writers in these two books are my friends. But if you put us in a room together, Pennsbury connects us. It was a large school, even back in the 1960s. Nearly 1,500 students jammed the old Pennsbury High in 1965. Maybe I knew a couple hundred. What has bound us together over the years is the shared experience of attending and graduating from one of the best high schools in Pennsylvania. Then and now.

As students, we barely knew who our teachers and school administrators were. They were older than us. Everyone seemed old when we were young. But not as much older than we thought. Quite a few of our teachers were still in their 20s when they came to Pennsbury. Others were in their 30s or 40s. Many were parents who went home to their families after school duties were completed. In the 1970s, we met a few of our old teachers at our local bar, Puss 'N Boots, where we finally spoke to them as equals. They were nice people who worked hard! Just like us.

We dedicated *Glory Days* to our parents because they were our first teachers. *Pennsbury Forever* is dedicated to the teachers and administrators who guided us through high school. They took us along the road through the 1960s when our quiet world became a little noisy. English teacher Bill Donaldson, now 85, writes in his chapter about the day JFK was murdered, the official announcement of his death coming just 15 minutes before school was to end on a Friday afternoon. Should the Medill Bair principal tell students over the loud speaker what had happened? Over at the high school, we knew before school ended.

Girls cried. Busses lingered outside school. Most of us went home to our safe haven that day.

As stories came in, I decided to divide this book into three parts. We honor our teachers and administrators in Part One. We tell "Life Stories" in Part Two, and in Part Three we write about extracurricular activities, sports mostly. You can blame me and my new pal Kevin Lendo for all the sports! But it turned out for the best because several younger alumni volunteered to write about their experiences in sports. Brien Martin, Class of 1980, tells the story about how he served as Coach Chuck Kane's football "stat man" in the late 1970s. Kane always told Brien, "You are a member of this team" and Brien never forgot how the coach included him in the program. To a teenager, that one kind gesture by Coach Kane was a life-changing moment. To Chuck Kane, it was just how you treated your students, and your football players.

Pennsbury aimed high from the start, as you start to see with Chapter One, a tribute to one of the early senior high principals, Donald Henry. His story came to us through Warren Knop and his brother Steve, who reached out to me with their tale of the World War II veteran who told his future wife Joan that if she could shoot some acorns off a tree limb, he would ask her to marry him. Joan did and they were married for 70 years, until Mr. Henry, as we knew him, passed on in 2021 at the age of 97, still playing poker to the end, according to his obituary.

Patricia Gordon, Class of 1964, tells a wonderful story about History teacher Al Matuza Sr. in her chapter, describing how the former Chicago Bears lineman stepped in to prevent her from dropping out of school. And then in 2004, Trish's work took her to a nursing home in Yardley where "Big Al" was living out his final days. You have to read her chapter to get the full impact of this story.

Bill Katz, a basketball star at Pennsbury and Rider College, writes about how he went into teaching and then administration. He capped his career with 15 years as principal of Pennsbury High. What could be more fitting than to hear the story of an Army brat who rose to the top of his alma mater?

I can't thank my "friends" enough for sharing details of their lives. Those little details are the essence of living. This book tells us how numerous teachers came to Pennsbury and stayed for the duration of their careers. It reveals more life stories from alumni now in their 70s and their 80s. The book also explains how extracurricular activities impacted our lives as teenagers.

We even learn about the "Forgotten Era" in Pennsbury sports. Who was Reggie Turner? That sports question stumped me, until Kevin Lendo provided the answer.

I hope you enjoy the book!

PART ONE

The Educators

A CHANCE TO SAY THANK YOU—At the Pennsbury High Class of 1964's 50th reunion, former school administrator Howard Stringer danced with all the girls and received a New York Times commemorative book featuring front pages for every year of his life. All classmates in attendance signed the book. Stringer had been honored 50 years earlier when the Class of 1964 Yearbook was dedicated to him at the seniors' award ceremony. (Photo by Barry Miner)

AN AMERICAN HERO—Willis Donald Henry dropped out of Lehigh University to become a World War II combat pilot. Less than 20 years later, he had risen to the job of principal at Pennsbury High School.

CHAPTER 1

'Mr. Henry' Lived a Very Full Life

(EDITOR'S NOTE: If there were a Mount Rushmore for Pennsbury High School icons, Willis Donald Henry would be positioned front and center, his chiseled features a perfect fit on the face of a mountain.

Think of it. Don Henry, at the age of 21, piloted a B-24 aircraft over the skies of Europe during World War II. He coached Pennsbury's varsity basketball team to its first Lower Bucks County League championship in 1956. In 1964, the lanky school administrator took over as principal of Pennsbury High as it began transitioning to a new building in 1966. Henry would move on to become Director of Secondary Education before retiring in 1982.)

By Warren Knop, Class of 1974

My access to Mr. Henry came through a friendship with his son, Tom. We were both trying out for freshmen football at Charles Boehm in 1970. Our family had just moved to Yardley from the coastal town of Atlantic Highlands, NJ.

Mr. Henry became one of the great mentors in my life. From the first time I met Mr. and Mrs. Henry in 1970, they treated me like a son. They were always there for me, during good and difficult times. In 1974, as a college freshman, they drove down to North Carolina to bring cheer to their adopted son.

To this day, 52 years later, Tom Henry and I remain close friends.

Don Henry passed away at age 97 in October 2021. His obituary was written with a light touch and told us how the former school principal lived out his years with grace.

Here is an excerpt of the newspaper obit that highlighted some of Don (Hank) Henry's life:

The formidable Willis Donald Henry, known as Don to some, Hank to others, and Hop Pop to his grandchildren, died on October 13 in Roaring Gap, NC.

Hank was a man of deep intelligence, integrity and humility. He was a respected veteran, educator, and an athlete with a strong pull to competition, on and off the field. He hit a hole-in-one at age 87, and was still winning money at the poker table until the end of his life. Don had fierce loyalty to his loved ones, a tender streak, and a subtle, sometimes sneaky sense of humor.

As much as he was a man of his generation, Hank would not have appreciated all of this talking about him. He didn't wear WW II hats or have bumper stickers on his car. He liked to win but he didn't celebrate. He did the right thing in the moment, and then he moved on.

Born in 1924, Hank grew up near Allentown in eastern PA, in Amish country, in a house that lacked indoor plumbing. Hank took to hunting, fishing and playing baseball. His father owned a small flour mill, and his mom was a teacher. Hank's grandfather on his father's side served in the Civil War.

As a child, Hank trapped mink and sold the skins for a dollar apiece. He was out there with his trap line in the dark before he walked to school, and if he happened to catch a skunk, he had to change his clothes and perhaps be late for school.

Hank's dad, with whom he was close, died young from tuberculosis, and this is a story Hank told most in his life. It was his biggest hurt. He would tell people his dad died when Hank was "only" 15. This, says his wife Joan, was the source of Hank's tenderness.

During his freshman year at Lehigh, 1942, Hank enlisted in the Army along with most of his fraternity. He became a lieutenant and a pilot, serving with the 16th Air Force Wing of the Army Air Corps, flying multiple missions while stationed in Italy from May 1944 until November 1945. He sometimes told a story about the engine shutting off during one flight. His crew wanted to parachute out of the plane. Don remained calm amid the chaos and finally got the engine running.

After 2 ½ years in the Army, Hank returned home, graduated from Lehigh, and hoped to take a crack at professional baseball. But the time away from the sport had proven too hard to overcome. So Don decided to combine his passion for sports with a career in education.

Hank met his wife Joan in grad school. Joan noticed the tall, handsome, athletically built fellow sitting in the back row of class, reading sports magazines. But she was more impressed when Hank defended women teachers in their desire for equal pay.

Hank courted Joan by taking her to all of the state parks within driving distance of Trenton. Hank eventually *took Joan to the family property, and they went for a walk with .22 caliber rifles in hand.*

"Hank didn't know I had grown up shooting rats in the barn," Joan said. "I was an excellent shot."

Hank pointed to a branch on an oak tree nearby and said, "I'm looking for a girl. If you can knock those acorns off that tree, I'll marry you." Joan shot down the branch and with it came the acorns. Hank asked Joan to marry him on the spot. And they were married for 70 years.

Joan went on to become director of the special education program for the Bristol Township school system. She was also very social. "My mom would walk into a room of 100 people and literally know everyone within 10 minutes," Tom Henry said. "Meanwhile, my dad had a list of peoples' names in his pocket."

As the years moved on, Hank Henry weathered two teacher strikes during his time as principal at Pennsbury High. In 1968, the U.S. State Department asked Hank to lead a team of distinguished educators on an exchange program to Russia, East Germany and Czechoslovakia. The former Army Air Force pilot had returned to Europe 23 years after the "Big War" had ended.

After he retired, Don and Joan retreated to the family cabin in the Poconos. It was here that the family recharged, where they entertained, and where a young friend of Tom's stayed up all night to watch for "snipes," at Hank's urging.

Hank had a special relationship with his sister, Charlotte. They were best friends who would just disappear in the Poconos. They'd be up and out by dawn, and spent the whole day walking, hunting and fishing. And talking.

The "snipe hunter" was me, a victim of Mr. Henry's sense of fun. He kept an eye on me as I tried out for the Pennsbury football team in 1970. I started at nose tackle during my junior and senior seasons. Pennsbury went undefeated in 1972 and lost only one game in 1973. And then they went undefeated again in 1974. Because of mentors like Coach Kane, Max Micsion, Joe Lowe and our defensive line coach, Al Matuza Jr., I was fortunate to morph into an all-state nose tackle. I made the same all-state team as Joe Montana!

If not for the success of Pennsbury football, my college options would have been limited. I went on to play football at Duke University and started at nose tackle in 1977. None of this would have been possible without my great coaches and teammates. A big part of our record-setting defense in 1973 was my teammate and future Pennsbury teacher, Cliff Stout.

I would like to give a shout-out to

Pennsbury faculty, including Bill Donaldson, Cissy Duda and my favorite sister in the whole world, Karen Wisen, who retired this year after a wonderful career in special education. I want to thank my brother Stephen, too.

Don Henry was always a man of faith, but his love for God only grew stronger as the years passed. His son Tom graduated from Furman University and went on to become a long-standing preacher in the Charlotte area. Tom has often reflected on his dad's blossoming spiritual side, which was witnessed in his actions more than his words.

Tom and I had some fun times at the family cabin on Promised Land Lake in the Poconos. One time, we "borrowed" Hank's canoe and packed it with a case of beer, taking turns jumping out of the canoe as the day progressed. The park rangers were unhappy with us. And there was Hank on the shore, yelling out, "I don't know those guys."

We put the old guy through so much torment through the end of high school. I never saw Hank with a bigger smile than when Tom went to college. When Hank retired from work in 1982, he spent much of the next 40 years golfing, fishing, hunting, reading books about the Old West and watching westerns on his TV set. Hank enjoyed spending time with his grandchildren. He liked to go bird-watching and take daily walks with Joan.

In closing, I hope this story reminds Pennsbury alumni one more time of a great man and educator.

CHAPTER 2

Bill Katz Went from Student to Principal!

By Bill Katz, Class of 1967

In 1954 I started kindergarten at Fallsington Elementary School. It didn't go well. Shortly into that year I got into trouble at recess. The teacher on duty caught me cutting into the line waiting for the sliding board. I had to stand in the corner of the playground. When students returned to the classroom I was still in the corner.

1964-65 FALCONS—Bill Katz, fourth from right in top row, started as a sophomore on this basketball squad. He led the Lower Bucks County League in scoring as a senior. Team members are, standing, left to right: Bill Hoffman, Kevin Lendo, Dwight Kerr, Ed Dugan, Gary Krapf, Barry Taylor, Jim Simpkins, Bill Katz, Lester Katz, Rich Olson, Assistant Coach Dave Mulholland. Kneeling: manager Dave DeDonato, Bob Matuza, Head Coach Joe Gavin.

Part of the full day kindergarten program was nap time. My teacher saw my blanket had not been picked up. She looked outside and saw me playing in the playground. She ran outside screaming my name. Trying to get away from her I ran to the fence and began climbing.

She grabbed my legs, losing her glasses in the process. The principal arrived, I was put in the back seat of a car and driven home. My mother was told by the principal that I wasn't ready for kindergarten.

Fortunately my father was in the service and we were due to move. I attended grades one through six in New York, and then Texas, back to New York, Alaska and Oklahoma as he continued to get new assignments. We left Oklahoma and returned to Pennsylvania during sixth grade.

I had learned from my mistakes. My academic record was good and there were no behavior problems. I was also fortunate that kindergarten was not required so there was no school record of that incident. I finished sixth grade at Fallsington and after our family resettled for good in Levittown, Oxford Valley became my final elementary school. By the way, many years later in a social setting for Pennsbury administrators, I found myself sitting next to the principal that handled the kindergarten incident. I had just been hired at Pennsbury and I reminded him that he threw me out in kindergarten. As we talked I found out that he never knew the teacher had left me unsupervised. He thought I was trying to run away from school. He wanted to know why I didn't tell anyone and I told him nobody asked.

Now that we had a home in Levittown, my mother told my father that she was not going to travel during his remaining five years in the Army. I went through two years at William Penn, two years at Medill Bair and 11th and 12th grade at Pennsbury High School. That format is gone today. Pennsbury now has three middle schools grades 6-8, and one campus high school (two buildings 9-12). I'll write about the campus high school later in this chapter.

I was a good student at Pennsbury but my favorite time was when I played basketball. Kevin Lendo is writing about Pennsbury basketball in another chapter so I'll leave most of the basketball story to him. However I do want to reveal that my basketball career almost never started. With my father stationed overseas, my mother took a full-time job at WT Grant. When I asked her if I could play basketball in 7th grade she said no. She wanted me home after school because of my younger sister, Dorothy, and brother, Alan. I guess my older brother, Lester, wasn't as reliable.

In eighth grade I again asked if I could play basketball and the answer was the same, I was needed at home. I couldn't bear going another year not being on the team. Since my mother's day off was Thursday I told the coach that she worked on Thursdays and I needed to be home to supervise Dorothy and Alan. He had watched me play basketball in gym class and knew I would be the best player on his team. He agreed to add me to the team and give me Thursdays off.

Things went well until my mother found out I was playing. On what must have been a slow sports day the local newspaper put the score of the William Penn basketball game in the paper and I was listed as the leading scorer. I was nervous when I read it but figured it wasn't a problem because my mother never read the sports section. That weekend my mother, the article in hand, confronted me about playing basketball. I tried once again to get her permission. I'm good enough to get a college scholarship, I said, but she wouldn't listen. She told me I could join the Army when I graduated and they would pay for college.

Heading to school on Monday I knew I had to tell the coach I couldn't play anymore. I wondered how my mother had found out. Did a neighbor see the article and congratulate her? Did a disgruntled teammate, unhappy with reduced playing time, spill the beans? I was close to tears when I told my coach I couldn't play anymore. That day was my worst school day ever, even worse than getting kicked out of kindergarten! I went home expecting additional punishment for what I had done. Instead, my mother said she changed her mind and was going to let me play. Our assistant coach had heard me explaining what happened to my coach. He called my mother, told her I was the best player he had seen at my age and I could earn a scholarship if allowed to play. I guess it took an adult telling her things I had told her but I didn't care. I was going to play basketball for Pennsbury!

After two years at Medill Bair we were scheduled to start school at the new Pennsbury High School built near Medill Bair. Instead we were told the school wasn't ready. We attended school one day and the seniors attended on the next day in the finished upstairs classrooms while construction went on in other areas of the building. We were able to go back to an everyday program with the seniors later in the year. The gym wasn't ready until my senior year so practices and basketball games were at Charles Boehm in 11th grade. Graduation the next year was at the football stadium at Charles Boehm.

I took part in Sports Nite both years and it was one of my favorite non-basketball activities. I took a sophomore to the senior prom and attended a second prom two years later when she was a senior.

I want to give a shout-out to the high school English Department and the teachers who made us stand up in front of the classroom and deliver speeches. I hated it then but years later I realized how much I benefited. It helped me when I was hired as a classroom teacher. Later I ran faculty meetings, spoke at awards programs and at Sports Nite. Graduation had huge crowds. Thank you for preparing me for a future in public speaking.

As my senior year came to a conclusion I was honored to receive The Falcon Award. It was a total surprise. I had a good career and outstanding senior year playing basketball but I only played one sport. Most previous Falcon Award winners excelled in multiple sports. It was a great way to finish my time at Pennsbury.

After graduation I attended Penn, played freshman basketball, and also played after transferring to Rider. I ended up scoring almost 1,200 points at Rider in two and a half years. I missed half a season because I had to sit out one year when I transferred. I was voted into the Rider Basketball Hall of Fame. Penn and Rider never would have happened without basketball scholarships.

My next stop was coaching basketball and teaching social studies at Delhaas High School in Bristol Township. I returned to Rider to add a Master's Degree in Educational Administration. I received the MA after about three years but had to wait until I had five years teaching experience to apply for and receive my principal's certification. My goal at that time was to become an athletic director.

As I neared the end of my seventh year teaching, my position was eliminated due to declining enrollment. Fortunately I had my principal's certificate and was hired as an assistant principal at Delhaas. I did teacher observations but the main part of my day was spent handling student discipline. Remembering what happened in kindergarten, whenever a student was sent to my office I made sure to ask for his or her side of the story.

Two years later, Delhaas closed but I was transferred as an assistant principal to Truman High School which was the new name for the high school that now combined Delhaas and Wilson students. Dr. Joan Henry, a special education supervisor, stopped in to see me as the school year started. We talked about legalities involved with disciplining special education students. Before she left, she told that she and "Hank" used to watch me play basketball at Pennsbury.

I had a good year at Truman but there were still talks of budget cuts and possibly eliminating administrative positions as well as additional teaching positions. It was stressful and I searched for available positions but none were found. Near the end of the year, Dr. Henry entered my office and closed the door. I figured I messed up handling a special education student and she was going to tell me the steps I needed to take to correct the problem. Instead she told me she felt guilty about what she was going to say because of loyalty to Bristol Township but she also knew my position had not yet been renewed for the next year. Next she told me that "Hank" had an opening at Pennsbury for an assistant principal and no inside candidates had applied. He was hoping I would be interested.

Finally I knew who "Hank" was. He was Don Henry, a former basketball coach at Pennsbury, my high school principal, and current Director of Secondary Education for the Pennsbury School District. I applied, interviewed and was offered the position. I accepted and 15 years after my Pennsbury graduation, I was returning to the school I loved.

As the new school year opened one of my responsibilities was to observe and evaluate teachers. I had moved from sitting in the classroom of my former teachers as a high school student where they graded me, to sitting in their classrooms and grading them. Additional responsibilities were student discipline, being in the halls when classes changed, supervising lunch duty and building the high school budget each year. Assistant principals had to attend sporting events, school activities and Sports Nite. Graduation involved being on the field and chasing down beach balls that had been inflated and floated around during the lengthy ceremony.

When Don Henry retired and Duane Bair moved to Fallsington—which now housed the district administration, Naomi Kelly became Pennsbury High School's first female principal. My interest in becoming an athletic director was gone. I wanted to be Pennsbury High School's next principal when Naomi retired. The only assignment I never had was student scheduling. I had watched assistant principals work on scheduling and felt it was the harder than anything I was doing. Wanting to complete my preparation for a future position, I asked Naomi for that assignment. She agreed and I took on the high school schedule.

I felt that computer scheduling programs would make my job easier but that wasn't the case. These programs attempted to create schedules with the fewest conflicts. Sounds good but conflicts need to be resolved. Telling a student signed up for AP Physics that there was a conflict and they would have to choose a general science course instead was never going to work. The high school schedule was built by hand and potential alternatives for honors and AP classes had to be prioritized.

There were eight class periods in a Pennsbury school day. The majority of students had six classes, a study hall and a lunch period. Some gave up their study hall for a seventh class. A few even requested an eighth class with no lunch. Fortunately we had an excellent staff and many were willing to allow a student to bring a lunch to class if they had eight classes. The typical teacher schedule was five classes, one duty period and one planning period.

Midway through my ninth year as an assistant, Naomi retired. I felt my time had come but when Naomi retired, Pennsbury had a superintendent who came in from Philadelphia. He wanted to bring in a colleague to fill the position. Duane Bair was given the additional title of acting principal because the superintendent did not want to give me an unfair advantage when interviews started. Duane's responsibilities at Fallsington were great. He would stop by and see me from time to time and was confident I could handle things. His visits decreased and I basically became the acting principal but never got the title.

When interviews were finally scheduled it was something I never saw before and it never happened again. Instead of central office administrators and other principals, the interviewing team consisted of the superintendent, the director of personnel he had brought in, two board members, one being his biggest supporter, and two other administrators. It was a loaded deck. Somehow I got three votes but the resulting 3-3 tie resulted in no recommendation for the next principal. It appeared to me that his new plan was to leave the position vacant and bring in an acting principal of his choice to fill the void. Once again I began to look elsewhere.

Things changed right before the end of the school year. Even though the high school principal position wasn't on the board agenda, the new president of the school board said it was unacceptable that we did not have a high school principal and she nominated me for the position. There were only eight board members present and five votes were required for approval. Three board members, all supporters of the superintendent, voted no but by a 5-3 vote I was appointed as the next principal at Pennsbury High School.

I had the strong support of high school staff when the new school year started. Unfortunately I lost an assistant principal in the budget process so I elected to continue doing the high school scheduling along with all my new responsibilities. It was stressful at times but everything went well until graduation. Due to the size of the senior class the stands at Falcon Field had to be filled on both the home and visiting sides to accommodate the attending crowd. Seniors were given six tickets for graduation, three on the home side and three on the visiting side. Since the graduates faced the home stands, seniors had to choose who got the three tickets to see their faces during graduation and who got to watch their backsides.

The program began. Students marched in to Pomp and Circumstance and took their seats. I welcomed the audience and the roll call of graduates began. Seniors names were called. They walked up to get their diploma covers and returned to their seats. (We only gave them covers because with so many students the chance of receiving the wrong diploma was great.) After the ceremony they would go back to their assigned rooms, return their caps and gowns and get their actual diploma.

By the time the last name was called everyone was getting restless. I made my initial comments and introduced the first student speaker. That was when the beach balls came out. Just like previous years the balls would float over the seniors. Teachers and assistant principals would try to get them and students would knock them away. The crowd began to cheer for the beach balls and speeches were disrupted. In my eyes based on what I had seen the past nine years, it was a typical Pennsbury graduation and I was thankful I had gotten through my first year as principal.

The next day I was called to Fallsington to meet with the superintendent and board members. I was told that graduation was a disgrace and I needed to make sure what happened was never repeated. I listened respectfully but silently I was thinking, "Why me?" Why hadn't this been addressed in the past?

Searching for a solution I met with selected staff and broke down the graduation ceremony. How could we improve it? We came up with some changes to address the problems.

The first problem we looked at was the length of the ceremony. My feeling was that most of the problems occurred because they were sitting too long and the beach balls were brought out to break up the waiting time.

We came up with some major changes. We shifted the seats to face the end zone instead of the home stands. All six tickets seniors received were for either the home side or the visiting side of the stadium based on which side of the field the senior sat. On the processional instead of marching down the middle of the field, students walked along the track right past the stands where their family and friends sat. Before sitting, the names of graduates were read, they received their diploma covers and then took their seats. This saved a significant amount of time and we were on the way.

While these improvements were all good, the beach balls and other potential disruptions had not been addressed. I dealt with that during graduation rehearsal. I explained the changes to the students during the rehearsal. I told them typical graduations had disruptions like the ones we faced but Pennsbury was going to be different. We would hold a first class graduation and seniors would be allowed to celebrate at the end of the ceremony. They could all exit together instead of marching off the way they marched in.

I told the seniors that we would graduate them one day early and distribute their diplomas after the ceremony. Once they receive a diploma they are done for the year. However, if there are disruptions of the ceremony the diplomas would not be distributed and they would have to go to school the next day to pick them up. I also warned them that teachers in their assigned rooms would be looking for items such as deflated beach balls that could be inflated and disrupt the ceremony. Items would be confiscated, the senior would be pulled from the line and family and friends would not see them graduate. It worked. All future graduations ran smoothly, the new format was a hit and the seniors were great. I had gotten through my first crisis!

When I became principal I didn't see the need for change. We had many graduates who had done well, including myself. However, my experience handling scheduling created some concerns. With our eight-period day, we were expecting our students to learn six different things each day. Some were trying to learn seven or even eight things every day. Was this the best way to teach our students?

I spent some time with Dave Hottenstein, principal of Hatboro Horsham High School, at a national conference in New Orleans. His school was using "Intensive Scheduling." Basically it was four classes each day instead of the typical high school schedule. I felt it was something we should look at. I found two basic formats, one where students had four classes one day and four different classes on the next day. I did not like that format because students were still learning eight different things. The other format had four classes for the first half of the year and four different classes for the second half. That was what Hottenstein was doing and it made more sense to me.

Dave invited me to visit his school and I took Don Harm with me. Don was one of my assistant principals when I became principal and he moved on to an administrative position at Fallsington. After our visit we decided block scheduling was something Pennsbury should look into.

We felt strongly that all students would benefit from more time per class and fewer classes to study at any one time. There was also an advantage for teachers. Instead of having five classes, a duty period and a planning period, they would have three classes and a longer planning period. We removed duty assignments from their schedule.

It wasn't an easy change. While we had teachers who were on board from the beginning, we also had veteran teachers who saw no need for change. Much of our classroom instruction was delivered via classroom lecture. Studies showed that wasn't the best method for long-term learning. Working together in groups, doing projects and presentations seemed to be a better approach. Teachers who delivered their subject matter by lecture would have to change. Lecturing for almost 90 minutes, three times a day, was almost impossible. I wanted teachers to approach their classes more like coaches. Put students in groups, assign projects and "coach" them instead of lecturing all day. We sent teachers to other schools using block scheduling and brought teachers in to work with our staff. It took time but eventually we were able to go to the board with a request to approve block scheduling.

When the board approved block scheduling, I requested another year to fully train our teachers for the new program before we started. Credit goes to all who worked hard to create and prepare for this major change. After implementation it was wonderful to hear when our graduates returned and said they felt block scheduling better prepared them for the fewer courses and longer classes in their college programs.

After the move to block scheduling there was one more major change that needed to happen. Something had to be done about the 9-10 high school and the 11-12 high school format. There was some talk of having two 9-12 high schools but not enough support to move in that direction. Medill Bair was officially considered a high school but the students didn't see it that way. It was time to try something different. I sent a proposal to Ralph Nuzzolo, our superintendent, for a 9-12 campus. All four grade levels for each subject would be offered in one of the buildings. Students would travel between the buildings for their classes similar to what takes place in a college setting. Also, all subject area teachers would now be in the same building for the first time. The longer classes created by block scheduling allowed us to dismiss students a few minutes early if their next class was in the other building. Since we had two principals my proposal was not to have one principal in charge. Instead I proposed naming an Administrative Principal and a Curriculum Principal who would work together to run the campus. Based on available space, more subject areas would be housed at Medill Bair but both buildings would house students in all four grades. The proposal was fine-tuned and the 9-12 campus was created. English, Math, Art and Instrumental Music classes were scheduled at Pennsbury while Social Studies, Science, Foreign Language, Business, Family and Consumer Science, Tech Ed and Choral Music classes were scheduled at Medill Bair. Phys Ed and Special Ed classes were in both buildings. An internal road was built and buses were used to transport students from one building to the other. Students also had the option of walking if weather permitted. Security guards monitored student behavior during the change of classes and kept students moving.

One final decision had to be made. What would we call the two buildings on the 9-12 campus? Separate names were needed so students, parents, visitors and mail could get to the right location. This topic was discussed at a secondary principal's meeting. I didn't want to lose the name Pennsbury and suggested we follow the lead that Central Bucks and Council Rock used when adding high schools. Pennsbury High School was farther east and Medill Bair was farther west. There was agreement and the 9-12 campus opened as Pennsbury East and Pennsbury West!

A lot of things happened during my 25 years as an administrator. I feel that changing the graduation ceremony, moving to block scheduling and creating the 9-12 campus were all major accomplishments. We also had great opportunities for students outside the classroom. Two that I want to highlight are the Pennsbury Marching Band and the Pennsbury prom.

I sometimes jokingly referred to our

band as the Mickey Mouse Band. That was not meant to degrade them. Instead it was used to point out that the Pennsbury Marching Band has performed in every Disney ark ever built. No other high school band in the country can make that claim!

Participation in the Orange Bowl and Rose Bowl parades included performances at nearby Disney World and Disneyland. When I was an assistant principal, Naomi Kelly accompanied the band to China and a performance in a Disney park that had recently opened. When I became principal, a picture of the Pennsbury Marching Band on the Great Wall of China was hung right over my desk!

I still remember when Disney officials came to visit Pennsbury and officially invited us to perform at their new park in France—now called Disneyland Paris. I welcomed them and in my comments I stole a line from Field of Dreams. I said "If you build it, we will come!" I also kiddingly suggested they consider building a park in Hawaii.

The trip to Paris was my first with the marching band and a great opportunity. The band had exceptional performances and the attractions we saw will never be forgotten. Years later, band director Mike Grothman told me the band had been invited to perform at the King Kamehameha parade in Oahu, Hawaii. Disney didn't build there but the marching band did get a trip to Hawaii. That became my second trip with the band.

As I approached my last year at Pennsbury, Frank Mazzeo, who had become the marching band director, told me that Disney was building another park in China and he was trying to set up a trip. It turned out the park wasn't ready for our performance during my final year. Instead of China a trip to California for the Monterey Jazz Festival was arranged. Our award-winning jazz band performed at the Festival and before returning home we went to San Francisco. After a visit to Alcatraz, a day was spent exploring San Francisco. We were walking in the city and Frank apologized to me for not being able to go to China before I retired. My response: 250 marching band students in China or 23 of our top students performing at the Monterey Jazz festival, I'm happier with this trip!

The Pennsbury Marching Band went to China and performed in a Disney park the year after I retired. The arrangement with Disney continues, if you build it we will come.

———————

The Pennsbury senior prom in my opinion is second to none. I took a sophomore to the prom in my senior year. Two years later, I attended my second Pennsbury prom when she was a senior. I enjoyed both proms but never really understood how much time and effort was put into producing the Pennsbury Prom until I returned as an assistant principal. I saw that the prom happens because of a cooperative effort between parents, students and teaching advisors. A prom theme is chosen after the new school year starts. In January, students and parents begin making plans based on the chosen theme. Parents transform the prom entrance, cafeteria and surrounding halls with lavish decorations. Students are responsible for the gym and surrounding halls. The prom is held on a Saturday night and all day Friday students work on their assigned area. Parents start at the end of the school day. By Saturday morning it would be hard to believe that what had been created was in a high school building.

On the afternoon of the prom the doors are opened and the community is given a chance to see the transformation. It is always spectacular. A sign-in book allows visitors to leave their comments. Reading those comments from year to year was a pleasure.

The evening of the prom, hundreds of spectators gather to watch the prom arrivals. Students build floats or choose other creative arrival methods. Harry Ettinger, a classmate of mine at Pennsbury, called me one year about a special arrival. He worked at Action News and wanted to use a helicopter. I checked it out, we got approval and we had the first aerial arrival for couples at the prom. After he dropped them off he took me up for a view of prom arrivals I never saw before. As far as other arrival requests I only remember denying one. It was arrival by hot air balloon! Too many potential pitfalls.

ROBERT COSTA
...Sunday morning caller

Michael Bamberger, who covered golf for *Sports Illustrated*, published a book about our Prom in 2005. When we first spoke, he said he had heard about the prom and wanted to write a story, not for S.I. but for some other magazine. His idea was to spend time at the high school and identify some seniors to write about—balancing their school work and prom preparation. He would also write about their plans after graduation and steps they were taking to get there. I was interested because I was very proud of our prom and felt an article in a magazine would showcase what a great event it was. Halfway through the year, Bamberger told me he wasn't going to write a story for a magazine. Instead, he would be writing a book.

While the initial approach was to write about seniors, one of our juniors played a significant role. That was Bob Costa, who became a successful journalist after graduating from Pennsbury and is co-author with Bob Woodward of *Peril,* a book about the last days of the Trump presidency. I remember being at home one Sunday morning when I answered my phone.

"Hello."

"Mr. Katz?"

"Yes."

"This is Bob Costa."

"Yes."

"I do the morning announcements at Pennsbury."

"I know who you are, why are you calling me on a Sunday morning?"

"I want to have a rock concert after school on Thursday."

'Bob, we don't really do that."

"Come on, Mr. Katz, this is a group that's going to be big."

"Let's talk after tomorrow's announcements."

The next day Bob told me the band was on tour, had a performance in Princeton Thursday night and had agreed to stop in at Pennsbury and perform before their evening show.

It was going to be after school so it wouldn't disrupt classes and open only to Pennsbury students who wanted to attend. I agreed to give it a try.

That Thursday I met Adam Levine and Maroon 5. They performed and our students loved it. Maroon 5 went on to become a popular band, winning multiple Grammys and other awards. I'm sure that appearance at Pennsbury paved the way!

Later in the school year Bob had another rock star that he wanted to perform at Pennsbury. It was John Mayer and he wanted him to sing at the prom. I told Bob we didn't have the budget for a rock star to perform and I would not raise ticket prices for our students.

Bob said he met Mayer after a concert, told him about our prom and asked him just to stop by and sing a few songs. There wouldn't be any charge.

As the prom approached, Bob was having difficulty contacting Mayer and was disappointed that his calls weren't returned. John Mayer did not perform at the prom!

The following year, Bamberger's book was finished. He returned to the high school to introduce the book, *Wonderland.* In the book he writes about Bob Costa trying to get Mayer to perform. He writes about Bob's disappointment and that John Mayer is no longer his favorite rock star.

With the release of the book it was also revealed that a major company had secured movie rights. Over the years the movie possibility has been re-examined including a visit to the prom after my retirement but nothing has happened to date.

A few weeks later, I drove up to Boston on a Friday to pick up my son Steve who had just finished his school year at Boston University. That year's prom would be held on the next day. On the way home I got a call from my secretary, Mary Ellen Rickerl. She told me I needed to find a place to stop and make a phone call. When I called I found out that John Mayer wanted to stop in at tomorrow's prom and sing a few songs. It was never revealed why he decided to come that year. Maybe Bob Costa, now senior class president, had finally got through. My theory was someone told him about the book, he heard there was talk about a possible movie and wanted to write a new final chapter where he showed up and performed at the prom.

SURPRISE PERFORMER—Popular singer John Mayer stopped into Bill Katz's office before giving an impromptu concert for Pennsbury High students prior to the 2004 Senior Prom.

We kept Mayer's performance a secret because we didn't want a large crowd crashing our prom. Bob met him at the Burger King across from Pennsbury and brought him to my office. I made an announcement that we were delaying the next dinner sitting and everyone needed to go to the gym. I took the microphone and Mayer was waiting outside. I chose to introduce Bob Costa and let him introduce John Mayer. When Mayer came in, the crowd went wild. His performance is still available on YouTube if you go to Pennsbury Prom, John Mayer.

When we returned to school on Monday, Mayer's performance was getting national attention. I received calls from radio stations in Texas and Oregon. On Thursday I was at meeting with the superintendent and other administrators at the Yardley Country Club when my school phone rang. I excused myself to take the call. It was Mary Ellen. She said Entertainment Weekly had called and wanted to know if we could get pictures of John Mayer singing at the prom. I said okay but before I returned to my meeting I remembered I had sunglasses in my pocket. I put them on, opened the door and said, "Sorry, I had to take that call, it was Entertainment Weekly."

The Pennsbury prom is usually held on the third Saturday in May. Over the years sometimes the prom and my birthday fell on the same day. In my last year at Pennsbury a student asked if I could drive them to the prom in my golf cart. When we moved to the campus setting a golf cart had been provided so I could easily go back and forth between the two buildings. That evening I drove the golf cart to the beginning of the access road where the prom arrivals started. They made sure that the golf cart would be first in line. This would be my final prom as principal and it was also my birthday. I led the "parade" and pulled up to the entrance. Immediately the crowd all began singing happy birthday. I got out of the cart and the Philly Phanatic appeared and gave me a big hug. What a way to go out!

Over 25 years there was so much that happened that I didn't include. I was asked to write a chapter, not a book. I benefited from an outstanding staff and some wonderful students that I'll never forget. A special thank you to Mary Ellen Rickerl, the best secretary a principal could have. She made my job easier on a regular basis. During my time as principal both of my sons were born exactly three years apart. Dan went to MIT and Brown. Steve went to Boston University. Both are doing well today and despite my busy times as principal I always tried to be there for them. After an embarrassing start in kindergarten, I turned it around and I'll forever be proud of the opportunities presented to me by the Pennsbury School District as a student and as an employee!

CHAPTER 3

A Lifetime Spent In and Around Pennsbury

By Nyla Mack Houser, Class of 1966

Pennsbury has been my life. I grew up across the street from the "old" high school on Makefield Road, received my education at various schools, came back after college to teach here, raised my children here, retired here, and still pay my taxes here. There are quite a few of us who have done this, such as the Yantz brothers, and Joe Marrazzo, to name a few, and we are the devoted Pennsbury people who continue to love the district that raised us.

The Pennsbury School District of the early 50's was different than it is today. New schools were being built as fast as the builders could build them. Five elementary schools suddenly appeared on the scene to accommodate the influx of workers coming to work at US Steel. But my father came here before the mill opened, and found little to no housing available. There was no Fairless Hills, and no Levittown. The choices for housing were only

SWEET MEMORY—Warren Breece, who would die in the Vietnam War, often spent time with his friend Nyla Mack when they were kids.

Lower Makefield, Yardley, or Morrisville. Houses in these areas were older, established homes, very few of which were newly-constructed. The schools in these areas were old. The only new school in Lower Makefield was Quarry Hill, but even that was newer than the rush to build schools elsewhere in the district.

The older schools were Yardley, Makefield, Fallsington, and the "old" Edgewood, all of which were at least 35 years old. Even the "new" high school was originally completed in 1951 to accommodate all 6th through 12th graders since the building in Fallsington (where they had been housed) was not large enough to house the numbers. The original Pennsbury High School graduated 14 years' worth of students before yet another new high school was needed. Two "junior" high schools were built where the biggest growth was taking place, (William Penn and Medill Bair) while only one such building was built near the high school (Charles Boehm). Suddenly the need for teachers to fill these classrooms became a driving force, and the push to hire teachers began. Pennsbury was growing by leaps and bounds in the 1950s and 1960s!

The teachers hired by the newly-formed district were largely housewives who had gone back to teaching, and men who had taken advantage of the GI Bill. They were not paid competitive salaries, even though a college degree was required. There was no "protection" for their jobs, and they were truly at the mercy of the school boards. Each new building needed a principal, so many of the male teachers acquired their administrative certificates and became new principals…men like Tom Menzies, Howard Houser, Bill Herr, Larry Callahan, and Harry Noblit. Some women became principals, like Cora Holsclaw (who later became an administrator), Marie Hobson, and Ruth Draper, but they were in the minority. The teachers' association was much like a social club, where teachers socialized and met teachers from other buildings. A comradery existed among teachers from around the district, the only distinction being whether they were elementary or secondary. They celebrated weddings, births, and life happenings. Retirement was not a lucrative option, so many left the profession to seek jobs with options for retirement that were better suited to their needs.

As students in Pennsbury, we had no idea what a great education we were getting. Our teachers were conscientious, and had the goal of educating our young minds at the forefront of their jobs. Pennsbury was a forward-thinking district, utilizing up to date teaching methods and curricula to best suit our needs. When in college, in a "methods" class for teaching, the professor kept asking who in the class of 80 students had certain teaching text books while in high school. My hand was the only hand in the class that went up for every one! PSSC Physics, Green Version Biology, SMSG Math, ALM French, to name a few. Finally he looked at me and said, "You must be from Pennsbury!"

As the population continued to shift, redistricting became common place. For our graduating class, I probably attended the fewest number of buildings from K-12…I attended five: Makefield, the old Edgewood, Charles Boehm, the old high school, and the new high school. For those going to Medill Bair, it could have been even more, with no less than four secondary buildings!

Pennsbury enrollments were growing incrementally. By the mid to late 70's, graduating classes were over 1,100 students, and elementary buildings were adding "modular" classrooms to increase space and try to keep class size down. We were bulging at the seams! The School Board was always trying to figure new ways to configure the district, and re-districting was always an option. The biggest change came when it was decided ALL ninth graders would come together in the Medill Bair/William Penn building, following the building of a "new" William Penn Middle School in Lower Makefield. Now, all 6th, 7th, and 8th grade students would attend the three middle schools in the complex between Makefield, Big Oak, Derbyshire and Roelofs roads, and starting in 9th grade, all would go to the now "Medill Bair" building complex. That complex is now called "West" and the high school is "East."

Pennsbury continued to grow, and became renowned for many of its programs. One such program, the music program, became a beacon in the state, sending many representative students to state bands, choruses, and higher qualifying forums. Mrs. Caroline Keller and Mr. John Mack were instrumental in bringing the music program recognition on a state level. Mr. Mack had connections with bands in New York, and the Stage Band was privileged to use the scores from those well-known bands. We had representation in state and national choruses. Mrs. Keller trained our voices to do well in auditions for county, district and state groups.

Our music department continued to shine, and eventually the "Long Orange Line" traveled to China, playing on the Great Wall, and has been featured in the Tournament of Roses Parade. They traveled to Europe, and were popular in many countries for their precision.

Representatives of Pennsbury traveled to academic, forensic, and thespian competitions on a national level, ranking high in the competition results. Even teachers in the district became set apart in the state for their innovative negotiating of contracts which became examples around the country. Negotiating teachers created teaching videos for those bargaining for their salaries and benefits.

The teaching profession in general changed dramatically as the years went by, and Pennsbury was no different than the rest of the nation. I was hired in 1970, along with over 200 other new teachers to the district, many of whom had graduated from Pennsbury. New teacher orientation felt like a Pennsbury reunion! Teachers were in demand, and I was offered a contract immediately following my interview in April of my senior year of college, as were many of my colleagues.

I was assigned to Penn Valley in first grade, and subsequently taught in Makefield, Edgewood and Eleanor Roosevelt, ending my career teaching kindergarten while having release time to be president of the Pennsbury Education Association. The Association was the bargaining unit for all Pennsbury teachers, and as such brought the salary level of teachers in Pennsbury up to a competitive level.

Teacher unions have become a controversial issue nationwide, and Pennsbury's was no different. The Pennsbury teachers first went on strike in 1972, and became big news as one of the first districts locally to do so. Teachers walking a picket line seemed unheard of, and my "management" father was offended by it. That strike lasted eight days, creating tension that was not easily settled. Four years later we went on strike again, in 1976, and this one lasted through the end of October when the teachers went back into the classrooms without a contract. The contract was finally ratified in December, just in time for Christmas. The results of that strike were far-reaching, affecting retirements, and friendship across the district for years to come.

But the story doesn't end there. Peaceful negotiations continued through many years, even though the school board and the teacher association did not always see eye to eye. Pennsbury became a pillar of the state with its salaries and successful negotiations, maintaining high standards of teaching and leadership. Students thrived, and a working rapport was established between teachers and parents. Contracts were settled but not always amicably. Many 12th hour negotiations narrowly averted labor issues, especially as more demands were put on the teachers' time, education, and requirements. The videos created by our original negotiating teachers were being used on a statewide level, and once again Pennsbury was set apart from the norm.

As President of the union, I was in the leadership position during the third and most recent teacher strike in Pennsbury. The breakdown of the rapport between the community and the teachers was monumental, even among teachers, taking a great toll on all within the Pennsbury community. Many teachers felt their close, positive relationship with the parents would bring out support from the community for our cause. Of course, it did not!!!! The disruption of daily life was more than many in the community could bear.

With the advent of laws regarding teacher strikes, the children still received their 180 days of instruction, but in a very different format than the normal school calendar. The community had trouble seeing that. No matter what side you were on, it was devastating. Was it worth it? It depends on who is answering the question. For me, well, I retired at the end of that year.

It's been said that my blood runs Orange and Black (our school colors). I grew up in Pennsbury, watching 14 years of seniors graduate from what is now "Pennwood," and eventually being in the first class out of what is now called "East." I taught my whole career in Pennsbury, teaching in four elementary buildings. Teaching now is different than it was in the 70's. At the end of my career I was teaching in a half day of kindergarten what I had taught in a full day of first grade in 1970. I was an officer in the association for many of those years. My two children graduated from Pennsbury, one going to Georgetown University, and one going to Drexel. I own my home in Pennsbury, and continue to willingly pay Pennsbury taxes.

I've seen two more schools built in Lower Makefield, (Afton Elementary and William Penn Middle School) three schools sold, (Yardley, Brookview and Fairless View), and one turned over to the Intermediate Unit, (Village Park). Pennsbury has truly been my life, and I will continue to support it as long as I am able. Has it changed? Oh, yes, dramatically! And hopefully it will continue to change with the times, as well it should! I am proud to say I am a Pennsbury graduate and a retired Pennsbury teacher, and a lifelong Pennsbury supporter.

CHAPTER 4

Phys Ed Dept. Stocked With Legends

By Terry Nau, Class of 1965

In researching this chapter on the early days of the Pennsbury physical education department, I finally learned that Vic Napolitano had been a three-sport star at nearby Trenton High in the mid-1940s. And one of his top rivals was Joe Gavin. Both would become head coaches at Pennsbury and end up in school's Athletic Hall of Fame, along with Vic's wife Ginnie, and several of their colleagues.

"Coach Nap" signed to play pro baseball with the St. Louis Cardinals after playing three sports in college at Temple University, including goalkeeper on the 1951 NCAA championship soccer team.

When the major league baseball dream dimmed, Vic decided to visit his hometown friend Joe Gavin, a physical education teacher and basketball coach at Pennsbury High. This would have 1956.

"Vic stopped by Pennsbury to say hello to Joe," Ginnie Napolitano, now 90, said in the winter of 2022. "They had played ball against each other while growing up in Trenton. I think Joe played for Trenton Catholic and Vic went to Trenton High. Then they went to Temple together for four years before Vic signed to play baseball and Joe went into teaching.

"Joe said to Vic, 'Hey, we need a phys ed teacher. Would you be interested?' Vic said yes. Joe took him over to see the superintendent, Mr. Currier. That was on a Friday and on Monday morning Vic was teaching phys ed at Pennsbury."

Ginnie soon became friends with the new teacher from Trenton.

"I liked Vic right away," she said. "He was just a good guy. We started dating and were married within a year and a half. We had two daughters—Vicki and Lauri. In those days, you could only work for around five months when you were pregnant. I went on leave in March of 1960 to have Vicki. Cora Clinton took my place. I never got my job back at Pennsbury because while I was out, the School Committee passed a rule saying couples could not teach in the same district. I did some substitute teaching at Pennsbury and then in 1971 I went back to teaching full-time at Villa Victoria Academy in Ewing Township."

HONORING 'COACH NAP'—Pennsbury High re-named its baseball field in honor of former coach Victor Napolitano in 2019. Participating in the ceremony, left to right: Head coach Joe Pesci, Vicki, Ginnie and Lauri Napolitano, and District Superintendent William Gretzula. (Photo courtesy of Pennsbury High)

Vic became the head baseball coach in 1965, replacing "Cy" Bachman. He would coach baseball for 29 years, earning 403 career victories, 13 league titles, three District One championships, and one PIAA Final Four appearance.

"During baseball season, Vic would leave the house at 7 in the morning and sometimes he would not get home until 7 or 8 at night," Ginnie admitted. "I didn't get to see a lot of his games because I was teaching full-time, officiating three sports, and being a mom.

"Vic never enjoyed being in the limelight. He was quiet but he did have a good sense of humor. He was not calm during Pennsbury games. His players knew when Vic was upset because he would take off his hat and start talking into it. That seemed to calm him down. Then he would say what he needed to say to the players or the umpires. Our daughters would laugh when they saw Vic take his hat off at home!"

Pennsbury High seemed like a pretty informal school in the late 1950s. Student enrollment was growing but not yet out of control.

"It was an enjoyable time," Ginnie Napolitano said. "There may have been 600 kids overall in the entire building. We had 35 or 40 students in a typical class. I taught phys ed and general science. All the phys ed teachers taught a health class and we had to change out of our gym clothes into regular clothes to teach outside the gym class and then change back for gym classes."

In those years before Title IX attempted to balance the ledger between boys' and girls' sports, teachers like Ginnie Napolitano could influence their students as both a teacher and a coach. After she was hired in January 1955, Ginnie began coaching field hockey, one of the few organized sports for girls in Lower Bucks County. Pennsbury captured the LBCL championship in both 1955 and 1958.

"I signed a contract to teach health, physical education and general science to students in grade 1-12," Ginnie said in her 2013 Pennsbury Hall of Fame acceptance speech. "In addition, coaching was required: field hockey, basketball, softball or cheerleading were part of my daily routine. Until 1959, women were not paid a supplemental fee for coaching, and my salary was $3,000."

Joan Marcotte, Class of 1958, wrote about her role models in the book *"Glory Days"* that was published in 2021.

"Ginnie influenced me," Marcotte recalled. "As my physical education teacher, and my varsity coach in field hockey and basketball, she was my inspiration and gave me the push I needed to pursue my dream of becoming a physical education teacher. I can tell you this. I loved Ginnie as a teacher and a coach. She knew how to get the most out of her students and athletes. To me she was the attentive mother I didn't have. Don't get me wrong. I loved my mother and all that she did for me but Ginnie somehow filled a void that a high school girl like me needed."

Joan's athletic career at Pennsbury almost got off on the wrong foot.

"In my first day of school as a ninth grader, I did not know there would be try-outs for field hockey right away. I did not come prepared to practice. I did change into my gym suit but didn't have sneakers. Ginnie let me try out in my loafers. Right away, I knew I would like this coach. Over the next four years, my respect for Ginnie would grow as she twice coached our field hockey team into champions of the Lower Bucks County League. It was during that time that my desire to become a physical education teacher grew even stronger. I wanted to be just like Ginnie!"

Marcotte recalled how Ginnie made her a better student, too.

"I was never a very good student but after many talks with her, I knew I had to bring my grades up. It was because of her interest in helping me that I began to buckle down and look for a college. I give her all the credit for my success as a person, an athlete, a teacher and coach."

"Joan and I remain great friends," Ginnie admitted. "She came all the way from her home in Las Vegas for my 90th birthday party last year! Joan has often told me how I influenced her to become a teacher. That is really a feather in your cap when you hear something like that."

Marcotte taught and coached both before Title IX and after the long-overdue law passed through Congress in 1972. She worked 33 years at Pennsbury before retiring in 1998. Like Ginnie, Joan is a member of the Pennsbury High Athletic Hall of Fame.

"I still see some girls I taught," Ginny admitted. "We were talking recently and laughing about how the girls had to take a shower every day after phys ed class ended. Showering was mandatory in those days! The girls had to undress, get into the shower, and then give us their names as they left the shower. A teacher would be posted there and take the names. It was embarrassing for the girls and for us."

Pennsbury's physical education staff grew like every other department at the school in the 1960s. A quick check of the Class of 1965 Yearbook shows a staff of eight—Vic Napolitano and Joe Gavin, football coach Erle Baugher, soccer coach Ben Kennedy, and field hockey coach Cora Clinton. Rounding out the staff were Marcotte, Martha Willits and Gloria Krellman.

Clinton influenced many young girls who harbored dreams of playing field hockey. Cora ran youth field hockey camps in the sport that she coached for 29 years at Pennsbury, during which her teams won seven LBCL championships and finished second nine times.

In 1962, Clinton organized and coached a girls' track team at Pennsbury. Three years later, she did the same thing for gymnastics, laying the groundwork for those sports in the pre-Title IX dark ages.

Clinton also directed or co-directed Sports Nite at Pennsbury from 1960-91. She was so popular with students that the Class of 1970 dedicated its yearbook to Cora.

In 1988, the Bucks County Courier Times honored Clinton with its 50th Annual Twin Sports Award.

Ben Kennedy impacted the life of Vern Von Sydow, Class of 1958, a star football player looking to land a college scholarship.

"I was about six feet tall and 205 pounds in high school," Von Sydow recalled in a Pennsbury book about the Vietnam War called *We Walked Right Into It*. "I played tackle and linebacker in those days. Ben Kennedy asked me if I would be interested in attending the Naval Academy. He said he had a friend down there who could help me get in. I had to go to a prep school for a year but I got into the Academy in 1959 and graduated in 1963."

Kennedy became coach of a strong soccer program at Pennsbury and was a no-brainer choice for the Hall of Fame.

Joe Gavin coached varsity basketball for

15 years and helped many of his players get into college. (See more on Joe's coaching career in the basketball chapter.) Gavin had an easy-going teaching disposition with a good sense of humor.

All of the physical education teachers seemed to impact their students and varsity athletes in one way or another.

From those early beginnings in the 1950s came the core of teachers and coaches who began setting high standards for Pennsbury students and athletes. Joe Gavin, Ginnie and Vic Napolitano, Cora Clinton, Joan Marcotte and Ben Kennedy built the foundation that Pennsbury has added to over the past 65 years. They were all Hall of Fame teachers and coaches.

CHAPTER 5

A Story of Ed and Diane

By Diane Fritsch-Cochrane

Confession: I graduated from Allentown's William Allen High School in 1964. My school had an extensive intramural program for hockey, basketball, and softball. There was only one varsity sport for girls—basketball. They called it the "Honor Team." In those days, girls had positions called rovers who were the only ones allowed to cross the half-court line.

It wasn't until 1971 when William Allen allowed all five girls to play full court. Because of the school's extensive intramural program, we only practiced once before each basketball game in a small gym with no room for spectators. As you can see, I came from a school where women's varsity sports definitely were not equal to the men's programs. William Allen had varsity sports for boys in football, basketball, baseball, swimming and track and field and just basketball for the girls.

After graduation, I went to West Chester University and majored in Physical Education. It was a wonderful experience.

WINNING TEAM—Ed Cochrane admits the smartest thing he ever did at Pennsbury was marry his fellow teacher, Diane Fritsch.

West Chester had every sport you can imagine. I played field hockey, basketball and lacrosse. Lacrosse was definitely my favorite.

I loved my college experience at West Chester. When I graduated in 1968, time had come to begin looking for a teaching job. A good college friend of mine, Ruth Logan (Pennsbury, Class of 1964), had already been accepted by Pennsbury to teach Physical Education. I remember her telling me what a great school Pennsbury was and that I should apply there. When I interviewed for the job, I remember sitting down at the table with Don Henry, who was then principal at the high school, and George Jarmoska, the athletic director. The interview went very well and I was offered the job.

My first impression of Pennsbury was unbelievable. It had a beautiful school and campus. The pool, football field, tennis courts, softball, baseball, hockey and soccer fields were all outstanding and well-maintained…something which I never had at my high school. At William Allen, we had ONE FIELD for all the girls' outdoor sports.

There were two women in the Physical Education Department at the time. Cora Clinton served as head of the department. She also coached hockey and was Director of Sports Night. The second female teacher was Martha Fillman, who coached varsity softball and junior varsity hockey. These two teachers helped Ruth and I fit right in.

They helped us with the "do's and don't's."

I was very impressed with Pennsbury, which had a strong physical education department and varsity sports program. My first-year coaching experience involved varsity gymnastics and junior varsity softball. I went on to coach field hockey, basketball and cheerleading.

Pennsbury was great with all the sports they offered the girls. The practice times and gym usage were fair. There were some problems with coaching salaries but that's another issue.

In 1976, I married Ed Cochrane, who was Pennsbury's boys' basketball coach. He had an outstanding career with over 200 wins while at Pennsbury. Ed's teams won the LBCL championship four times between 1973 and 1980.

We used to go to a lot of our students' sporting events. I would always talk to them in class the next day about how they played and how proud I was of them. But there were also students who didn't go out for sports. Maybe they didn't have the ability to compete, maybe they had a job after school, and maybe they just didn't want to. This is why Sports Nite is so wonderful. It is not just for the athletes. It's for everyone!!! It's a chance to compete with your fellow students. A chance to compete in front of a crowd that is screaming and cheering for you. Win or lose, we all come together at the end and become ONE TEAM of PHS!

After Cora Clinton retired, I became Director of Sports Nite along with Kenny

Alston. During my time as Director, we made a few changes. Dressing rooms were always a problem. One team would change in the cafeteria—which was fine—but the other team used classrooms (not a great situation). So we changed the dressing rooms to the auditorium…soooo much better.

We also changed the music we used. The students were now responsible for picking their own music and altering it to the way they wanted…with a few restrictions. If I had to pick my most favorite moments at PHS, it would be very hard. I've had many. One would be when I introduced William Ingraham, a former Pennsbury Superintendent, to the Orange and Black Teams at the 50th Anniversary of Sports Nite. Dr. Ingraham created Sports Nite in 1949 when the high school was still located in Fallsington.

The other favorite moment would be during my last Sports Nite. Mr. Chuck Knight, our Assistant Principal, presented me flowers in front of the teams and all the students there wished me a happy retirement. I was very moved by that!!!!

In closing, I just want to say how proud I am to have been a teacher at Pennsbury High School. Even before Title lX, Pennsbury's Physical Education program was far ahead of most schools. I want to reach out and thank all my students, faculty and administration for the wonderful time I had while there.

Ed Cochrane Came From Central PA

By Ed Cochrane

What was the smartest thing I ever did at Pennsbury? That's easy. I married my wife (Diane Fritsch)!

I don't really like to talk about myself much. I came to Pennsbury in 1972 after my Tyrone High team had an undefeated season in the Mountain League in central Pennsylvania. You could say I was a hot commodity as a young coach. I applied for two jobs—Upper Saint Clair (near Pittsburgh) and Pennsbury. I heard about Pennsbury from Tom Frederick, who I met walking down the hallway in school at Tyrone. Tom was a behemoth from Lower Bucks County. He played football for Bishop Egan and Penn State. When I met Tom, he had just been cut by the Detroit Lions of the NFL. We became good friends before Tom went back to Lower Bucks to coach football at Bensalem High.

I knew nothing about Lower Bucks or Pennsbury but Tom told me the Pennsbury basketball job might be coming open. So I did some research and I came down to interview three different times. I got the job but they probably wanted to fire me when we lost our first nine games! Then we won 11 of 12 to finish the season. Almost qualified for the playoffs.

Steve Neilsen and Wayne Emme were good players on that first team. Then we won three Lower Bucks championships (1973, 1974, 1978) and a fourth in 1980.

The 1980 team had to be our best during the years I coached. We had a kid who scored over 1,500 points in his career (Jack Pepper) and one who probably still holds the all-time school rebounding record (Rick Block). And our third excellent player was our sophomore guard, Gary Jones, who would make all-state before he graduated. Gary played in the prestigious Roundball Classic out in Pittsburgh. Jack Pepper was a great shooter and a terrific game player. He would pass up an open shot to get the ball to a teammate for a better shot.

Did Diane and I see each other during basketball season? Of course we did. Diane coached the cheerleaders' squad and sometimes our team and theirs would ride the same bus to the game. It was no problem. We both went about our business.

———

POSTSCRIPT: Ed Cochrane coached Pennsbury for 15 years, from 1972-86. His teams won four LBCL titles. They qualified for the PIAA tournament 11 times in those 15 years. His 1980 team was ranked No. 1 in SE Pennsylvania and No. 3 in the state. They lost in the state quarterfinals in double-overtime. Cochrane retired from teaching in 2006. He is a member of the Pennsbury Athletic Hall of Fame.

CHAPTER 6

'City Kid' Takes a Chance on the Suburbs

By Bill Donaldson

*BILL DONALDSON
...an empathetic teacher*

I am a city kid at heart. I grew up on trolley cars, buses and trains. Big! That is what my environment was in Philadelphia—a high school of 4,000 students, Temple University at 40,000, and lots of neighbors living close, very close. The prospect of moving to "rural suburbia" had caused some hesitation. This story is about my living and working in the new environment.

After two years of graduate school, I enrolled in a certification program that placed liberal arts graduates in public schools after one summer of training. This was a program at Harvard and Temple fueled by a Ford Foundation Grant (FFG) as a result of the Soviet Union launching a satellite (Sputnik) into space in 1957. I was placed at Pennsbury for the summer and offered a full-time teaching position for the fall. That is how I landed in Bucks County which was in transition from rural to suburban atmosphere.

On Tuesday, September 6, 1959, the day after Labor Day, I drove up US 1, from Philadelphia into Bucks County, took a left on Oxford Valley Road, to Big

Oak Road, and I drove into the parking lot at Charles Boehm. That was the first day of my 23 years at Pennsbury. This first year served as training for the years that followed; I made mistakes of commission and omission, but a patient administrator helped me "right my ship" by year's end. Richard Currier, Director of Curriculum and Instruction, was a significant influence in my development and throughout my tenure at Pennsbury High School. His mantra was, "What's good for kids?" Those four words made it easy to focus on my planning and to understand what teaching is really about.

A year later, in September 1960, Pennsbury opened a new ninth and tenth grade building, Medill Bair, under the leadership of Principal Stan Beuchler. The faculty was a combination of new hires and teachers from all the secondary buildings to balance experience across the buildings. I was one of the "experienced" teachers, when in reality I had a chance to make a clean start. Mr. Beuchler led us with a gentle hand while challenging us to excellence in teaching and learning.

Medill Bair was a happy place with a committed faculty. Everything was new. Almost immediately, we had a student newspaper called the Bair–O–Net, new teams with new uniforms and coaches, and Bairlympiad (the Orange and Black field day). Student faculty basketball games became traditions. All was well with our world in Lower Bucks County!

It did not take long for the ugly side of mankind to make its move on history with a single shot. President John F. Kennedy was assassinated on November 22, 1963. Americans still can recall where they were when they heard the news. It was a Friday afternoon and I was about to open the door to the school office, when the cafeteria manager came out and told me the President had been shot. With only 15 minutes left in the school day, and in the absence of cell phones and other communication devices, students were unaware of the news. A decision had to be made whether to dismiss the kids with or without making the announcement of the news of the President. I don't remember who decided what, but I do remember that there was a quick, silent exit by all staff.

By the time we resumed classes after a weekend of mourning, it seemed as though shock, anger, and sadness had moderated slightly. Being back in the building seemed almost normal. Folks continued with plans for the Thanksgiving holiday. But the decade of the sixties was not through with us yet. Rather, it was but the beginning of circumstances that repeatedly tested our faith and resolve as a nation. I thought, how could this teacher (me) prepare his students for what we had yet to experience?

One of my attempts at preparation came after an assembly of mock debates between the two candidates for President. The 1964 election pitted the sitting Democratic President, Lyndon B. Johnson, against the Republican challenger, Barry Goldwater, in a contrast of political postures. The great majority of students committed for Lyndon B. Johnson in a mock election assembly. Hoping to make it all a teaching moment, I told one of the students during our walk back to class that I was going to deliberately provoke the LBJ group with questions that evoked emotion and passion by using my tone of voice and body language. Well, it worked! Some students were actually angry with me because they felt I was not being objective with my questions and I was favoring the Republican candidate.

Finally, I asked the student to share with the class what I had told her I was going to do. There were sheepish grins and a few students smiled knowing they had reacted emotionally, not intellectually. I believe (hoped) they all realized that they needed to know more about issues before making their decisions. They were bright kids who liked to learn.

After the 1964 election ended in a landslide victory for LBJ, Vietnam commanded more and more of the headlines. It became evident that students were watching news, paying attention, voicing their opinions, lining up with students of like positions on issues. At the same time the culture of protest was penetrating high schools across the country.

Student use of drugs grew exponentially as the decade transitioned into the 1970s. I found it sad and angering as I saw kids go downhill academically, athletically, and socially. Dealing with the developing drug issues on campus was a new experience for administrators and teachers. Strategies within the law were formed to address the problems that drug use brings to a community.

As an example, one community (outside Lower Bucks) lost a court case where the principal had opened a student's locker without his knowledge and found drugs. The defense was that the locker had a rental fee and claimed that it was his private property and no one could enter without his knowledge. The court agreed! At Pennsbury, at a teacher's meeting, it was suggested we change rental to maintenance fee, which would allow us to enter the lockers because they would be the domain of the school. It never became an issue at Pennsbury because most students were probably unaware that this was an issue anywhere.

A strategy at Pennsbury was to have one outside person serve as a student teacher for an extended period of time. He was looking for information about suppliers. One day he was gone, never to be seen again! Of course, observation by all staff was a major source of information on users in the school. Pulled fire alarms and bomb scares were occurring more frequently to the extent that even students were complaining about the disruption of classes. Most people were blaming the drug culture for these problems as well.

While all these circumstances were developing, Pennsbury students and staff moved into the brand-new high school building in Fairless Hills, a few hundred yards from Medill Bair's campus. Well, not exactly. The move was into only one half of the building. Only the second floor was finished, and it was all classrooms. Cafeteria, gym, auditorium, and many classrooms were unfinished on the first floor. Determined to open on time, it was decided that we would skip a day, where juniors came one day and seniors the next. That lasted three weeks! Then we moved downstairs and normal school days began.

We had survived eating lunch in classrooms, a student from each room going for lunch milk (shades of kindergarten), no area for student socialization, separation of juniors from seniors, and of course, missing seven or eight days of education during skip-a-day. I suppose we could rationalize and say skip-a-day was an advanced look at college schedules for faculty and students.

All the while, situations nationally and internationally were ramping up toward a frenzy, and our country was becoming more deeply divided, especially over Vietnam.

It was during the latter half of the sixties that the Vietnam War came to Bucks County, specifically Pennsbury, with all too much frequency. Too many grey cars pulled up in front of a home and a military officer got out. Too many lives changed forever from wounds. Too many relationships were severed because of strong political differences. Too many young men left for Canada to avoid the draft.

When I consider my time at Pennsbury High School during the sixties, I think of my first year and its struggles, my tenure and professional growth, and particularly the many students who sat in my classroom. I also remember the destruction caused by the growing social culture invading our student body. Vietnam overrides it all, long after the war ended.

As a teacher, you never stop worrying about your students, even after they graduate. We were sending them into a chaotic world, armed with lessons and experiences they had learned in the Pennsbury school system.

CHAPTER 7

A Principal's Memories of Sept. 11, 2001

By Norman Gross, Class of 1968

The day started like most others. I took my post at the intersection of two first-floor hallways at Afton Elementary School and greeted 630 kindergarten through fifth grade students as they passed by on their way to their homerooms.

Pia Miller, the school's art teacher, whose classroom was adjacent to those hallways, approached me, visibly shaken by what she had just seen on the television monitor in her classroom. Her exact words still ring in my ear. "Norm, you're not going to believe this, but a plane flew into The World Trade Center." I left my post and walked with Pia back to her classroom…and watched.

I have often described myself as a Pennsbury lifer—13 years as a student, 11 years as a teacher, 26 years as an elementary principal. Nothing could have prepared me for that day. There was no manual.

I should provide some background. Afton was the newest of the Pennsbury School District's elementary schools. It opened in 1997 and I was honored to be its founding principal. Prior to my retirement I spent the last 13 years of my 50-year association with the district at Afton. It felt like a crowning achievement! The teaching staff and support staff were exceptional, even

NORM GROSS—Pennsbury 'lifer'

before Day 1, all pulling together to make it right for the student population that would be coming from four existing schools through Pennsbury's redistricting model.

The newly-formed Afton Parent-Teacher Organization (PTO) was equally up to the challenge. Our banner head in those early years was "Creating New Traditions." Eventually the mantra evolved to one befitting a school of such high academic standards: "Creating a Tradition of Excellence." Parents, students and those of us who worked at Afton knew we were in a special place.

The Afton PTO could not have been more supportive of the school's goals. Among the many things the parents did for the school was to maintain a welcoming bulletin board in Afton's front lobby. During the school's first February they created a fitting theme, not only posting the PTO's monthly upcoming events but pictures of the American Presidents, from Washington to Clinton.

As a joke, someone posted a picture of me right after Clinton's. As it turned out a PTO mom was bringing a neighbor to Afton one morning. The visitor had a young child who would be attending kindergarten the following year. "This is Mr. Gross, Afton's President," the veteran parent remarked, then corrected herself with a blush and a nervous laugh. I quite liked it and told the parent, "Sometimes that's the way I feel."

Playing on that theme, every year thereafter at September's annual Back to School Night, I would reference that story and then address the parent population with my "State Of The School" speech. It was good for a laugh before venturing into the very important agenda of underscoring our school's mission: "Your child's academic well-being is our first priority!"

The events of September 11, 2001 shook me to the core of my beliefs. Nothing would ever be the same.

Pia and I were soon joined by guidance counselor Merrick Sirota and the three of us watched in horror as United Airlines Flight 11 flew into the second tower; the meaning became self-evident. Many of the Afton staff had the monitors on in their classrooms, even as the children were still filing in. In a two-story building, I still recall Merrick's command, "You take the downstairs; I'll take the upstairs!" We sprinted to each classroom directing teachers to turn off the monitors to best safeguard the children from the horrific news. Thankfully, most of the staff had already made that decision.

The rest of that day was a blur, but many elements remain crystal clear to me. By 11 a.m., after a plane flew into the Pentagon, the district was in lockdown. No one was allowed to enter the buildings; no one was allowed to leave. Parents were frantic to get to their children, yet the doors were locked.

After a while I recognized the absurdity of the mandate and began releasing children to their parents upon request. Happily, the district followed suit. As things began to settle in my head, I remembered that there were Afton staff whose spouses worked in New York. Ellen Armes was a second grade teacher. I later learned her husband, an FBI agent stationed in Manhattan, was running toward the danger while the civilian population ran the other way. Like all the Afton staff, Ellen put aside her fears and went on with her teaching day.

Many of the children, mostly residents of Lower Makefield Township, had parents who worked in New York. The staff did a phenomenal job in shielding all their children from the terror. My own children were both in Washington, D.C., yet I didn't have the time to call and later learned from my wife that it would have been fruitless to try, as cell phone communication was disrupted. They were fine, but it was only after I learned that a fourth plane, quite possibly headed toward the White House, went down in a field in Pennsylvania, that I realized how much danger my own children were in.

I cherish the memory of those brave souls who took the terrorists down on Flight 93. In the days that followed I spent much of my time patrolling Afton's exterior with walkie-talkie in hand, keeping the school safe from land-based terrorists. As absurd as that now seems, staff member after staff member approached me to say how comforted they were that I was on patrol. Our sense of safety and well-being was enhanced by the presence of our local police department and the District's own security staff. Normalcy eventually returned and curricular-based teaching and learning resumed.

But a lasting impression was made on me those days following September 11. Learning cannot be realized when a child doesn't feel safe in their environment. This post-9/11 message shouldn't have been a revelation to me and perhaps it really just underscored something I knew but had lost in the fervor of trying to maximize curriculum and instruction. Whether it's a child who is neglected or abused at home or an LGBTQ student who is struggling with their identity, or a myriad of other issues, a school needs to be a safe place for a child to learn.

In September 2002, I gave my State Of The School address, but this time making "Your child's feeling of safety and well-being is Priority No. 1," for without it, learning is difficult at best.

PART TWO
Life Stories as Told by Alumni

PLAYING WITH BILLY PENN—To help fill up the Class of 1965 Yearbook, Stephen Trudnak captured this whimsical photo of classmates Joe Fioravanti, Rigmor Lyssand and Ed McGurk gathering around the statue of William Penn on the front lawn of the old high school.

CHAPTER 8

Of Super-Heroes and Second Chances

By Patricia Gordon, Class of 1964

My story and memories are quite different than so many of my friends and classmates. I didn't play sports, although watching and cheering the Little Leaguers at Magnolia Pool and at the school were high priorities. I never grasped the finer points of football or basketball (baseball I could manage), but that did not diminish my desire to be a part. It was so important to be included!!! I had absolutely no appreciation of the sacrifice my parents made or the efforts they expended to give us such opportunities as newly-minted Levittowners and future Pennsbury graduates.

My family came to Levittown after living my elementary school years in a Norristown row home which was owned by my father's cousin. Looking back, I have near certainty that my father came home from WW II with a palpable case of PTSD which lasted for more than a decade. Being the mother she was, my mom shielded us from the turmoil, but I now recognize not only what she had to contend with but also the burdens my father faced every day.

A word here about my parents, George and Elizabeth Gordon, neither of whom had more than a 10th grade education. They

PATRICIA GORDON
...never give up

never felt or acted deprived or inadequate. Both learned and overcame obstacles that I will most likely never know. My dad, like almost everyone else's dad, was drafted into WW II, U.S. Army, but then, because of his extreme natural intelligence, he made it into the Army Air Corps and became a bombardier. This means that in less than a year he went from playing football on the streets of Germantown to flying newfangled aircraft over the skies of Europe and Germany. If you don't understand the role of a bombardier, read the book *Unbroken*. Its description is spot on. Now, that is what I'd call an education, literally on the fly. As a kid, this was completely lost on me. All I knew what that my dad could solve any math problem I ever brought home. His methods were less than traditional but his answer was always right. Now, that's intimidating!

As to my mom, she always worked. I remember her working as a waitress when I was in elementary school. The significance is that most 50's moms were stay-at-homes. Looking back, I'm sure that was a huge reason why we had a roof over our heads. However, something big was about to happen that would change everything for the better, forever. That "something big" was that my aunt, uncle and cousin (Enid Showaker Hadfield, Class of 1961) moved from northeast Philadelphia to the Vermillion Hills section of Levittown. I was convinced that they were SO rich but didn't understand why they didn't have a phone or grass! Nonetheless, Sunday dinners in Levittown were a weekly adventure. My cousin not only had her own bedroom but the entire second floor of their Jubilee home. Good grief, I shared a bedroom with my brother (George Gordon, Class of 1965) and sister. Suddenly, I felt the weight of the world's inequities. Maybe I couldn't have an entire second floor but my own bedroom? (Well, that never happened but I didn't have to sleep in the same room with my brother after we moved to Levittown!).

Our Sunday dinners in Levittown were really a job-hunting expedition as my parents scoured *Courier Times* want ads for the job that would make the big move possible. After a few months, my dad found a job at Paterson Parchment Paper in Tullytown where, in short order, he became Union President and, from there, he was on a rocket ship. Within five years, he was tapped by the International Union and became an international organizer. He was amazing. When my father died at 50 years old, we couldn't believe he had become this really important man! To us, he was just dad, but it was clear when he saw the chance, he stepped up to the opportunity and literally knocked it out of the park. Now, that's a role model.

At this point, another word about my mom. Never challenge her and expect failure—just wouldn't happen. After my dad's job was secured, mom went into high gear. We were moving to Thornridge! A dream come true.

PENNSBURY FOREVER

We were not "original Levittowners." We arrived in 1958 so we missed the mud and the corner phone booth and other pioneer events endured by "the originals." What I much later learned, however, was that my parents needed $100 to complete the house settlement, and believe it or not, my mother stopped off at the Household Finance Company on Route 13 on the way to Ostroff Realty for settlement and borrowed $100 to close the deal. Try that today in a computer society. Like I said, give mom a challenge and she would find a way.

Looking back, it's clear we didn't realize the role models that our parents were becoming. Despite their lack of formal education, each climbed to the top of their careers. My dad with the Union, and my mom at A&P where she became the first-ever deli manager—female at that!

So, moving day came on January 2, 1958, in the midst of a blizzard and sub-zero weather. Within a month, another blizzard took down the electric lines, and we had no power for nearly a week. My mom cooked dinner in the fireplace. Nothing like it! After dinner, we played Monopoly by candlelight. I'm sure it was a real challenge for our parents, but we kids loved it. Finally, Vermillion Hills got electricity so we trekked over to my aunt's house. My cousin was like my big sister, and I thought she was so glamorous! She probably thought I was a pain but such is life. In the end, we were true friends.

As to Pennsbury, my siblings went to Penn Manor but because the school lacked a sixth grade, we bussed to Fairless View for that one year. This was my first experience with a truly great educator, John O'Byrne, who set me on a course for success. When I arrived, I was woefully behind grade level. I was an A student in Norristown, but the problem was Pennsbury, even in those early years, was breaking through every barrier and offering educational opportunities far in advance of the older districts. Mr. O'Byrne, bless his heart, understood that I had the ability but simply had not yet been taught higher skills. His solution—morning instruction for me with the class, then he tutored me at his desk in the afternoon while the class worked on their assignments. He also crafted special homework for me to get to grade level. Mission accomplished. By Easter, I was working with the class at grade level. I had no idea that I had just met one of those fork-in-the-road mentors, who impacted my life dramatically for the good. He was my first male teacher and my first Pennsbury super-hero.

That summer, we discovered the next Levittown "luxury" that became our daily summer haunt—Magnolia Pool. Every day I'd quickly get my chores finished so I could go to the pool and hang with friends. We watched Little League teams play ball on an adjacent field. We had no idea those boys would go on to win the World Series in the summer of 1960, but they did. We'd lay and sunbathe the day away until it came time to go home for dinner. Then it was eat, wash dishes, get cleaned up and return to the pool to hang out at the basketball court or at the baseball field with, of course, our transistor radios and the ever-present O'Boyle's ice cream truck. Those summers were the best with then and now friends—Bobby Cusanno, Nancy Ryan, Vince Tanzola, John Quattrocchi, Wayne Guenther, Jody Crosby, Elaine Clark, Donlyn Sabbath, Steve Toff, Doreen Susser and so many others. So many great memories.

While others played sports, I always had a job. First, it was Dairy Delite on Route 13 (started at age 13—try that now). My salary was 35 cents an hour (no tips). I worked there until the summer I turned 15 when Mr. Cusanno offered me a job waitressing at his Italian restaurant/pizza shop on Haines Road. I think that was also 35 cents an hour, but I got tips which meant more money for clothes! Bob Cusanno worked in the kitchen and was the best pizza dough spinner I ever saw. Vince Tanzola, Bill Chadwick, Steve VanderGast and others were the pizza delivery boys. Can you imagine all those kids working together? No wonder Mr. Cusanno kept an eye on everything from the kitchen. Primarily, it was just us and Mr. C, although Mrs. Cusanno came in every day with her beautiful homemade cakes and pies for the restaurant. Lord, that woman could cook and cook she did. Every time we were at Bob's house—it was the No. 1 hangout—Mrs. C would start cooking and feed us until we went home. My memories of that house on Elm Lane are so good. We knew, without exception, we were welcome.

By high school, we were driving cars. Our horizons expanded. In addition to the pool, we now had Gino's on Route 13. Nancy Ryan had her own car. I often times got the family car (what were my parents thinking?). Evenings were now spent hanging out in Gino's parking lot until they told us to leave, and then we basically went "over the wall" to the train station. Again, music, kids and clean fun. No one got into trouble. The most larcenous thing we did was disconnect the car's odometer and refill the gas tank with pooled change (remember, gas was just 29 cents per gallon in those days) so our parents wouldn't know how far we really drove. Nancy Ryan and I were partners in crime on this one.

The firehouse dances and Hugh Carcella were also big events. Now we were able to meet students from Bishop Egan and Woodrow Wilson, some of whom became life-long friends.

Freedom, however, sometimes brings unpleasant consequences. I learned the hard way that poor judgment generally leads to bad results. And that is exactly what happened to me early in our senior year. By Christmas, I knew I was pregnant and the times then were not very forgiving for girls with such poor judgment. The first impact? A pregnant girl could not attend

PENNSBURY FOREVER

TO THE RESCUE—Al Matuza Sr. cast a giant shadow at Pennsbury High for many years.

school and had to leave—whatever that meant. To say my parents were furious is a real understatement. I had one choice and that was to get married. So I did.

There were few options for girls who made this mistake. Some had "mono" and were gone for a time. Others "hid" it until graduation, while others just left school. That seemed the only option for me. I remember the day I went to the school office with a note from my mother essentially giving "permission" for me to quit school. By today's standards, I still want to scream, "Are you kidding? What were you thinking?" Here is where another fork-in-the-road event took place, and a true Pennsbury hero stepped in.

When I arrived at the office with my "note," I was met by Principal Rohrbaugh, who was very displeased with me and told me how I had thrown my life away. He pointed out my class rank and "squandered potential" and was probably about to send me on my way. However, fate intervened in the form of "Big Al" Matuza, a history teacher who stood 6 feet, 2 inches tall and weighed well over his NFL playing weight of 200 pounds.

This former Chicago Bears football player came into the office, couldn't understand what was happening, demanded an explanation from the principal (Can you imagine?) and got it. He took the note from Mr. Rohrbaugh and tore it up, bellowing (in his booming voice): "Like Hell! She's not going anywhere! I'll tutor her and she WILL graduate." At this point, Mr. Howard Stringer appeared, came up to speed pretty quickly, and tried to reason with the principal, who, with all possible charity, I suppose, was only following district policy, despite its stupidity. It was the times. Nothing further needed to be said. However, these two super-heroes took over, told me to go home, and they would be in touch. I have no idea what transpired in that office after I left but I'm sure it wasn't pretty, and I do know that the Matuza/Stringer team prevailed. Thanks to Big Al Matuza, I did graduate. This man, after teaching his entire day and fulfilling all of his other obligations, met with me in a small conference room three afternoons a week (after school dismissal, of course) and tutored me in every subject that I needed for graduation. If not for him, I would have been a high school dropout.

By the time the Class of 1964 graduated, I was living at Fort Carson, Colorado. I was homesick, afraid, very pregnant and primarily alone, because my husband was training to go to Vietnam. It was a sobering experience but a really bright point was that periodically I received a note from—yup, you got it—Big Al Matuza. Every note contained his signature phrase, "You go, Girl." The man was light years ahead of his time. He saw equality long before Gloria Steinem.

After two years, I returned with my son, moved back into my mother's home, and got a job at Pennsbury. I became secretary to the Assistant Superintendent and eventually the Superintendent. I became the recording secretary to the School Board, and I was barely 20 years old. Here I had the privilege of working with Dr. Ingraham, Mr. McInerney, Mr. Orr, Mr. Jarmoska and Mrs. Reynolds (who was the real power behind the throne in transportation). And, yes, I had regular calls from Big Al, always with a "You go, Girl."

Eventually, I moved on to another job, got a divorce, and became a single, working mom, which is a lot for anyone, let alone a barely 20-year-old who was completely on her own. Over the years, Big Al stayed in touch. Years later, I went to work for a state-level education association and things really began to happen career-wise for me. Ultimately, I became an expert in special education and school finance and went on to work for the Governor of New Jersey. My job entailed testifying before legislative committees and other state and federal decision-makers. Occasionally, items would be in the paper with my picture or name after which I usually got a Matuza phone call telling me, "You did good." By this time, Mr. Matuza was long retired but I did hear again from him after I graduated from Trenton State and before leaving for Dickinson Law. He had seen an article in the paper about my having graduated first in my class at TSC, and he called to tell me how proud he was of what I had accomplished and what I would be doing in law school. This man was a true educator. He changed lives, and he claimed no credit for himself. He loved what he did, and he loved his students. We were his pride, and he showed it in so many ways.

In 2004, when I was practicing law, I had reason to visit a Yardley memory care facility, and a doctor told me Mr. Matuza was a patient. This time, I went to him. He didn't know me, but as I talked, I said my name. I said Pennsbury. I said Class of 1964. As he looked at me without recognition, his aide said he didn't recognize anyone anymore. It broke my heart to see this once-formidable human so dependent. As I stood to leave, I gave him a hug and, when I stepped back, he looked at me and quietly said, "You go, Girl." I have no idea what he did or did not know, but I knew at that moment that Big Al was still there. His essence of goodness wasn't overcome by illness or disease. Two days later, Mr. Matuza died at the age of 85.

The beauty of this story is that I knew for sure that I was absolutely his most special student in the history of time. However, all you need do is say the name Mr. Matuza or Big Al, and it seems like every Pennsbury alumnus of a certain age will relay his or her own story of how they were, without a doubt, the most special student to have ever crossed Big Al's path. You will hear how he saved them or made them see futures they could not even imagine. And I thought it was just me! Big Al was a brilliant, gifted educator, but he was also one of the kindest, most caring individuals I have ever met. With Mr. Matuza, I was never a girl with a problem. I was a girl with a challenge, and he was there to meet the challenge and to ensure that I did as well. Now, that is a teacher!

As to the other super-hero in that story, Mr. Stringer, I had the great opportunity at our 50th reunion to spend quality time with him. It was a bit strange having a glass of wine with our former disciplinarian, but it was a blast watching Mr. Stringer dance with every "girl" at the reunion. He loved it. We loved it. And, again, an educator for the ages. We were his product and his pride, and he had no problem telling each of us how special we are. I can't fathom the number of us he rescued from ourselves and our mistakes, and we will never know because, like Big Al, Mr. Stringer did not draw credit to himself for all the good he had done for so many students. Now, that is an administrator who never lost sight of the ball.

The bottom line on my story is that I, despite myself, always had someone in my corner. I've had second chances I probably didn't deserve but, when presented with an opportunity, I did the best I could. I had parents who, despite limitations, struggled, worked, and achieved. Good role models.

And, from what could otherwise have been a high school dropout, I have two Associate degrees, a BS in Political Science and Economics, a Masters in Public Administration and a J.D. I've gotten to places in my life that I could not have imagined without the help and intervention of educators like John O'Byrne, Howard Stringer and Big Al Matuza. There are so many others, but these are my standouts for all time. I've tried to pay it forward, especially with women and girls in crisis, clients battling addiction, and others who needed guidance. Sometimes I saw the result; sometimes I didn't. The best I could do was to try. Thanks to teachers such as these, I've had the opportunity to try, and that would never have happened without their support, intervention and commitment.

An irony is that, many years after that fateful day in the school office with my mother's note, I had the privilege of being part of the group that instituted retention and in-school education along with childcare for girls who face this issue today. As a result, so many more girls have stayed in school, graduated, and even gone on to college and/or graduate school, despite being teen moms. It's better for them, and it's better for their babies. A chance is given where one easily could have been lost. Such a simple solution, but one that didn't exist in 1964. Thankfully, we are now more enlightened, and the times have definitely changed for the better.

And, to think, none of this would have happened if my mother hadn't gotten that $100 HFC loan on the way to their real estate settlement and a new life. Thanks, mom.

CHAPTER 9

Looking Back After All These Years

By George Strachan, Class of 1966

It's hard to believe I've reached a time way beyond Pennsbury. Well past the roots established in Levittown and well past all the usual nonsense that growing up entails. Others have detailed the industrial boom of U.S. Steel and the housing boom of Lower Bucks County. The two went hand in hand and provided much of the foundation of my life and for so many others. Where our lives would take us after high school was a mystery and one that unraveled in different ways for all of us.

TIME TO REFLECT—George Strachan pauses while crossing the famed Swilcan Bridge on the St. Andrew's golf course in Scotland.

Certainly better for some than others, but who is to judge another's life when our own lives took so many extraordinary turns?

The timing of my high school graduation offered three obvious options for someone like myself: working at the mill, going to college or waiting for the call of the military. The war in Southeast Asia had started to heat up and was not being looked upon favorably by many. That number would grow as bombings increased and the death toll mounted. Those circumstances pushed the military to the back of my list of options. Working in the steel mill offered a young man decent money and seemingly a way to support himself and a family when the time came. It also offered difficult work in dangerous conditions.

College provided an opportunity to pursue the mystery of higher education in the hopes that new avenues would open for me. What those avenues were and where they might lead, I didn't know, but with teachers and family promoting this option, off to Penn State I would go.

Before I went to college, I did experience life in the Rolling Mill division of Fairless Works. I saw enough to know that it wasn't terrible, but nothing I wanted to do long term. Four summers at the mill, including one in the dreaded Open Hearth, went a long way to paying for my college tuition and room and board. Dirty, hard work and a lot of overtime allowed me to escape the student debt that shackles so many young people today. Thank you, U.S. Steel.

Penn State offered a new beginning—along with the uncertainty of "What the heck am I doing here?" I was the first one on both sides of my family to attend college so there had been no mentoring going on. Just the nudge and hope that if you went to college, something good would happen. A university of 40,000 students swallows up many and my first term raised some misgivings for me. I did well enough in class and made some friends. I also kept remembering my other options of blue collar labor or the olive drab of the Army. Penn State was an easy decision.

Going back to school after the Christmas holidays of my freshman year opened up some new social options for me. I was able to rush fraternities and naturally a Pennsbury and steel mill connection came into play. I had worked that summer of '66 with Joe Napkori, Pennsbury Class of 1963. "Nap" was an interesting and funny guy and made his house, Kappa Sigma, sound like fun. Fun it was and it allowed just enough time for studying to keep the education part of Penn State alive. Our house was made of all kinds of people, including many guys like Nap and myself who came from blue collar stock.

In ways that no one anticipated nor planned on, our group of Kappa Sigs learned to take care of each other and provide support. Things learned there became an important part of my life. Fraternities are often known for parties, and believe me we had them, but we usually managed at least a small amount of decorum. Better make that damage control.

There was an inordinate amount of pressure on male college students at that time to stay academically sound. If your grades fell below a standard that wouldn't lead to graduation or you became a part-time student, you could expect to hear from the draft board. I still remember our local draft board was on Farragut Street in Bristol and I didn't want to hear from them.

In the late 60's and into the spring of 1970, the conflict in Vietnam had heated up immensely. As I was awaiting graduation, the country suffered from war protests and the horror of the killings at Kent State and Jackson State. The first draft lottery, created to lend some sense of order to the selective service process, had taken place and I drew a sufficiently high number that allowed me to plan a life outside the military. I was engaged to be married so finding a good job was now at the top of my agenda. The girl I married is my wife now of 51 years. Ann Hilferty was from Penn State and Doylestown. We would embark upon the adventure of married life together. I think our 51 years together is a testimony of something good. Well, mostly anyway. Perhaps you should ask Ann.

I took my first job in pharmaceutical sales. It had a big salary of $750 per month along with a company car and expense account. We thought we were living high! Starting with an apartment in Lindenwold, N.J. and moving into homes in Delran and East Windsor, my career began. I branched off into medical sales and later into marketing management. Living in Jersey was okay, but we both yearned to get back to Bucks County.

The 1970's were a hectic and frenzied decade. Watergate, the end of the war in Vietnam and the energy crisis all had the country's attention. Political differences spawned and stirred things like never before. The power of the media was just starting to evidence itself. That troubled me then and troubles me more today. I prefer to develop my own opinions rather than take those of others thrust upon me.

The 70's also brought the birth of my son, George L. Strachan IV. A glorious day, that was only to be matched by the birth of my daughter, Lauren. She was unburdened of a title. Responsibilities of parenthood were jumbled with trying to grow a career and make sense of a world clamoring for civility. Upheaval was everywhere and solutions for it nowhere. The 70's were difficult and unharmonious. And speaking of unharmonious, did I mention Disco? Couldn't Doo Wop and Motown live forever?

The 1980's brought inflation and record high interest rates. Mortgage rates rose to 18 percent. With economic uncertainty crushing America, naturally I decided it was a good time to go into business for myself. I had a good job with the American Express Company and a defined career path that would have pleased many, but to stay with Amex at that time would have meant working in New York City or undergoing corporate moves every two years. With a 3-year-old and a 1-year-old, and still the itch to get back to Bucks County, it seemed the time to see if I had really learned anything at Pennsbury and Penn State.

In life we all begin at the same starting position but once life takes off, many different directions are followed, some by choice and some by directions of others. This was to be my choice.

Long story short, I used my connections at Amex to improve a point of purchase sales effort that had been around since the 1960's. It was a successful venture that I thought I could pursue until I had a new and more glamorous idea. The first idea provided enough success and time for me become the type of father I wanted my children to have, to be home with them, to coach their athletic teams and to participate in the community. Idealistic to some, but important to me. Oh yes, my community now was Upper Makefield, back in Bucks County.

We were excited to live in our new home and community and anxious to be part of it. The kids went to a terrific school and Ann and I dove into the things that young parents do. It was a prosperous time for many. My business was growing and allowed us a life that kept us warm and dry. That was important to Ann and I and good for the kids you hope would never know another way. You want your children to have a nice life, but you also want them to know what it took to get there. That can be a difficult message to communicate.

Well, adversity did show up for our family and it showed in a way that you never envision. My son, George, was diagnosed with Ewing's Sarcoma at age 11. Ewing's is a rare type of bone cancer that when diagnosed is usually found in adolescence. We knew that this would be a tough ordeal but we were prepared to fight it to the limit. We went to Sloan Kettering Hospital in New York for treatments and also endured many difficult rounds of chemotherapy at Children's Hospital in Philadelphia. George had his ups and downs and even through his sessions of chemo, he still insisted and was able to play ice hockey and baseball. He displayed a toughness and will that gained the admiration of many. Unfortunately, in August of 1989 at 12 years old, he succumbed to his illness.

It's amazing how death exposes the lie that there will always be time. George ran out of time. He was the toughest guy I will ever know. Life went on, but never as good as it was before.

As a family, we limped into the 1990's and I finally admitted to middle age. Business continued to be good, but my zeal to achieve was no longer as strong as it once had been. Life had shown its fragile side and it wasn't easy for our family to deal with. I still wanted to achieve, but in new directions. It took time, but I found some. Not the kind that might stand out to others, but the kind that would substantiate and support me and our family.

America was in need of support as well. The Gulf War had been explosive, as were the riots on the streets in Los Angeles following the Rodney King verdict. A precursor to what is happening today. Is this an issue that can never be resolved? It is an issue that continues to be divisive for our country. Can we ever put politics aside and work to a common goal that is good for all? Color me guardedly hopeful. The 1990's did give us Viagra, just in time for many baby boomers.

The much anticipated new millennium came in without any significant issues. The concerns about all things computerized being rendered unusable didn't really manifest themselves. No upheaval proved too costly to withstand. That was to be short-lived.

The terrorist attacks of 9/11 on the World Trade Center, the Pentagon and the plane crash in western Pennsylvania struck close to home. Many Pennsbury graduates had their roots in that part of the state. Numerous Pennsbury people had friends and family working in the World Trade Center. We all suffered the significance of the attack on the Pentagon. There was no one that could ignore the violence and arrogance of the attack. Yardley was particularly hard hit by this act of terrorism. People we knew and cared about were killed and others were impacted in ways that seemed unimaginable in a civilized society. Events and services were held to recognize and remember those lost. Monuments were built and a Garden of Reflection appeared to help remember, but who could forget? As a country we didn't forget and two years later we entered the war in Iraq. The war was ostensibly to oust Saddam Hussein, a brutal dictator, which was done. It is hard not to think part of it was to go back to biblical values—an eye for an eye! Not judging, just observing.

Even with the turmoil of terrorism and war, the country was enjoying great prosperity. Tech stocks sent the stock market skyward and advancing IRAs made many feel economically comfortable. There seemed to be no end in sight for prosperity. Until there was. False promise in stocks became too evident and many of them dropped off a cliff. Real estate values followed suit. Should regular people like ourselves panic and sell or stay the course and hope for recovery? We all knew people who chose from these directions. Some took the proverbial beating by selling low, while some—paralyzed by fear—just held on. Conventional wisdom that normally would seem sound to people like ourselves no longer felt quite as wise, just as we were planning for retirement. The value of a solid pension all of a sudden had enhanced importance to those of our vintage. As you age, more bad things seem to happen and this certainly was one of them. It was a time for strength and resolve, something many of us had shown before and would need to show again. Those that were able to hold on to their investments had their decision, if not their faith, rewarded. Our values of trying to do the right thing and thinking things through, as best you could, still seemed valid.

At 60 or so we can no longer claim middle age and we grudgingly accept the next stage of life. Some things that once seemed important now seem frivolous. Things we once wanted to have are not things you care to have anymore. Those things that are most desired by us are often out of our control. Your children and grandchildren may no longer be partial to your company. Your partner may no longer be with you. It's as if life conspires against us as we age. When young, I remember older people saying that things were fine "as long as you had your health." Now I don't believe that good health is everything, but it is sure a great place to start.

Our daughter, Lauren, married in 2009. Lauren graduated from Council Rock High School and Penn State. My son-in-law, Patrick, graduated from Pennsbury and Penn State. We think that is a strong foundation for a successful marriage. 2010 brought the arrival of our first grandson, George Patrick O'Leary. Named after his late uncle, he is our fifth generation George. Our granddaughter, Lana Kate, came along 3 years later. She will create her own legacy.

The last 10 years or so have gone by in a blur. There hasn't been any real mourning of the passing of our youth, but I can say I was of the opinion that the front side of life was brighter than the back side. Then I had cataract surgery and realized that modern science did have some powers of rejuvenation. Things were bright again!!

I know that life has no clear outline, no calendar that allows us to follow. If we all knew our check-out time, would we be better off? Life would be like an episode of *The Twilight Zone*, but without Rod Serling directing, we would self-direct. I'm not sure that would lead to a better result. We can't go back and change our beginnings but we can start where we are now and direct the ending. We can do things that gives us a sense of purpose and self-worth. We've earned that. Let's just try to make that ending farther away.

CHAPTER 10

From South Philly to Levittown's 'Land of Oz'

By John Quattrocchi, Class of 1964

Born in St. Agnes Hospital on Broad Street in South Philly, lucky to be the second son of two great parents, Rosario and Lee Quattrocchi. My dad, like many others, just out of the Marines after serving in the South Pacific, got home to my mother and brother in November of 1945, and lo and behold, on August 19th, 1946, I was born. You do the math. A war baby to say the least.

My parents' best friends lived two doors down the block on 16th Street. The Tanzolas, Vince and Lois, would change the direction of our lives forever. They moved to the Elderberry section of the great suburb of Levittown around 1952 or so, and we would drive, seemed like forever, with no expressway, to visit them.

My father got a job at the *Levittown Times* and we moved to the brand new Birch

ALMOST GREAT—*The 1963-64 Pennsbury basketball team finished with a solid 14-8 record despite losing a handful of close games. Team members include, left to right: Bill Hoffman, Art Lendo, John Quattrocchi, Bill Houser, Jack Dale, Rich Olson, Bob Matuza, Jack Tanner, Mike Burns, Joe Shickling, Tom Mazenko.*

Valley section. What a difference in living conditions! It was like the beginning of the movie *The Wizard of Oz*, where it starts out in South Philly in black-and-white and, suddenly, we are in Technicolor…Levittown!

Because we lived in a new community that lacked neighborhood stores, we were barraged by milk and bread companies giving us free deliveries, hoping to get our business. Very cool!

The only recreation I remember in South Philly was in the summer some folks would open the fire hydrants and stop up the drains to fill the street with water to run around in. In Levittown, we had fields and playgrounds and even a few fire hydrants. The developers planted peach, apple, and pear trees on each property. Our neighbors were friendly and positive. We went to Catholic services at the Edgely Fire Station until St. Michael's was built, attended Fallsington Elementary, and became the first students at Penn Manor Elementary.

We had a sandlot field to play ball on. Later in life, I saw the movie *The Sandlot*. It was an accurate depiction of kids playing baseball on a quirky field. Our neighborhood also had a basketball court, and a huge swimming pool. Our sandlot evolved into Levittown American Little League's home field, future home of the 1960 World Series Champs. I had the honor to play with some of this phenomenal group the year before, in 1959.

Interesting enough, I think that magnificent team's belief system, that they could win the World Series, was seeded in 1955 when my brother Ben's All-Star team lost to a great Morrisville team that went all the way to Williamsport and won the World Series. Morrisville beat Levittown American in an early round by edging our fire-balling young pitcher, Vaughn Ward, 1-0. Only the great Joe Mormello from the 1960 team had a better fastball than Vaughn. Also, on that 1955 team, Josh Kalkstein, who was the only player I ever saw steal home in Little League. Morrisville gave Levittown's Little League the belief they, too, could become champions. And in five years, Lower Bucks County had a second World Series champion!

In 1959 we had a great All-Star team, too, but would have to go through Morrisville if we won our first tournament game against Trevose. We beat Trevose handily 12-3, setting the stage for a showdown with Morrisville. We were ready for them. Our lineup included Tom DiIorio, Dave Neeld, Dwight Kerr, Jim Simpkins, Joe Mormello, Jack Mack, Steve Evans, Kevin Murphy, and myself.

The game was played at Morrisville's Island Park diamond, which was like Connie Mack Stadium compared to our Magnolia Field. Morrisville had the first grass infield we ever played on, a lighted scoreboard, and a dangerous cement wall instead of a fence.

I was, with my teammates, out to avenge the 1955 loss. To Morrisville we were just a steppingstone in their World Series quest.

It was a great game, well-played by both teams. I was fortunate enough to out-duel their pitcher, 3-2. Our team had to come from behind to put us ahead 3-2 going into the bottom of the 6th with the top of their order coming up. To this day, one or the highlights of my life is striking out the side to help beat Morrisville.

Most embarrassing was that as the game ended my dad charged on the field, picking me up and planting a kiss on my cheek. Embarrassing then, but one of my fondest memories of my dad.

We got the revenge. Thanks to my teammates, and my standout friend, Tom DiIorio—a five-tool player. Unfortunately, we ran into a particularly good Pennridge team in the next round and lost, 6-0, ending our dreams.

But in 1960 it all came together for Levittown 'A.' A talented team at every position, with a great manager and coaching staff. Roger Witt, who helped coach the 1960 champs, had been my manager and pitching coach in 1959. Bob Cusanno and I were honored to have pitched and caught some batting practices for the 1960 team up until they won the State Tournament.

Happy Days at William Penn and Medill Bair

Attending William Penn was a coming-of-age experience. We now went to school with new classmates from other parts of Levittown and Fairless Hills. I played soccer, basketball, and baseball there and met new teammates. Notably Tom Mazenko, Bill Houser and Jack Dale, who all went on to play Varsity Basketball with me in 1963-1964.

Entering 9th grade we were among the first classes to attend Medill Bair, then a Junior High. Sports were important but attention was interrupted by, of course, girls! We had class dances once in a while and canteen on Saturday night, which included 9th through 12th grades at Pennsbury High. I am sure my brother Ben was thrilled to have his little brother along for the ride to the dance. He was my idol and off-the-books educator. He laughed at my timidity around girls but tolerated me and my lack of sophistication. A caveat he gave me, him being a senior and me a freshman, was that "Dancing is a vertical substitute for a horizontal desire." I did not totally understand its meaning at the time. Girls were still a mystery to me and now at age 75 they still are.

Ben and I used to stop at St. Anne's Church every now and then to go to confession so we could receive Holy Communion on Sunday. Probably should have gone after canteen with all my sinful thoughts. Little-known fact is that I may be the only one you know that was thrown out of confessional. Imagine that! Yes, my brother and I went into St. Anne's to confess, and I came out white as a sheet. Ben asked why I was acting funny after confession. I was quiet and dumbfounded.

The next morning my mother asked what was wrong. She always knew. I told her I went into the confessional and said, "Bless me, father, for I have sinned. It has been six months since my last confession." The priest blurted out, "If that's all you think of your faith in this church, just get the hell out of here!" Which I did.

Unfortunately for that priest, who will remain anonymous but not unscathed, my mother told my father. Very rarely did my father show his anger but we all knew the consequences. With my brother as a witness, my father found that priest and without words slightly manipulated him by the neck and explained what he would never do again!

I remember what great parents everyone seemed to have and am thankful for mine.

As Ben went off to college in Kentucky, in tenth grade I was somewhat on my own without a big brother, who was my protector and one of the baddest guys in the valley, Delaware Valley that is. I was fortunate to have a lot of friends. My oldest friend from South Philly, Vince Tanzola (before there was The Fonz, Vince was The Tanz!). Next was Bob Cusanno, whose house I hung out at, and whose dad had a luncheonette in West Philly. Alphonso Cusanno would get us up at 3 a.m. and take us to work with him, stopping at Donuts Galore to buy donuts to resell at his restaurant. Boy, was that wholesome fun at 4 a.m.! We got to the luncheonette before breakfast. Mr. C cooked and worked all day. It was always a wonderful day, unlimited playing records on the jukebox for free, super double burgers for lunch, and the coming-of-age part!

Mr. C would give us cab fare for Bob and I to go downtown Philly to the movies. Guess what? We didn't choose Abbott and Costello. I am sure it was Bob's fault, but we bluffed our way into a Brigitte Bardot movie. We were 12 and you had to be 16 to be allowed to watch that movie. I think I learned how to sell from my friend Bob. After that, on to Connie Mack Stadium to see Willie Mays, Hank Aaron, Duke Snyder, and many others. One day we even went to New York to see Mickey Mantle and Roger Maris! Talk about happy days!

My other best friend was Wayne "The Brain" Guenther. (Yes, he was and is smart.) Wayne and I would smell up his house using his chemistry set many times. I envied Wayne for having a complete set of Encyclopedia Britannica's. Most of us had the cheaper ones that could be bought at Penn Fruit, our local supermarket. Wayne was well-known at our house for showing up "unexpectedly" almost every Thursday for spaghetti dinner and my mother's southern iced tea.

On a sad note, my friend Vince Tanzola passed away in 1988. Bob, Wayne, and I remain close friends.

In 1961, a girl from the class ahead of me got a letter from Dick Clark's American Bandstand television show in Philadelphia. She received tickets for six people to go on the show. I apologize for not remembering her name (a Joe Biden moment.) She invited me to go with four of her friends. I danced on TV that day. My parents got a kick out of seeing me on Bandstand. I was not hard to find in the dance crowd as I seemed to be much taller than the regulars on the show.

The guest singer that day was Jimmy Soul, who sang his popular tune of the day, which included the lyrics, "If you want to be happy for the rest of your life, never make a pretty woman your wife." Wow! Somewhat prophetic for me.

At Medill Bair we had to play our Pennsbury rival, Charlie Boehm Middle School. I had heard about this guy Art Lendo from a baseball and basketball article in the paper. I was looking forward to playing him and got the chance in 9th grade. Since he was their outstanding player, I wanted to see if I could shut him down on the basketball court. We lined up next to each other, Bob Purcell out-tapped Jack Dale. The tap went to Art. I backed up to defend him, ready to block his shot. Unfortunately, no one told me he was left-handed, and Art blew right by me to my right for the lay-up. Needless to say, Boehm beat us. Only Tom Mazenko kept the game close for us.

Off We Go to Pennsbury High

In 1963-64 I was happy that Art was now my teammate. We were a scrappy team, no one stood over 6-foot-1. Team captain Art "Lefty" Lendo, Jack "The Ripper" Dale, Tommy "The Bomber" Mazenko, Bill "The Oz" Houser and me, affectionately nicknamed "Cuban Reuben" by my friend Tom DiIorio (because I was so tan all summer, he said I looked like the shortstop for the Phillies at the time, Ruben Amaro). And, of course, Bob "The Kid" Matuza, of the great Pennsbury family. We played against giants. I may have been tall on the dance floor but 6-foot-1 in basketball was just an average height. Bristol had a 6-foot-7 center named Woody Woods who I had to guard. Woodrow Wilson had two 6-foot-5 players—Gary Steele and Dick Davidson. We scrimmaged a team from Princeton High in Jersey whose center was over 7 feet tall. He got every rebound but then Tom Mazenko or I would steal the ball from him and we beat them.

Our team compiled a 14-8 record. We lost six or seven games by only one point, including four in overtime! Coulda, shoulda, woulda.

My classmates Art Lendo, Ken Medlin, and Bob Peresta are all in the Pennsbury Athletic Hall of Fame and I am proud to say they are my friends.

In the social part of my life, great times are remembered of the St. Mike's Fair and Carnival in the weeks leading up to July 4th. We cruised around the carnival (not much money for rides or games) just looking at girls. I did knock the high-and-dry clown into the dump tank with one pitch, before he could insult me.

Of significant mention is my friend Bob "Bobby" Kotz, a great golfer in our class. I knew nothing about golf, except Arnold Palmer was my favorite professional player. I caddied, which means I carried Bob's clubs and handed him what he told me, at the Trenton District Amateur championship final in 1964, where he defeated fellow Pennsbury alum Denny Milne in sudden death to become the youngest golfer ever to win the tournament.

Bob teed off on the playoff hole and hit out of bounds. The match seemed lost. But then Dennis Milne hit wide left of the fairway. Bob dropped where his ball went out of bounds, took his penalty, and was still away so he shot next. We were about 150 yards from the pin. Bob calmly addressed the ball and gave it a whack. I could only see the flag. As the ball landed, Bob looked at me surprisingly and said, "I think it's in the cup!" I thought to myself, "You are nuts!" but he was my friend, and I went along with it.

We walked to the pin and there it was, the darndest stroke of luck I have ever seen. Years of practice had something to do with Bobby's "luck" that day. I wouldn't say Milne was shook up but he missed the green and took three putts. It didn't matter. Bobby won with a spectacular par from 150 yards away. Luck comes from a lot of practice and Bobby's hard work paid off in a memorable triumph. Bobby became the youngest player ever to win the New Jersey Junior Amateur. All with my help, of course.

The Class of '64

The Class of '64 produced maybe the only high school jazz band to appear on the Johnny Carson Show. Led by my great friends Barry Miner and John Byzek. It was a thrill seeing your friends on maybe the most popular late-night show of all time.

After Pennsbury

After high school, I got a job at Gino's. Gino Marchetti, Hall of Fame defensive end for the Baltimore Colts, opened a hamburger joint to compete with McDonald's. I applied for the job which paid $.75 an hour. The manager asked me one question, which was, "how much is 5 x 15?" Since I took honors math, I proudly said, "75." He said, "Great, you are hired! You are a window man!" Thanks, Mr. Eisenhart, for my math skills.

Attending and not finishing college, the U.S. Air Force, and Southeast Asia are a story for another time. Although I love the line in Jimmy Buffett's song "Send you off to college, just to gain a little knowledge, but all you want to do is learn how to score!"

A popular song in 1964 was "*Can't Buy Me Love*" by the Beatles, which was proven wrong on my first night in Bangkok in January of 1968. Who says money can't buy you love?

"As my lack of education hasn't hurt me none."—Simon & Garfunkel

The Johnny Q Hall of Fame

I would like to end with recognition to some influential places and people in my classes growing up.

Places

To Levittown in general, the LPRA and Magnolia Pool; the Towne Theater; Levittown Shopping Center, mostly Pomeroy's where Lois Tanzola worked; Sun Ray Drugs (which had the best ice cream sodas of all time); Greenwood Dairies, of course my brother finished the Pig's Dinner Ice Cream (10 high scoops of great ice cream); The Feed Bag Steaks & Pizza, second only to Alphonso's on Haines Road; Grant's, where I went to check out Jody Crosby before she met Milo; the Great Pennsbury School System.

Friends

I cannot mention all my friends for I am blessed with many. If I did not mention you, you may cuss me out next time we meet.

Gail Ellis and Beverly Briegel, who made fun of me every day in Latin IV class for sounding like a stuttering Porky Pig when trying to translate Latin for Mrs. Carfagno; Corrin Grossman and Doreen Susser; Pat Gordon; Doris Bradfield, my prom date; Jim Barnes, who turned out to be maybe the greatest wrestling coach in South Carolina's history; Les Hoffman; Paul Weinberg; Linda Peebles; Ruth Ann and Mary Beth Logan; Margie Robinson; Joan McInerny; Lorraine Zack; Maureen Ziaylek; Cindy Marcotte; Alice Brooks; Ted Sims; Elaine Guida; Mike Burns; Dick Byrnes; Nancy Noah; Karen Banks; Lorraine Goodwin. Lastly, my good friend and comic relief Robert "Bob" Haviland, of whom our physics teacher, Pete Kundra, said would never smell the gates of college. Uncle Pete, he proved you wrong!

And I would like to thank Art Lendo and Joe Fioravanti for saving my son's life!

Teachers and Coaches

Medill Bair: Mr. Donaldson, Ms. Overly, Ms. Lanning, and Mr. Eisenhart. Coach Campbell, Vic Napolitano, and Vice Principal Howard Stringer. Mr. Stringer was our Marine Drill Sergeant. And we loved him! Our yearbook was dedicated to him. We invited him to our 50th Anniversary Reunion as our Honored Guest.

Pennsbury High School: Mrs. Carfagno, Ms. Hoffer, Mr. Kundra, Mr. Matuza, and Mr. Kennedy.

Mrs. Carfagno was an Ivy League graduate. She was an exceptionally refined, sophisticated professional. She enjoyed enormous respect among the students. We were lucky to have her in our young lives…a Hall of Fame role model.

Little League Coaches: Mr. Cook; Mr. Di Iorio; Chet Gardner Sr.; Mr. Roger Witt, my manager and pitching coach who taught us to be our best!

'64 Classmates

Stu Thompson, Carey Vonada, Ralph Wells, Gene Stacer, Jim Tarity, Fredi Verker, Jack Volz, Hank Hoffmeister, Carol Hoffman, Billie Ingraham, Sam Hulings, Roy Freeman, Margie Bott, Larry Patchell, Chuck Carver, Rochelle Boxman, Don Bigioni, Terry Bloomingdale, Steve Battershell, John Armagost, Pete Jacobus, Jeanie Kettler, Russ Kaufman, Bob May, Kinter Koontz, Joyce Lisbinski, Sue Little, Joyce McCann, Barbara McCusker, Diane McGinley, Bob Miller, Kathy Morris, Craig Monaghan, Dave Neeld, Noreen North, Larry Patchet, Jay Phythyon, Jake Rees, Ralph Rhodes, Diane Rothman, Jon Rounds, Kathy Seymour, Penny Reynolds, and Jimmy Spahn.

If I were Bruce Jenner I would put on my ruby slippers, click my heels three times, say "there is no place like home," and go back to 1960's Levittown for a few days. Since I am not, I will say Levittown was the greatest place to grow up for this kid from South Philly. Truly the Land of Oz for many of us.

(Dedicated to my family: Rosario, Lee, Ben, Linda, and Bob Quattrocchi)

CHAPTER 11

A Most Challenging Year at Pennsbury High School

By Kevin Lendo, Class of 1966

Having so many excellent teachers and coaches at Pennsbury was a huge influence in my becoming a career teacher. I started my time as a student with kindergarten at Makefield School and ended up in 1966 at the new Pennsbury High School, which was a school year like no other. More about that later.

My family moved to Yardley in 1953. Our home was still being built, so we stayed at the home of Dr. Cardall and his family in Woodside for a few months. That area is still known as Cardall's Corner. I can recall Dr. Cardall landing his own plane in the field behind the house. Not too long after that, he crashed and died on a foggy day

SAFE AT HOME—Kevin Lendo slides across home plate to score a run for Pennsbury High. (Bucks County Courier Times archives)

approach. His landing strip is now part of the Makefield Highlands Golf Course. On Fairway Drive, we were the second house that was built on the street. We lived in a modest one-story home with no garage. The family car was always a Chevy. The best part of that location was sneaking out before dusk and playing a few holes of golf at the Yardley Country Club. On a few occasions, I had to make a hasty exit upon seeing the patrolling Country Club Jeep.

I attended six different schools until my graduation from Pennsbury. In 1958, St. Ignatius School opened up right around the corner from our house. My four years at St. Ignatius were a unique period. I mostly had the same 30 classmates and had nuns as teachers, the same nun in three of the four years. Whatever the educational limits there were, I certainly left Ignatius with a solid foundation in the basics. I also got to play CYO basketball for three years. That set up my return to the Pennsbury school system at Charles Boehm in ninth grade. I can recall the adjustment quite vividly. I needed help from other students on how to follow the rotating schedule that had me on the move throughout the enormous school between classes. Seeing former classmates from Yardley School was comforting. Having gym class in what had to be the finest high school gym in the entire region was a daily highlight.

Having to attend three different Pennsbury Schools in my last three years was hectic. (Boehm, old high school, new and unfinished high school). Junior year was another milestone in my education. I would get to meet half of my classmates for the first time. I did know a few students from Medill Bair through sports. In homeroom, I saw Lou Pica, who I had played baseball against in Frosh and JV Baseball, Boehm versus Medill Bair. Because of overcrowding, juniors didn't get their own locker. Lou and I shared. Bringing a full gym bag on most days made for a very crowded locker. The juniors had an assembly in the spring where we learned that the new high school under construction in Fairless Hills would open its doors to us in September.

The first hint that my final Pennsbury year would be different came in August of 1965 when I read the headline in the Courier Times: "Pennsbury High School to Go on Skip a Day Schedule through September." In homeroom the first day, I got copies of three schedules—(1) if the school was finished; (2) If we were still at the old high school; (3) For the Skip a Day schedule which we followed. I went to school every other day that first month and we just stayed on the second floor. In October, the first floor opened up. The auditorium and gymnasium wing did not open until much later.

So much was different that year. Having no cafeteria until December meant packing a bag lunch. For Phys Ed class, we reported to a large room with empty bookshelves that would become the Library by the end of the year. On Mondays in the fall, we would watch the film from the recent football game. Football coach Erle Baugher would narrate. Study hall was an evolving event. For a short time, study hall was spent outside of the high school. I had to go to my locker and get my coat. Then get on a bus for the short ride over to William Penn. I would find my assigned seat in the William Penn auditorium. After a few minutes of study time, it was back on the bus and back to my locker before going on to my next class. We did finally have gym class in late May. There must have been some waivers about Phys Ed from the state Department of Education. I sure know I didn't go to school 180 days! The auditorium opened in June of my senior year. The school was a construction site for the whole year. I will never forget the day that we could smell smoke drifting throughout the school. Sadly that day, a worker was electrocuted and lost his life.

Competing in varsity basketball and baseball meant I would miss quite a bit of my senior English class. All sports participants had to leave their last period class 20 minutes early every day to get the athletic bus over to Lower Makefield. All sports took place that year at the old high school. Football was still played that year at the 4,000-seat Falcon Field, as was graduation. I believe the stadium had a varsity life span of seven years. That concrete stadium would later be demolished.

Sports was such a big part of growing up in Lower Bucks County. My father, Alexander Lendo, was the commissioner of the Pennsbury Athletic Association where I started playing baseball in the Little League. In 1960, the Pennsbury Little League opened All-Star tournament play at Morrisville's Island Park Field. What were the odds that the first team (Levittown American) we would meet would go on to win the Little League World Series in Williamsport? My Dad also started a CYO basketball program at St. Ignatius and was my coach there. The Little League fields had to be moved to make room for the construction of the football stadium. Previously, Pennsbury had played home football games at Morrisville High. At the time of that construction, I could also observe the Charles Boehm Junior High going up. That massive gymnasium stood out. It was such a great experience being able to play four years of scholastic basketball in the finest high school facility in the entire region. I also got to see up close events like the Harlem Globetrotters, and preseason and regular season NBA basketball in that 3,200-seat facility. Ten future NBA Hall of Famers played on the same court where I played for the Falcons. The *Courier Times* headline for the NBA preseason game on Oct. 20, 1959 stated "Warriors Nip N.Y. 124-123. Wilt Chamberlain stars before 2,700 at Boehm."

At basketball practice, we had 12 individual baskets that we could use. And while we practiced, both balconies were used by other activities. Winter track would be in one balcony, while the cheerleaders would be practicing in the other balcony. Boehm is now a middle school. Sports Nite is still held there every spring.

The Pennsbury Falcons participated in a historic high school doubleheader on February 9, 1963. A *Courier Times* headline on February 9, 1963 declared, "2,900 Fans See Wilson, Falcons win." My brother is in the picture. The Pennsbury Falcons drew a bigger crowd than Wilt Chamberlain!

Working was also a big part of growing up in Lower Bucks County. My first official paying job was at the Pennsbury football games. Athletic Director George Jarmoska entrusted members of the basketball team to direct traffic and parking. Once most of the cars were parked, we would then head in and watch the rest of the game. That was usually shortly after kickoff. The big exception was the 1964 Neshaminy game during my junior year. Four thousand temporary bleachers were added to Falcon Field for that game. With standing room, there must have been close to 10,000 in attendance. After finding parking for so many cars, it was almost halftime before we got into the game.

For summer work, I served as a counselor for two years at Pennsbury Recreation. It was good preparation for my future teaching career. But having to help pay for college brought about a big jump in the summer of 1968. There was the possibility of a strike at U.S. Steel on August 31. One thousand summer jobs were brought on to build a stock pile. I celebrated the good news that I did not get assigned to the Open Hearth. However, the Bar & Billet Warehouse that I was assigned to worked on a six-day week. With a shift schedule, I had very few days off. The continual weekly overtime helped me earn $1,800 that summer. That was 80 percent of my full cost of a year of tuition and room and board at Rider University in 1968. After that difficult work, the following summer I went for a different job. A new General Cinema Theater opened on Olden Avenue in Trenton. I wore an usher's blue blazer, which was quite different than my work attire at U.S. Steel. I did get a promotion there. Every Wednesday, I made the popcorn. That meant a $.25 an hour raise for that day. I also could eat all the popcorn that I desired. I have not eaten popcorn since then!

In 1970 I started my teaching career at Burlington Township High School in New Jersey. It was interesting to step into a four-year high school that had "only" 780 students. That was almost the same total as my high school class. Basically, I knew every student in my new school. How ironic, that after playing for the Pennsbury Falcons, I would end up coaching for the Burlington Township Falcons. My four years of basketball at Pennsbury were great preparation for my coaching career. The three state championships we won at Burlington Township are lifetime highlights for me.

PENNSBURY FOREVER

Growing up, I had great role models in my teachers, coaches, and especially my parents. In looking back on my school years, a disappointing part for me was that I never got to meet half of my Pennsbury classmates until junior year. I had only known Medill Bair students as rivals on the athletic fields. I wish I had more time to get to know more classmates. I do not know who made the decisions to build the magnificent Boehm Junior High School in 1957. Those school officials deserve a lot of credit. But that Boehm planning is in sharp contrast with how the senior year for the Class of 1966 was allowed to unfold. However, I can say, I was in the only class that attended both the old and new Pennsbury High School. Despite a school year like no other, I value my years at the Pennsbury schools from kindergarten through 11th grade.

CHAPTER 12

Pennsbury Is a Piece of Home For Me

By Terry Nau, Class of 1965

My one major regret about high school is not getting involved in activities after school. All my fault. I tried playing baseball but that was an easy thumbs-down call for Coach "Cy" Bachman. Anyone could see that a 5-foot-5 infielder with no speed should probably be joining an after-school club requiring typing skills, not athletic talent.

Based on my future life course, I should have joined the student newspaper, the *Pennsburian*, but instead took the bus home to where I felt most comfortable, away from the bustling crowds of high school. Looking back, I was more comfortable in smaller groups within the neighborhood than in a crowded school. Some of my classmates seemed super smart and that was intimidating to me. Teenage anxieties were and probably still are very much a part of high school life.

On my own, I enjoyed taking our hunting dog for a run in the woods after school. Sometimes I took a nap. Sleep seemed very important in my teen years. Why did school start so early? I often would wake up around 11:30 at night and watch Johnny Carson or Steve Allen until 1 in the morning. And then the next day I would sometimes nod off in classes. My grade point average hovered around 2.7, right in the middle of the pack.

KEEPING BUSY—*After 40 years in the newspaper business, Terry Nau turned to writing and editing books in retirement.*

Without a language class to screw up in 12th grade, I made the Honor Roll, surprising my homeroom teacher who sort of chuckled to the class when noting my name on the hallowed list. Like Rodney Dangerfield, I never got any respect!

In a fateful piece of planning, I took a year off after graduation to work and save money for college. My parents matched me dollar for dollar. The plan was working just fine until I got drafted into the Army during Orientation Week at Penn State in late September, 1966. I wasn't a Fortunate Son. Nor were many of my classmates. I have counted as many as 55 of us from the Class of 1965 who personally experienced the Vietnam War. Two did not return home alive—Eddie Beers and Pat Roy. War and the conscription draft were major problems in the 1960s, especially if you put yourself in the crosshairs, as I did. I don't blame anyone for how they managed to avoid the military. Vietnam was not our fight.

I came home in 1968 and melted back into suburban life. Began my freshman year at Penn State-Ogontz, worked nights as a copyboy at the Philadelphia Daily News, and when that got too wearisome, I accepted a part-time sports writing job at the *Courier Times*. My dad, who died early in 1969, would have been happy to see me writing. It was in eighth grade I told him that I hoped to become a sports writer. No wonder. Dad bought four or five newspapers into the house every day. He let me grab the sports pages first. I read them before laboring over my homework. If I could have remembered math and science theorems the way I could absorb batting averages from the Sunday paper, I would have graduated No. 1 in my class.

My eighth grade teacher, Royce Walters, encouraged me after I wrote a book report about (surprise) major league baseball. It took a teacher to get me thinking about my future. And now, at age 75, the future is limited. The past extends almost forever.

Somewhere along the way, I learned a few things not taught in schools.

- A good local newspaper feeds family scrapbooks.
- Serving in the military can be an eye-opening experience.
- Family is everything.
- You can go home again.

As a small town newspaper sports editor for 40 years, I understood that our daily editions filled many family scrapbooks. Parents often complained about the coverage, but they clipped stories from the paper and laminated photographs for their children.

Before the Internet killed newspapers, those daily editions recorded the life of a community, from birth announcements to death notices and a few things in between. Newsmen considered their work important, and a privilege. My various job assignments took me away from home, first to State College, and eventually to Rhode Island for the second half of my life.

And yet my first byline came at home in September 1969 when *Courier Times* sports editor Dick Dougherty sent me to cover the Bristol football game at Morrisville. Before U.S. Steel changed life in Lower Bucks, these two schools were on a par with the existing Langhorne and Bensalem schools as high school sports powers. Much had changed during the past two decades. These teams from long-standing communities simply did not have enough players to match the larger suburban schools like Pennsbury and Neshaminy.

Bristol won the game, 12-7. After talking to both head coaches and sensing dismay among the losers, I described that scene in the first paragraph of my story. Morrisville players took this narrow defeat hard. A few cried.

Dougherty wrote a terse headline for the story.

'Morrisville Sick.'

Newspaper analysis: Dick's page layout cast my story in a small corner that could fit only a two-word headline. He backed himself into a hole of his own digging. Bulldog fans took the headline literally. And of course I soon bumped into a Morrisville coach at a local bar. He matched my red hair to the reporter standing on the sidelines. Damn that red hair! Long story short, I told him I didn't write the headline. The controversy passed in a few days, as do all sports arguments.

Back in the 1950s, the only daily newspapers printing in Lower Bucks County were the *Levittown Times* and *Bristol Courier*. Those two papers soon merged to share the challenge of covering a rapidly-growing market. The *Courier Times* followed every game of Levittown American's march to the Little League World Series championship in 1960. Local news meant a lot in those days.

If you made the Honor Roll, or went off to college, your name and perhaps even your picture might land in the *Courier Times*. I remember when my brother Tim and I were in the same American Legion baseball photo but the caption switched us around and blamed Tim for missing the catcher's throw when it was me who waved at the bouncing throw. Newspapers never get everything right!

I worked at the *Courier Times* for nine months in 1969-70, taking phone calls three nights a week in the sports department and often reporting on a weekend sports event. There was a formal atmosphere in the newsroom. Male workers were supposed to wear a tie, although some of us ignored the rule on the night shift. I left Lower Bucks for Penn State in the summer of 1970. It was time to make my mom happy and get that degree. I had become a decent student in college, and a bit more serious about school after spending nearly two years in the Army. A lot of veterans are better students when they get home from the military.

During the middle years of my life, while living in Rhode Island, I would watch my girl friend's father head off to reunions of his World War II unit almost every summer. And I would say to myself, "That will never happen to me."

Vietnam veterans did not, for the most part, stay in touch after they returned home and settled into their lives. We all went home separately, perhaps with a few phone numbers tucked inside our wallets. I called a couple of my comrades in my first year home and then put the memories of Vietnam aside. Thirty years later, when I finally figured out how to find people on the Internet, a dozen of us started having reunions every other year until the pandemic came along. Those renewed friendships became an important part of my life, 35 years after we left the war zone. With each reunion, this group of veterans from all over America grew closer, and eventually we shared our most difficult war memories.

A few of these old artillery soldiers shed tears as they described events that dropped them to their knees at the ripe old age of 20. One fellow from North Carolina recalled being sent to the scene of a mine explosion where five new recruits, in country for only a few days, died before they reached our unit out in the field. That soldier, Larry Smith, wept as he told the story of a nightmare that never left him. He could still see those soldiers in his bad dreams—blood and flesh soiling their brand new green fatigues.

After a few reunions, I began to understand why Bill Britland went to see his buddies every summer, growing sadder as death took away his pals, one by one, until only two remained. Bill might have been the last one standing. He died in 2003 at 82. Bill had been shot down behind enemy lines and spent nine days in Austria before the underground network found a way to get him back to safety. You don't forget stuff like that. Bill carried the memory with him to his grave. His war service defined Bill as a person.

In my waning years, I know that Vietnam did not define me. What does define us? I guess we all have a different answer.

The war gave me self-confidence that had been severely lacking during my teenage years. I worked in a fire direction bunker with eight soldiers in our unit, most of them my age or older. Because I could quickly add up numbers in my head (thanks to my work on batting averages in the Sunday papers), I was promoted to section chief after six months. I took over during the Tet Offensive in 1968. Doubts raced through my mind because I worried whether the other guys would accept me as their leader. I grew into the job and had my bearings within a month. If you can do the work, people will respect you.

My newspaper career would be similar. I usually worked with a staff of two or three sports writers. We all worked together. We shared the work. The Army proved a great teacher for the rest of my working career. Soldiers must work together as a team. We took pride in our work and we complained about our bosses. I was ready for the real world!

It seems odd that one year in my life could reverberate through the years and into my old age, where it seems even more important. After retiring from newspaper work in 2012, I decided to address the subject in the only way I knew—by writing. I self-published two books about soldiers who died, 15 of them from Pennsbury High, 21 more from my adopted hometown of Pawtucket, R.I. It was an emotional journey because I dealt with families of soldiers who had died in combat. They were left to deal with a wound that never healed. I learned to think of Vietnam in terms of those Gold Star families and the incalculable losses they had suffered.

My research for a book about Pennsbury High's Vietnam War casualties (*"We Walked Right Into It"*) brought me back home again in 2014 for an interview with Mike Yatsko, brother of Joseph, the first soldier from Lower Bucks to die in the Vietnam War. Mike proved a powerful interview, my first for the book, and I knew I could not turn back after hearing how Mike (who was stationed near his brother) escorted Joe's body home from Vietnam in a commercial jet stacked with silver coffins.

Since Joe Yatsko had graduated from Pennsbury in 1959, his name was familiar to younger people like me who read the sports pages. Joe wrestled for the varsity, 5-foot-5 and all muscle. We looked up in awe at those older student-athletes, like Joe and Vern Von Sydow, who would go on to play football at the Naval Academy and then serve three tours in Vietnam as a helicopter pilot who rescued downed pilots out of the Pacific Ocean. Vern and Joe lived a few streets apart in the North Park section of Levittown. They rode the bus to school. One came home, and one did not.

We grew up in a blue-collar community. Our parents wanted us to choose a field to work in. College might be the ticket to that kind of freedom. Everyone seemed to feel that way in the 1960s. Teachers encouraged us to schedule college prep courses. Not that a college degree guaranteed success. In my case, it earned me entry into a rather low-paying job field compared to most of my peers. But I loved what I was doing. And as the years passed, I saw my friends chase their own dreams. My neighbor and good friend living three houses down the street, Bob Burke, became a much-loved school bus driver for Pennsbury. Bob never had children so the kids who climbed into his bus were substitutes. He was a bear of a man who would protect those children from anything and anyone. I think of Bob often when the subject of loving your life comes up. Bob loved what he did.

When I visit from Rhode Island every few months, several places remind me of home—the old steel mill property, our family home on Cardiff Road in Fairless Hills, and all the Pennsbury schools I attended from 1952-65. The mill is gone. Our home was sold four decades ago. But Pennsbury remains, continuing to educate the young people of today, teaching lessons that were not always appreciated in our teenage years.

When I drive by the old high school on Makefield Road, memories come flashing back. My heart grows warmer, and it aches a little bit, too.

CHAPTER 13

Cherishing Memories of My Youth

By Ralph D. Rhodes, Class of 1964

My experiences gained while growing up in Yardley in the fifties and early sixties remain my most cherished memories. My story of this time begins with my father. Ralph Ernest Rhodes lived through the Great Depression. Since money was tight, my father won an athletic scholarship to Alfred University, graduating with a degree in ceramic engineering. The rest of his life was spent on the mining, consulting, and selling of clay.

Like many men at this time, my father had to put these plans on hold. From 1942-1945, he married and served as a

KEEPING CLOSE—Ralph Rhodes, right, with son Will and wife Carolyn, is enjoying the fruits of a life well-lived.

meteorologist in the Army Air Corps. He was stationed as an officer in California when my sister Donna was born in 1944, and when his duty was over, I was born in 1946 in New York. My sister Kathy was born in 1948 in Cleveland when my father returned to his former job in Ohio.

In 1953, my father got a job at United Clay Mines in Trenton. My parents bought a three-bedroom Texas rancher for $10,000 in Pine Brook Farms off Dolington Road. Today, Realtor.com lists the house at $430,000.

Donna and I attended Pennsbury, a school district which had excellent teachers and many student activities. This was perhaps due to their considerable tax base from the new Fairless Steel Mill and the large homes south of Yardley. My sister and I spent ten happy years at Pennsbury and graduated from the high school on Makefield Road.

With the Depression and the War over, millions of babies were born, some of them running around our little Pine Brook world. It was a carefree time marked by a sense of freedom for most kids. I don't recall any curfews. Parents knew each other and cared about us as if we were extended family. Many mothers read Dr. Benjamin Spock's 1946 bestselling *Baby and Child Care* book which advised parents to be more flexible and affectionate with their children. He discouraged spanking, although my parents made sure this was never off the table.

In our neighborhood, there were enough boys to form pickup baseball and football games. Classmates Bill Austin, and Stewart Thompson lived on our little two-street development of 52 houses. With Hall's orchard on one side and Raab's farm on the other, we were surrounded by farmland and woods. Pheasants fluttered into flight when we walked the fields. We explored Hall's farm's mysterious deep and wooded quarry. We traversed the vast pines of the Scammell property, built forts to ward off invaders, erected small dams in Buck Creek, and played tag in Hall's field.

Yardley was a mere bike ride away. A towpath off North Main Street connected us with friends along the canal and the river. Our taste buds were satisfied by the cakes and cookies of Cramer's Bakery, which is still in operation today. Up the street, the Continental Tavern served a different clientele. When our school bus passed the tavern, we'd wave to the happy men who spent afternoons nursing their drinks on the front porch.

I got my bi-weekly flat top haircut at a barbershop off East Afton Avenue. In the early '60s, I noticed a lone protestor carrying a sign. I asked the owner, who had cut my hair for seven years, why he didn't cut Black people's hair. He said their hair dulled his scissors. When I was 16, I worked at the Yardley Inn as a bus boy. I was both surprised and amused the first time I heard the lady waitresses use language that I would later hear from my chief petty officers.

We shopped for school supplies, shoes, and penny candy at Yardley's finest: Phil Freedman's drug store, Louis Seplow's department store, and Len Murray's Five and Ten. But we went to Trenton to buy clothes or to go to the movies.

In those days parents encouraged us to attend school dances. My first date was when I was 12 years old. I asked Nancy Carter of North Main Street to go to a dance at the Yardley Community Center. My father drove me to her house and told me to introduce myself to her parents and be sure to open the car door for her.

With considerable shyness, I mustered enough courage to introduce myself to her parents. I walked Nancy to our yellow '57 Desoto with tail fins that resembled jet engines. I opened the back door and let her in and then quickly jumped in the passenger's seat next to my father. Later that evening my father suggested a more appropriate way to do this.

On a wooden floor the size of a football field, we wiggled our awkward bodies to Jerry Lee Lewis' "Great Balls of Fire" and acted out the lyrics to the hit song, "Flying Purple People-Eater." The alien in this song came to earth to be in a rock 'n' roll band. We were so sophisticated.

I started dating in eighth grade and got to know wonderful girls who taught me about relationships, about being kind, and having fun. In most cases I met their siblings and parents who widened my view of how other families lived. The Sheehy family was particularly bright and fun to be with. Each relationship in their own way, brought me out of my shell and taught me new things.

Ours was the first class of the baby boomers, so it was large. In fact, in the 1950s, Bucks County's population more than doubled. This was exacerbated in Falls and Lower Makefield due to the arrival of the steel mill in 1952.

As time passed Pennsbury ran out of classrooms. By fourth grade Makefield Elementary could not hold us. Those from Yardley enrolled in the old school on College Avenue. By 6th grade, we moved to a small overflow school in Woodside. By 7th, we went to William Penn in Fairless Hill while two new Junior high schools were being built.

We were taught by caring and demanding teachers, coaches, and music specialists. Mr. Ronald Seacrist, who taught math, identified some students in our Algebra class who did well in the subject and needed more challenging material. He gave us extra problems to solve and made time to go over them with us.

In 1957 Russia launched the Sputnik satellite. This encouraged Pennsbury to offer subjects like physics as early as the 10th grade. My talents did not align with physical science, and I was in trouble. I passed due to the kindness of my teacher who gave me an alternative project after my final exam on the physics of bubbles.

Pennsbury offered a smorgasbord of student activities, which my parents urged us to participate in. My father could be very persuasive. It's fair to say he was a driven man. He was president of his college student government and played first string on his varsity college basketball team. As an adult, he started in sales and ended as president of another company. When I was eleven, he asked me how long I practiced my drums each day. I told him half an hour. He said I'd be twice as good if I practiced an hour each day.

I also had some self-imposed pressure because my older sister got straight A's while being active in sports and music. Naturally I followed suit and got involved in the Pennsbury's athletics and music programs. These experiences allowed me to grow socially, but I never matched my sister's grades.

I began drum lessons in fourth grade and played in all the school bands from elementary school through high school. In ninth grade, I joined the prestigious high school marching band. As a lowly ninth grader, I was given the huge bass drum to march with. It wore me rather than the other way around.

Our marching band performed all kinds of complex maneuvers. We marched in rows of eight abreast. In my line, I had a cymbal player on my left and trombone player on my right. When we reached a certain part of the music, the entire line was to about-face and march two steps. Then we were to make another about-face and march down the field.

My first time with this maneuver was fraught with peril. When I wheeled around that big booming drum, I wiped out the cymbal player. On my second about face, I knocked down the trombone player. As the band continued to march down the field, two members were left sprawled on the ground, one with a badly dented trombone.

Director Smith was no doubt pleased that my participation in the marching band only lasted one year. Thanks to my sixth-grade teacher, Mr. Wescott, I tried out for the soccer team and loved it. I played that sport from 10th grade through my senior year at Pennsbury and for four years with the varsity team at Denison University.

My experiences in Pennsbury's music program allowed me to meet other musicians. In junior high, a bunch of us formed a Dixie band, and after the Beatles came to America, four of us formed a new band and played their music. We called ourselves "The Fops." I was on drums, classmate Jim Guest played rhythm guitar and supplied vocals. Bill Green played lead guitar and Dave Clark was on bass.

One of my favorite musical experiences occurred at Charles Boehm. Our new music director played in a professional band. Instead of rehearsing the week's concert music, he sat down at the piano and let me accompany him on a drum set. He was a talented jazz man. It was pure joy. I still play with a church band and credit him and my other music teachers for my sustained interest and enjoyment of the drums.

Though my mother's sense of fun and curiosity stamped much of my personality, my father was always there for me. Before I got my driving license, my father would pick me up after our weekly canteen dance parties. If we got into a meaningful discussion, which was often, he would take the long way home.

Something that really changed my life was being selected as an exchange student with the American Field Service during the summer before my senior year. Four students in my class became finalists among 22 applicants: Judy Parker, Theresa Mercurio, Kathy Seymour, and me.

They were all far better students than I. Our applications were sent to New York, and at some point, we were interviewed. In the National AFS competition, more girls than boys tried out. This may have worked in my favor as to why I alone was chosen. I had taken Spanish at Pennsbury and asked for a Latin American placement, but I was given Brazil, the only country in South America where Portuguese is spoken.

I was assigned to a family in a small coffee town hundreds of miles into the interior of the state of São Paulo. The father was the town's dentist. The family had a son who was one year younger than I and another who was nine. The older son spoke a little English, but the rest of the family only knew "Good morning." In fact, most of the town's residents did not speak English so I had no choice but to learn Portuguese.

One afternoon at the tennis club, I met a beautiful girl named Aldelisa, and we began to date. Actually, dating may be the wrong term. When I took her to the movies, the entire family went along. I always had a chaperone. Most of the time it was her fourteen-year-old sister. Neither of the girls knew a word of English; we got by with my broken Portuguese and by drawing pictures.

I made wonderful friends. Parties were full of music, and someone always had a guitar. They brought out percussion instruments and taught me the unique rhythm of the Samba and the Bossa Nova. There were dances—sometimes twice a week. My Brazilian brother taught me to do the Rumba, Samba, and Cha-Cha by dancing with a pillow.

Dances started at nine and lasted past midnight. We had to ask permission from the girl's parents if we wished to dance with their daughter. Afterwards, my friends and I would go with a guitar to the homes of the girls we danced with and would serenade them outside their windows. On the way home we'd stop at the town's bakery for freshly baked bread which we ate as the sun came up.

At the end of my six-week stay, my Brazilian family threw me a big farewell party before walking me to the bus. Some people carried large white sheets, hyperbolic tissues to show how sad they were that I was leaving. When the bus came, I went to the back seat to look out the rear window. My friends and family were waving goodbye while pretending to wipe their tears with the sheets. I made farewell eye contact with my friends before turning my gaze to my Brazilian family. Then my eyes met Aldelisa. She had tears streaming down her cheeks. It was a long, lonely ride to São Paulo.

On the bus I opened a letter from my father. Ever practical, seldom sentimental, he wrote, "It might be sad to leave Aldelisa right now, but you will soon return to your final and busy year at Pennsbury. She will be thousands of miles away. Be realistic. You will never see her again."

Out of puppy love and a dash of spite, I began to write to Aldelisa every week. I slowly lost my fluency in Portuguese, and it became harder to decipher her letters and to write my own. Soon I was charmed by a varsity cheerleader. She was a wonderful and fun companion for the rest of my senior year. Aldelisa may have also found a new friend. Our letters gradually stopped.

When I returned to Pennsbury for my senior year, I got accepted into Mr. Richard Knippel's honors social studies class. His exemplary teaching methods stayed with me for life. When I attended Denison University, I majored in history.

When the Vietnam draft knocked on my door after I graduated from Denison, I credited my Pennsbury experiences for giving me the confidence to pursue leadership opportunities that helped me get accepted into Navy OCS. Sadly, I lost two friends in the war: Jim Guest, who was a key member of our band, and Bob Meiss, who I spent ten years riding the school bus with. I still carry some survivor guilt from that war. Why them and not me?

POSTSCRIPT: After getting out of the Navy, I attended graduate school at the University of Wisconsin, earning a master's degree in Curriculum and Development. I landed a job with the Council Rock School District where I taught history for 32 years, mostly to high school honors students. In 1988, at the age of 42, I finally married Carolyn, a special education teacher who blessed me with my son, Will. I currently play drums in my church's praise band and still correspond with my Brazilian family. Thanks to some dedicated classmates, the Pennsbury Class of 1964 frequently gets together to nurture friendships and relive shared experiences. We are a dancing class. Over the past sixty odd years, we still manage to hit the floor to dance to the compelling music of our time.

CHAPTER 14

My Life's Journey From Philadelphia to France

By Len Heitov, Class of 1965

When I was born in 1947, our family lived at Eighth & Ritner Streets in South Philadelphia. Both my parents had grown up in that neighborhood. My mother also born there. My fathers' parents had emigrated from Russia to Palestine in the early 1900s and my father and his oldest sister were both born in Palestine. Their family came to the United States in 1913, only months after my dad was born.

Because my parents' families lived close by one another, my mom became close friends with one of my dad's younger sisters and they spent a lot of time together. My dad was six years older than my mom, so I'm

BOLD MOVE—Lenny Heitov and his partner, Penny Hadden, bought a home in the south of France in 2001 and never looked back.

sure there were many times when this little girl playing with his sister was just an annoyance. Little did he know that this annoying little girl would later become his wife!

While we were still living in South Philly, my father owned a 5 & 10 store at 19th & Columbia Streets, now known as Cecil B. Moore Avenue, in North Philly. Long after he sold the store, this area became the epicenter of the racial riots in Philadelphia. I mostly remember loving to visit the store, which seemed huge to me, but really wasn't at all. Just inside the front door there was a glass enclosed fixture, similar to a movie popcorn stand, only this one was filled with chocolate covered peanuts, which I devoured at every visit.

The only employee at the store was a very nice African American woman named Grace. Several years after my father sold the store he decided to bring Grace to Levittown, to see our new home. I don't remember how old I was, but I was old enough to have a sense of unease as she walked from the car to the house because I was imagining what many of our neighbors who might have noticed were thinking and saying. I'd heard enough of my friends on the street and their parents often uttering the N-word to know how they felt. My father, as a young Jewish boy growing up in a very non-Jewish neighborhood, had heard plenty of religious taunts through the years and he instilled in his three sons a sense of tolerance for those not like "us." I've tried very hard to heed his words.

My father, like most of our fathers, fought in WWII, so he was able to take advantage of the GI Bill to buy a home in Levittown, which was still under construction. We moved onto Pebble Lane, in the Pinewood section, in October 1952. I went to kindergarten in Fallsington and Penn Valley Elementary School was completed in time for first grade in 1953.

Earlier that year there was a popular science fiction movie called Invaders from Mars.* The scariest part of the movie, especially for a five-year-old was that anyone, including a lot of kids, who were released by the Martians could be identified by a tell-tale mark on the back of their neck. During a dedication for our new school, we were all formed into lines outside for the ceremony. Much to my shock and surprise, the boy standing right in front of me, who will remain unnamed, had the exact Invader from Mars marking on his neck! I never said anything to anyone and somehow, he and I remained friends throughout all of our years at Pennsbury.

By sixth grade, Penn Valley Elementary School had become overcrowded, so they bused us up to Oxford Valley Elementary School in Fairless Hills. Two things stick out in my mind about that year. The first was this giant, 6-foot round, white canvas ball that we were occasionally allowed to

---

* When writing this segment I originally thought that the movie was War of the Worlds, but Google proved me wrong. Details like this often elude me.

push around the grounds and over as many people as possible. I don't know why or what it was for, but it was just there. The second thing was that one of my new classmates was a girl named Vicky Hadden, someone who has remained a close friend through all phases of my life and, as it turns out, eventually plays a big part in the latter part of my story.

Eighth grade started in 1960. We didn't know it at the time, but the 60's would turn out to be one of the most colorful, dynamic, and turbulent decades of the century. For some of us at William Penn Junior High School it began by celebrating the previous summers' Levittown American Little League World Championship. I had become friends with one of the heroes of that team, Julian Kalkstein, the year before, both from our classes together and playing on the soccer team. Julian and I made a habit of hanging back in the locker room before our soccer team practices so that we could skip running so many laps. We remain good friends to this day.

As a boy of 12, going on 13, I spent a disproportionate amount of time thinking about girls. Why not? One in particular was Merrily Evans and at some point in time that year I took a humongous leap of faith and gave her a ring. I think it must have been during the summer because I rode my bike from Levittown ALL the way up to Fairless Hills to do it. But being a boy that age, things changed quickly, and a girl who lived just beyond my back yard struck my fancy, so I rode ALL the way back to Fairless Hills and asked Merrily for my ring back. Fast forward a lot of years to our 50th high school reunion. I hadn't seen Merrily since we'd graduated, and I was happy to see her there. As we were catching up a bit on our lives, I apologized for being such a cad in eighth grade and I found out later she was touched by what I said. Thanks for being so understanding.

I think it was in the 10th grade that one of my classes was taken on a field trip to American Bandstand. That was exciting stuff back then. The guest singer was Freddy "Boom Boom" Cannon and he sang his latest hit, "Palisades Park." Later in the show they always had a slow song, ladies choice dance. Shockingly I was asked to dance, not by Justine or Bunny or Arlene*, as they all had their steady partners, but it was still a real shot of adrenaline and an ego boost for a 15-year-old kid from Levittown!

When President Kennedy was assassinated in 1963, it felt like the end of our youthful innocence. At the same time the civil rights movement was happening in the south, seemingly so far away from our sheltered lives in Bucks County. Then, when we graduated in 1965, the Vietnam War tore families apart and eventually tore the nation apart.

---

* Google helped out here too, as I really didn't remember the names of "popular" dancers. FYI: Freddy Cannon was the most frequent guest singer on Bandstand, with 110 appearances.

PENNSBURY FOREVER

After graduation I went to the University of Pittsburgh as an engineering student because math had always been my best subject. Pitt was on the trimester system, which meant we finished the school year in early April, so when I came home for the summers I was able to get my choice of jobs at the US Steel Fairless Works. I'm probably one of the few people who worked there for three summers and never got his hands dirty. I delivered mail after my freshman year, handed out parts from a warehouse sophomore year, and worked in their Industrial Engineering department junior year. They did offer me a job when I graduated, but I passed.

At Pitt in 1969 the job placement program consisted of a bunch of brochures from various companies. I picked one out and the first thing that caught my eye was "company car provided." It didn't matter that the job was as a Fire Protection Consultant, for which I had no prior training. The company car thing sealed the deal.

The company, Industrial Risk Insurers, had offices throughout the U.S. and I was supposed to work in the New York City office, but at the last minute something changed and I was given a choice of Charleston or Philadelphia. I chose Philly. I rented an apartment in Center City and soon found out that Vicky Hadden lived several blocks away. It was nice to have an old friend nearby and we hung out a lot.

I worked from my home, not out of the office, and as the years passed and as I got pretty good at my job, I found that most days I had a lot of free time. I had moved from my apartment and with my first wife bought an old Victorian house that needed work. I started buying various woodworking machines and tools, built an addition at the back of the house, and set up a workshop. In the 42 years that I had that house I turned out a ton of furniture and other woodworking projects. There are still numerous display cases of mine in a permanent exhibition at the University of Pennsylvania Museum and another at the Academy of Natural Sciences.

I'd mentioned earlier that Vicky had played a significant role in my life, so it's time to explain. Vicky is one of four girls in the Hadden family, with Cindy the youngest, then Vicky, Penny and Becky. During our college years, especially in the summers, we hung out together and, as Cindy is only two years younger, she became part of the group. This continued after we'd all started our adult, working lives.

The oldest sister Becky lived in New Holland, PA, and we started to spend quite a bit of time with Becky and her husband Jack. Jack was the brew-master at Schmidt's Brewery in Philly. They had a split-level home, with a big, cozy den. The garage was attached to the den and in the garage was a refrigerator with a keg of beer piped to a nozzle mounted on the wall of the den. Party central! Jack and Becky were always off skiing or sailing or something and that's when we had the best parties. So, three of the four Hadden girls were already long-time friends, but they swore there really was this other sister Penny out there.

Sometime in 1996 I visited Vicky at her home in Newtown, PA. At the time I had a time-share in the Cayman Islands and I asked Vicky if she and her husband Bob would like to join me there for a week. She agreed, but she did ask me if it would be OK if her sister Penny, who had just moved to Newtown, could come along too. I said that I thought it would be a good idea if I could meet Penny first. Penny was temporarily staying with their mother, who also lived in Newtown.

A short time later we did all get together at Mom's house and it went well, so we picked a date for our trip. It was only after Penny had bought her plane ticket that Vicky suddenly found a reason why she and Bob couldn't go. Hmm. So, since they had convinced Penny that this Lenny guy wasn't a serial killer and that we had a lot of things in common, she should still go. We did. We called it our "Blind Vacation" and we had a great time, and as they say, the rest is history.

Penny had just retired and was now living in her cute little house down the street from Mom and Cindy and not far from Vicky. She had worked for United Airlines for thirty years, mostly in the marketing end of the business. Several of those years had been in Amsterdam and London and she had fallen in love with Europe. By the time that we met she was already planning to buy a house in France and was searching the internet for houses and realtors. When she asked me if I would be interested in going to France, I said something stupid like, "Sure, I studied French in school, so how hard could it be to learn the language?" The answer to that question is "very hard."

I was still working, so we spent the next few years dating from a distance, as I still lived in my home in Philly. We traveled often and one of our first trips was to France, but just as visitors, not as potential residents. It wasn't until March 2001 that Penny had lined up a few realtors. We wound up looking at places in the south of France, specifically Provence, probably because we'd both read and liked Peter Mayle's "*A Year in Provence*." After several days and numerous uninteresting visits, we were shown a typical French farmhouse in total disrepair. Penny loved it, and as they say, that's all she wrote. We went back in November for the closing and found an architect who would act as the general contractor and oversee the project.

Work began in 2002 and over the next few years we made several trips over to check on things. The architect was this tiny French woman, respected by her crew who worked hard for her. We were never surprised or disappointed at what we found when we got there, unlike poor Peter Mayle. The main house was completed near the end of 2004 and we were there in November for the arrival of all the furniture from Penny's house and some from mine, including half of the farmhouse kitchen that I had built in my workshop. The second half of the kitchen was built and shipped the next year.

By 2007 we got tired of just visiting our French home so we packed up our two dogs and two cats and moved. I still owned my Philly home so we did have a place to come back to if we wanted. Across the courtyard from the main house was a big open shed building that was converted into my dream workshop. We had over an acre of land, filled mostly with olive trees.

About fifteen minutes from our farmhouse is a small town called St. Remy de Provence. The population is around 10,000 but there are more than 50 restaurants and twice as many shops—it's a popular tourist town. We went there for our weekly French classes and dined there all the time.

One day in 2009 Penny suggested that we look for a small house to buy in St. Remy that we could rent out on a weekly basis for some additional income. A realtor showed us many places, but none were at all interesting. Then he said that they had just gotten a listing for a place, but it was a family home, not the type of place we were looking for. We said why not see it, so we did.

As soon as we walked in the front door, our interest was piqued. Stone walls and stone floors, 14-foot high ceilings with massive wooden beams. This house and two other much larger connected houses were all originally built as a hotel, or townhouse, in the early 17th century. We walked through the second and third floors and it kept getting better and when we got to the huge roof terrace, overlooking the town and two mountain ranges, we were hooked. We looked at each other and said, "Let's buy it."

We'd left our farmhouse that morning with one thing on our minds and came back later that day thinking something completely different. We contacted the realtor and put it on the market. We loved our farmhouse, but what we both really wanted when we started the journey in 2001 was to live in a town where we could walk to everything that we needed. With the farmhouse we had to get in the car to just to buy a baguette.

It took a year and a half to sell the farmhouse, but by late 2010 we were into the St. Remy house. We had many projects as the house hadn't been updated since the 1960s, but we've never regretted making the move to St. Remy, or more broadly, to France. Fifteen years later we still sometimes find ourselves amazed at where we've wound up.

We've found that one of the most interesting and enlightening aspects of living here is the strong sense of camaraderie that we've developed with ex-patriots from England, Germany, Holland, and other countries, as well as our French friends and acquaintances. We generally find that all of our cultures have many interesting differences, but at the end of the day there's much more that we all have in common. Another perk of this life is that in the time it takes to drive from Philly to Pittsburgh, we can hop in our little Renault Twingo and be in Barcelona, Spain or Geneva, Switzerland. A seven-hour car trip to Paris only takes 2:20 by high speed train.

Do we miss living in the US? From time to time, of course. And we've always kept that option open by keeping a home there, although that situation changed drastically in 2017. I had been renting my home in the Germantown section of Philly the entire time, but the headaches of renters and general upkeep on a big, old house finally got to me. We found a nice, one-bedroom condo, located in the heart of the Historic District in center city Philly and we had the closings on both properties done in one day. We had been going back to the new apartment several times a year until COVID hit and hopefully, we can start doing that again in the near future.

Friends often ask us if we think we'll stay here or move back to the US. Our answer has always been and still remains *on verra*—we'll see.

CHAPTER 15

On the Road Again With Liza and Friends

By Liza Hamill, Class of 1965

Toward the end of my senior year in high school I had a stroke of good luck. My French teacher, Walter Cobb, "*Le Maître*," said he was taking his family to Europe for a month during the summer and asked if anyone was interested in going along as an *au pair* for the kids. Much to my amazement I was the only one who raised a hand. The deal was that if I could pay my round trip airfare to Europe the Cobbs would take care of room and board en route. A tightwad from my

ON THE ROAD AGAIN—Liza Hamill and her traveling companion, Kathryn, pose at the Potala Palace in Tibet.

89

early years thanks to a steady diet of Uncle Scrooge comics, I had saved every cent I'd ever been given for birthdays and Christmases and it just about covered the ticket. Uncle Scrooge stories always involved exotic travel so this seemed a worthwhile way to spend my loot.

It was late July when we left, back in those halcyon days when your family could go right to the plane to see you off. Nobody in my family had been out of New Jersey much so it was a big deal. I was shipped off with advice from my relatives such as not to talk to anyone and to eat a lot before I went because I wouldn't like the food once I got there. They were so wrong on both counts.

We started out driving around Ireland for a week and then flew to London for five days, then to Paris. We rented a car in Paris and headed south toward Italy. In Ireland, around day two of the trip, I was badly bitten by the travel bug and I've never recovered. We were driving through countryside and we hadn't seen a restaurant for miles. We pulled into a farm yard and asked the farmer if he knew anywhere to have lunch. He said no, but that the wife had a ham. That sandwich was not only home cured ham on homemade bread, it also changed my preconceptions of humanity. I couldn't imagine five strange people showing up at my parents' house unannounced and getting fed. I was clearly in new territory.

The whole trip was full of new experiences and places I'd never dreamed I would see. During one overnight at Mont Saint Michel I watched in horror as Mr. Cobb ate raw oysters, never expecting that I would learn to love them myself. The Changing of the Guard at Buckingham Palace was so beautiful I cried. In Monte Carlo the Cobbs somehow pulled elegant formal wear out of their tightly packed suitcases and went to the casino dressed like movie stars. I was awestruck. The trip ended for me in Rapallo, in northern Italy, because I was starting college in a week. They dropped me at a train which took me to Paris where I discovered that my four years of high school French were inadequate to my needs. I needed a cab to the airport and the helpful cab driver looked in my wallet and said that I didn't have enough francs for the fare but he would accept lira too and I had just enough for the ride. I flew home with just coins in my wallet. It took me over a year before I figured out I'd probably been fleeced but there are all kinds of lessons to be learned in the world and that was a useful one.

Fast forward through four years of college, eighteen months of marriage, twelve years of backpacking up and down the east coast, six jobs, five addresses, too many bad boyfriends to count and one day in 1991, in my mid-forties, I realized that once again I had enough money for a plane ticket. I was working at an advertising agency and while I was entitled to three weeks of vacation management didn't allow anyone to take more than one week at a time. One of my backpacking friends who had started traveling by herself after her husband passed away had been diagnosed with cancer but she still had things she wanted to do. We decided to take a trip together so if she had a bad day I could help. We scheduled a two-week trip to Botswana between chemotherapy treatments. I raised some eyebrows at work by telling management I was taking two weeks off but when I told them of the circumstances they allowed it.

At the time Botswana was just beginning to develop a tourism industry so not everything ran as smoothly as we would have liked. En route we were scheduled for an overnight in Lusaka, Zambia. Our ride met us at the airport and drove us past armed soldiers on every corner. I was nervous but Shirley wanted to experience the local ambiance and went for a walk. She was back in five minutes because people kept trying to buy her sneakers. The next day we were driven back to the airport to check in for our flight to Zimbabwe but our travel agent had neglected to provide the necessary tickets. I was told tickets were on sale at the far end of the airport. I set Shirley down with the luggage and ran as fast as I could across the tarmac to the sales office which was mobbed. There are some cultures in which forming a line and waiting one's turn just isn't done and this was one of them. I threw myself into the mob, everyone yelling. The man behind the desk saw one pale face in the crowd holding a fistful of American dollars. He pointed at me and I got the last two tickets. White privilege and a stable currency is a powerful combination. I was grateful to get the tickets for Shirley's sake but it was the first time I "got" white privilege and it was uncomfortable.

A couple of hours later we were landing in Victoria Falls, Zimbabwe, where the airport was an old military Quonset hut with a wind sock. It had not even a vending machine in the way of amenities, let alone a phone booth. We waited while the other passengers got picked up or just wandered away into the bush until we were the last ones there. The only other person was a young man sitting on a folding chair holding a sign that said "Hertz." Since his business was slow we paid him to drive us into town where we could, maybe, make contact with the civilized world.

The Victoria Falls Hotel was a remnant of the colonial era, like something out of an Agatha Christy novel. High tea was being served on the veranda. Vervet monkeys were dropping out of the trees and stealing cookies off plates. You could hear the falls in the background. But they had a fax machine! I dashed off a scathing message to our travel agent and then found the bar. By the time I'd finished my second beer a young fellow in safari gear came puffing up to us, all apologies, and led us to his Land Rover in which he drove us across the border into Botswana and dropped us next to a rudimentary airstrip out in the bush. He told us the plane would be along any time.

Half an hour later, in the hot sun, we were feeling like lion food when a bush plane landed and flew us to our camp in the Okavanga Delta. Our first wildlife encounter, a very lucky one, was a leopard sunning himself in the track between the airstrip and the camp. He was gorgeous and so was the camp. We stayed in tents, were summoned to dinner by the sound of drums, were served fabulous meals by candlelight. We enjoyed a fully stocked bar with a smiling bartender named Orbit. When we went to bed we found someone had put hot water bottles for our feet under the blankets. In the morning they woke us up by delivering a tea tray to the tent. Shirley and I were the only guests.

After that we flew to two more camps, each one a bit different but all lovely. They were run by old colonial ex-pats most of whom had very colorful stories. We traveled by open Jeep and could park right next to lions tearing apart a zebra and as long as we kept our extremities inside the Jeep the lions assumed we were part of the car. The elephants came right up to the dining hut and reached through the windows for snacks. Baboons hung in the trees over the shower enclosure and watched us, fascinated. I wanted to stay much longer but, alas, my two weeks were up. When we finally got back to Victoria Falls we'd been so far off the grid that it was the first we'd heard of the dissolution of the Soviet Union. Had I been home I'd have been glued to the news. In Africa it barely mattered.

Sadly Shirley didn't live to take another trip but having her as my inspiration I still had things to see. It had only been two years since I'd had the audacity to take two weeks off in a row so I booked a week's trip to Belize and Guatemala. There wasn't much to do in Belize besides some snorkeling and a rather sad little zoo. We were going to be in Guatemala only two nights but those nights made the whole trip worthwhile. We spent a day and a half in the Tikal archaeological site, a huge pre-Colombian complex which at one time was one of the largest cities in the world.

I didn't know what to expect but wanting to be an archaeologist since I was small (and having been told that it wasn't a job for girls) this place left me gobsmacked. I climbed the first pyramid we came to. And the second. The third one was huge, towering over the tree canopy. The view from the top was breathtaking and the sound of the howler monkeys echoed over the landscape. There were ruins poking up through the trees as far as I could see. I never wanted to leave and I never wanted to have to limit myself to a one week vacation again.

The following year I got a brochure describing a trip to Peru. Before the year was up I was putt-putting down the Marañon River, a tributary of the Amazon, on the Esmeralda, a boat that was in only slightly better shape than The African Queen. It carried 16 passengers and we were on it for a week traveling from Iquitos down through tiny river villages. Tourists seldom got to that part of the jungle. We fished for piranha (tastier than you'd think), paddled dugout canoes and saw pink dolphins. At the end of that week we flew to Cusco for the main event, Machu Picchu.

My cabin-mate on the boat was a woman who had worked for the State Department and spoke 6 languages, one of them Spanish. She helped me bargain at the markets and clued me in on local customs. She was great. Unfortunately the altitude affected her a lot more than it did me so once we were up in the Andes I was on my own a lot. One morning I had planned to climb Huayna Picchu, the tall spire of rock that towers over Machu Picchu, so I could watch the sun rise over the ruins. The trail was carved out of the rock by the Incas and it was almost nothing but switchback stairs going vertically up the side of the mountain. I gave it my best shot but it was grueling. I passed people much younger than I who were sitting beside the trail, weeping, and by the time I got to the top the sun was already well up but the view of the ruins was awesome and totally worth the climb. The train back to Cuzco was rustic. Each car had Andean flute music piped in. Something was wrong with the brakes which necessitated stopping the train every few miles to pour buckets of water on the undercarriage. A two hour ride wound up taking ten hours and the flute music never stopped. It's rattling around in my head to this day.

For my next vacation I could only get one week off again so I went to Costa Rica. We were busy at work and at the last minute my boss wanted me to cancel my non-refundable trip. I went anyway. I was often pretty cranky for the first few days of a vacation due to work stress and I guess I was especially cranky on this trip. We traveled from the Caribbean side of Costa Rica (spiders the size of my hand) to the Pacific side (volcanoes and scorpions) by boat, bus, and horse. At the end of the trip at our final dinner I was awarded a prize for "The One Most Likely to go Postal."

The job was clearly getting to me. It paid the bills but I had no autonomy or social life. All I did was work. I was pinching pennies elsewhere to double up my mortgage payments in an effort to pay off the house early and then quit. I was getting close to my goal when I received a brochure in the mail for a trip to Indonesia. It was a week in Bali, and then we'd board an old sailing ship that had once been used for cargo and sail through the archipelago to Komodo to see the dragons with lots of snorkeling along the way. It required three weeks. This was during Y2K and everyone was expecting the world to go off the rails. I went to Indonesia. (All these years later my boss still calls me up every six months or so to remind me that I am the only employee to ever have taken three weeks of vacation in a row. It still drives him crazy.)

This trip was transformative in so many ways. Aside from the beauty of the place and its people there's a spirituality that permeates everything. I decompressed instantly.

It was like there was Xanax in the air. We spent four days out in the countryside at the most exotic hotel I've ever stayed in and just before we were to board the boat I was introduced to my cabin-mate, Kathryn. For me this would be a three week vacation. For her this would be just a segment of an around-the-world trip. She had sold all her worldly goods in California, quit her job, packed a small suitcase and hit the road solo. She'd been traveling for months. Once onboard the boat I mistakenly picked up her passport and when I looked inside I realized that Kathryn and I had been born in the same hospital in Hackensack, New Jersey, exactly 30 days apart. I don't know if there's a word in Indonesian for "Holy Shit!"

We had gorgeous weather, we snorkeled, we drank copious amounts of beer, we sat on the deck and read, we swapped stories with the eight other passengers. We would go days without seeing other people. The food was cooked fresh every night in the smallest galley I've ever seen and one day when we ran out of white wine a couple of the crew took off in a Zodiac with a case of red wine. Three hours later they caught up with us with a case of white wine they'd traded, who knows where. Another day they caught a good size yellowfin tuna, enough food for a couple of days. Once they'd pulled it onto the deck they slit it open and the lucky fisherman who caught it pulled out the still beating heart and swallowed it. None of us had much of an appetite that evening.

Then it was on to Komodo and Rinca where the dragons live. A few locals live there and as we got off the boat we were issued pointy sticks as defensive weapons and told to head off into the jungle. Komodo dragons are scary beasts who live on wild goats and the occasional tourist. There is so much poisonous bacteria in their saliva that when they bite you and you run away they just wait because you're going to die soon anyway and then they can eat without all the drama. They're an endangered species but one gets the impression they can take care of themselves.

I've never been so upset to see a trip end. From Komodo we sailed to Surabaya where there's an airport and I had to say goodbye to my new friends. The unkindest cut was that everyone else was going on to Borneo to see the orangutans and I had to go home because my three weeks were over.

And just like that I was back at the old grind and dreaming of Bali. My boss kept reminding me as I worked late at night how lucky I was to have gotten three weeks' vacation in a row and that it wouldn't happen again. One day when I just couldn't stand listening to him any more I told him I'd be leaving for good.

I had a few more years of mortgage payments to make but I found freelance work in graphics that kept me going. And one day I met an old guy who built model railroads for people and he hired me to do the scenery. Imagine that. I spent three years playing with other people's toys and getting paid for it. Old Walt's vacation policy was a bit more lenient than I was used to and during that time my Philadelphia Zoo membership offered a two week trip to Kenya so I went. More zebras, more giraffes. One day our Jeep got bogged down in mud and we had to get out and push. Knowing there are predators wandering about really spikes up the adrenaline. And knowing I didn't have to go back to a job I hated made coming home so much easier.

I'd been home awhile when I borrowed a DVD of "Indiana Jones and the Last Crusade." The setting was incredible and I learned that it was a real place, Petra, in Jordan, and not a movie set. The very next day a brochure came in the mail with a picture of Petra on the cover, advertising a trip to Egypt and Jordan. I've always been a bit superstitious so I took this coincidence as a sign. The terrorists had been at work in both countries. The price was right and there were no crowds. It was better than I could have hoped. I hiked all over Petra. We cruised the Nile and rode camels. I got to visit King Tut's tomb. I felt like I was living a story from National Geographic. About a month after I got home the hotel where we stayed in Amman Jordan was blown up.

The Galápagos Islands were next, another boat trip. The wildlife was so friendly, the blue-footed boobies kept untying my sneakers. I went snorkeling with sea lions who barked at me under water and one "booped" me with his nose. And then there were tortoises. I got to meet "Lonesome George," the last of his species, now deceased.

It was about this time when something called "Facebook" turned up. I'd been on Classmates and had connected with some of my old high school friends but Facebook kicked it up a notch. I was browsing one day and who should appear as someone I might know but Kathryn, my runaway home girl from Hackensack. She had joined the Peace Corps in her 60's and had been living in Ghana. Thus began a friendship I cherish to this day. I was still traveling alone and she'd already been everywhere but she spent the summer months in her family cabin in the Endless Mountains of Pennsylvania where I tracked her down one day and we've been fast friends ever since.

I continued my globetrotting to Thailand and Cambodia. Uncle Scrooge had been to Angor Wat in one of his stories and the real thing didn't disappoint. The temples were spectacular and the people were lovely but the scars of the wars that have been fought there are still evident. Land mines are still killing and dismembering people. They were incredibly poor and I once again felt a little guilty for my luck in being born where I was.

The following year another brochure sent me to Morocco (best food ever) for a couple of weeks. The geology was fascinating, the country and architecture beautiful. One morning I got to ride a camel to watch the sun rise over the Sahara. It's not an easy place to be a woman, though. I saw some things I found disturbing. An adorable little moppet sitting in the front row of a madrassa we visited looked at us and drew her thumb across her throat. Death to tourists!

The next trip was Turkey, split between two continents. So many ruins. It's always been the antiquities that really capture my heart. While exploring Ephesus one of the tourists took the stage at the Roman theater ruins and sang an opera solo. The acoustics were phenomenal. The Silk Road passed through Turkey and the Asians, Romans and Greeks all contributed to the melange of art and food and architecture. You could get lost shopping in the souks. It made my head spin.

Then one day Kathryn called and suggested we go to Cuba. President Obama had loosened the rules and it was so close to home it seemed silly not to go. It was great having a travel buddy again and the people there were lovely. There was live music everywhere. They loved Obama. It was nothing like I expected. If not for the American embargo limiting supplies and blocking American tourism it would have seemed like paradise. Education, child care and elder care was free. The rum was amazing. I smoked my first cigar and liked it. Cuba Si!

Having survived one Communist country Kathryn and I decided our next trip would be a three-week trip to China. We started in Beijing, then rode the bullet train to Xi'an. En route Kathryn went to the bar car to get us a couple of beers and came running back to tell me there was somebody I had to meet. He was a young American doctor who practices obstetrics at Hackensack Hospital. Clearly he had nothing to do with our coming into the world but it was fun to meet him. Along the trip we saw pandas and the terra cotta warriors and cruised the Yangtze. We ate all manner of strange and wonderful food. (Smoked rabbit heads, anyone?) We flew to Tibet and spent several days in Lhasa. Once again some people ran into altitude problems. I found myself short of breath. Kathryn became quite ill. I went on a tour of the Potala Palace, the Dalai Lama's former residence, but Kathryn decided to stay in the hotel. When I got back she was in bed and hooked up to an oxygen tank. Apparently she had called the front desk, croaked the word "oxygen" and within minutes someone showed up with it. It must happen a lot. We were going to be there a few more days and as we were trying to figure out what to do Kathryn lifted her oxygen mask and quietly said "Are we having an earthquake?" And, in fact, we were. It was the same earthquake that caused such devastation in Nepal in 2015. We were all the way on the other side of the Himalayas and it was rattling our hotel.

About the only other place Kathryn hadn't already been to was Scandinavia so we set our sights on that for the next trip.

We hit Norway, Sweden and Denmark by boats, busses and trains. The scenery was spectacular. Everyone seemed happy. Everyone we talked to felt a little sorry for us as Americans with such a weak social safety net. In Norway there was an election coming up. Out front of the capitol building in Oslo each candidate had a little booth and anyone could go have a conversation with them. In person. And we did.

And then, against all odds, after living alone and liking it for most of my life, in my mid sixties I met a new travel buddy and main man, Rich Richardson, another Pennsbury alum, who soon became my housemate as well. While he hadn't done much traveling he was game to try anything. He had always thought he'd like to see Costa Rica so that was our first trip as a couple. Since I had already been there, I knew what to expect but it was fun seeing it through his eyes.

Since then we've been to Greece where the first gift shop I walked into was run by a Greek man who, I swear, used to sell used cars in Hackensack. We went to Iceland a few years ago, and we have made numerous trips to Mexico, the best of which was a 2-week tour of the Mayan ruins from Mexico City to the Yucatan peninsula. They are every bit as impressive as the ruins in Egypt or Greece but our Eurocentric system of education rarely mentions them. It was one of the most interesting trips I've ever taken and since I'm part Native American it breaks my heart that the pre-Colombian history of America is swept under the rug.

At this point in life I have climbed pyramids and mountains and hiked and tented all over the world and now, at 74, I feel like I won't be missing anything by staying in more civilized accommodations. Our most recent trip was to Italy and I picked up where I left off with the Cobb family so many years ago. It was wonderful. Venice, Florence and Rome by train. Amazing art and architecture. Such fabulous food.

These days airplane travel is more of a chore than it used to be. My carbon footprint is on my mind. I was lucky I got to travel as much as I did when I did and I doubt any of it could have happened if not for that trip with the Cobbs. I will forever be grateful and I had a chance to express my gratitude one night last year when I was browsing through Facebook and saw a comment on the "Morrisville Town Watch" page written by someone with the last name Cobb. I messaged her asking if her parents had taught at Pennsbury. Yes, they did. She was the little 7-year-old girl I looked after as we toured Europe in 1965. We met for dinner one night and looked at the photos I'd taken on that trip. It was wonderful to meet her again.

And Kathryn? She winters in Phoenix now and I'm headed out to see her in a few weeks. In May she'll be back at the cabin in Pennsylvania where we can sit in the boat house with our cocktails, check out places on our iPads and figure out where to go next.

CHAPTER 16

Salley Family Bleeds Black and Orange!

By Tammy Salley, Class of 1992

Orange and black runs deep through my veins.

I can remember as a little girl, my father walking me through the big front doors of Penn Valley Elementary School with familiarity, pride, and humbleness on his face. "Tammy Jean, this is where I went to school. I sat in these classrooms, I ate in this cafeteria, and I ran around this same exact playground when I was your age! You're going to love it here!" I didn't even question it, I could feel it. The journey was

A PENNSBURY FAMILY—It all started with Bob Salley Sr., standing in the middle. Left to right: Bob Salley, Jr. (Class of 1995), Josie Salley, Ellie Leimer (2026), Lori Salley (Neshaminy, 1972), Bobby Salley, Bob Salley, Sr. (1972), Tammy Salley (1992), Salley Kehan (2020), and Jim Kehan (2018)

about to begin and my love and dedication to being a Pennsbury Falcon would eventually come full circle.

My story is simple and very familiar to many who are PHS alumni. I am a 1992 graduate, the child of a 1972 graduate, a Pennsbury employee since 2006, and a Pennsbury parent of 2018 and 2020 graduates and a future 2026 graduate. This community is full of generations similar to mine; families who came to Levittown in the 1950s to build the American dream and passed down that orange and black sweater or jacket with a humble sense of pride.

My dad was the Pennsbury football star who married a majorette from rival Neshaminy a year after graduation. They had their first child a year after that and started one of the many Pennsbury generational trends. My brother Bob, a 1995 graduate, and I grew up in a community full of local roots and family tucked in every corner.

Education in the 1960s through the 1990s and the idea of community was much different than it is now. Teachers, administrators and support staff usually stayed in their positions for the duration of their career and often times stayed in their own back yard.

As I grew through elementary, middle, and on to high school I was very often greeted by someone in the halls of William Penn, Medill Bair and PHS who remembered my father.

Upon hearing my last name, they would say, "Are you related to Bob Salley?"

My answer was quick, "That's my dad."

The wonderful memories of a time before me flooded their faces instantly. They smiled as they remembered their career back then and my dad's involvement in football and the Falconaires choral group. Mr. Harry Jones in particular loved my father and his involvement in music as a popular football player. Mr. Jones quickly loved me the same and immediately treated me as family. The familiarity of the hallways, classrooms, and teachers made Pennsbury a second home. It felt like a big extended holiday gathering and I definitely became addicted.

In 1992 I graduated and moved on to college and Pennsbury stayed with me. I went to a state school and there were plenty of my PHS classmates alongside me for that journey. In their faces I felt "home" in a new, sometimes scary and unfamiliar place.

During my time at Pennsbury we were still separated by the train tracks until 11th grade. We were the Levittowners and the Boehmers. I was from Levittown and wore that badge of honor proudly. We told tall tales of the Boehmers and the things that allegedly occurred on the other side of the tracks and I'm sure they had their own stories about us. Interestingly, when we all met up at the high school in 11th grade most of us found that we weren't really all that different from each other. We laughed at the same jokes, used the same Aqua Net hairspray, pegged our jeans the same way, drank from kegs in different woods, and we were all pretty good at running from the guy in the white van. Ironically enough, I work with Pennsbury's beloved attendance officer (also a Pennsbury grad) Mr. Gary Campbell, who assisted the "van man" and his story might be a little bit different than ours.

In college my roommate was a Boehmer, Meredith Gray, and I loved her with my whole heart. We amazed people with the picture of our entire senior class sitting on the gym bleachers that hung with pride on our wall. There were plenty of people from rural parts of PA at East Stroudsburg University who simply stared at that picture with their jaws on the floor. "That's your senior class? All of those people???"

The emotions started to flood me again in those cinder block dorm room conversations and I held Pennsbury and my incredibly unique experience in my heart to carry me through college. Meredith and I also had the attention of our ESU peers when we told them we graduated together, but we really didn't know each other in high school. We never even said a word to each other in the huge hallways of PHS and a graduating class of over 1,000. We barely even knew the same people in high school. She was inarguably my best friend in college and it was because without even knowing her, she was part of my Pennsbury family.

The Pennsbury chosen family bond is strong. Although I met a PHS alum in college who quickly became my sister, my 2nd grade best friends, Sheri and Sherri, often visited me at college and to this day we sit and laugh about the recess "hot box" in elementary school and high school classroom shenanigans. My William Penn middle school partners in crime—Tricia, Jenny, Kim, and Amy—have stood the test of time, too. We all went to prom together, held flowers in each other's weddings, brought meals to meet each other's babies and dried tears during heartache, loss and divorce. We all meet for weekly dinners, cheer on each other's children in milestones, and religiously tailgate to watch the Prom Parade every year and wonder when we went from limos to floats. Our group text is named "PHS forever" and although we've moved on in so many ways, we'll never actually move on from the bond we built way back when.

When I got divorced and found myself a single mom of young children, I reluctantly moved back to Lower Bucks County. I needed help and support from my parents and friends. Unknowingly at the time I also needed the support of my community and my Pennsbury family. I was a stay at home mom, with an unused bachelor's degree in Sociology and kids I loved more than anything. I moved back home with just a car, a suitcase, and barely a dollar to my name. I had to think quickly about what I was going to do and I stumbled upon a job as a part-time school social worker for Pennsbury school district. It felt like a calling home. I wasn't qualified, I didn't have the education or certification necessary, but I felt drawn into the position like I was born for it.

In my interview with the Director of Special Education, I recounted my high school gym class experiences. Back in the early 90's, students with special needs were placed in a separate "squad" at the end of all the alphabetical squads in gym class. With the last name of Salley I was always in the last row and therefore I was placed right next to the "special education" squad. Although there was minimal talk of inclusion back then, it didn't sit well with my 17-year-old self that there was this separation and I quickly befriended the entire row of unique, fun, inspiring, and extremely special girls. I helped them learn their PE required dance, I invited them to eat with me and my friends at lunch, I attended birthday parties at their homes, and I even settled arguments between them in the hallways.

I truly believe that story and my love of Pennsbury landed me the job. Pennsbury helped me receive the emergency certification required and sent me on my way to get my Master's degree to keep the position long term. My first day of work, I met yet another influential Pennsbury alumni family member. Diane Ellis Marseglia met me at Eleanor Roosevelt elementary school to introduce me to the role of school social worker. We became fast friends and bonded in our love of social justice and the orange and black. I worked with Diane for years while she taught me how to support the families of our Pennsbury community and I could not have asked for a better mentor. Diane went on to achieve ultimate advocating status and became Bucks County Commissioner were she continues to serve members of this community and continues to make her Pennsbury family proud!

Once again my family of origin and my orange and black family was holding me up and together. I healed from my divorce, walked my children into the same big glass doors I walked into as a child with my father, and stumbled into the most rewarding career.

For 17 years I've worked with Pennsbury students and families as a school social worker and certified home and school visitor. I work to help support families I grew up knowing. I work with families that could have easily been mine back in the 1980's. I work with amazing teachers like my 2nd grade best friend Sheri Basalyga Flinn, who is fiercely dedicated to the orange and black and whose own children, like mine, are also products of Pennsbury. I work with administrators and support staff who walked the halls of PHS as students, many of whom have children who attend or graduated from Pennsbury. I now work alongside an extremely connected PHS alum on truancy issues who has a much cooler district vehicle these days. When the attendance officer, Gary Campbell, and I have to conduct a home visit; most of the time one of us knows the family and we connect with them right away because we are both fellow Falcons. We go out on assignment with a Pennsbury address on hand and no one ever has to give us directions because we both grew up in and continue to live in this community.

In 2018 I dove deep into nostalgia as my best friends and my family attended my son's senior year Sports Nite. We all sat in the stands and cheered on my son, their nieces and nephews, and other family friends. My father sat alongside his friend from elementary school and a Pennsbury teacher, Mike Barnes. I was blessed to sit with my best friends and we cheered through all the continued traditions.

Orange and black pom poms were raised to indicate the winners, dances and colorful sequined costumes energized the Charles Boehm gym, and the dizzy bat relay was still the crowd pleaser. 46 years after my father and Mr. Barnes participated and 26 years after my friends and I participated we were sitting in the stands watching the festivities move around us as if they never stopped. The crowd was alive with Pennsbury pride and the students, although part of a very large class, were as bonded as a small intimate family.

In the same year, my daughter was in the middle of her sophomore year on the PHS girls' volleyball team. Her coaches were two fellow Falcons and high school friends of my brother, Mike Falter and Justin Fee. Coach Fee is also a Pennsbury teacher and lives with his family in district. Sitting in the stands cheering the team on were various familiar faces in teachers, coaches, fellow alumni, and community members. As I watched my children grow through the same PHS hallways and experience the milestones and traditions that are rich in this district, I beamed with fulfillment knowing they would also carry the family Pennsbury pride. I am positive it will live in them forever and also shape their life experiences in many beneficial ways. Pennsbury is a home you carry in your soul.

Orange and black runs through my veins like so many others in this community. 1972, 1992, 1995, 2018, 2020 yearbooks grace my family's bookshelf with a spot for 2026. Pennsbury helped give me a life and then gave me my life back. Pennsbury educated me, questioned me and, at times, made me question myself. Pennsbury helped me find myself and grow in so many important ways over the past 42 years. Pennsbury supported three generations of my family.

Pennsbury gave me friends that have lasted a lifetime, gave me mentors that became my family, and gives me support professionally that goes way beyond expectation. Pennsbury created bonds way beyond the schoolyard swing-set.

Pennsbury is a huge, eclectic community that shows up for one another, that is dedicated to the past and the future, and that holds a place so much bigger than school in so many hearts.

Pennsbury is forever.

CHAPTER 17

Levittown Life Had Room For Fun

By Bob Kellagher, Class of 1968

In 1953 we moved from Ashland PA to Levittown and our own house in the suburbs. Moving day may have been the most exciting day of my life. I remember it in extreme detail. Large earth movers crawled through the muddy yards, planting a peach, apple and pear tree in each backyard. The moving truck never showed up so the first night we slept on bed sheets on the cool linoleum floor. It was heaven.

We knew that as early Levittown residents we were part of something new and

GUITAR MAN—Bob Kellagher came of age just as the Beatles and Rolling Stones changed the culture around the world.

exciting. My parents were thrilled with the concepts of good jobs at US Steel and affordable housing, and what those things would mean for them and their children.

My next clear memory is the excitement around entering kindergarten at Penn Valley Elementary School in September 1955. Mom balanced me on the handlebars of her bike and drove me to the school to register.

The first day of school I had just arrived and a young man jumped off his bus, walked up to me and said "Plenty early for school isn't it?" I agreed and a close friendship was born. I stayed in close touch with Alan Bruzel until we graduated from Pennsbury in 1968.

Our kindergarten teacher had the unusual name of Miss Wantz. She avoided teaching older grades for obvious reasons.

In second grade the teacher got a phone call, then faced the entire class with a serious expression. "Robert Kellagher, you have been assigned to attend special speech lessons each week to attempt to correct your speech impediments." I have thought about that moment every single time throughout my life when I have spoken in front of groups of people. I've been successful in that realm, and I think I owe it all to an insensitive second grade teacher who motivated me in a harsh manner.

The speech lessons were actually fun and a nice break from sitting in class. It turned out that my "impediments" were all related to the upstate "coal cracker" dialect that we had brought with us. The most fervent mission was to get me to pronounce the letter H correctly. In the coal region we said "haitch." I was eventually deemed cured. Even while it was happening, I felt sorry for kids who did not live in Levittown. It seemed like there were 100 kids on every block, and some game or pastime was always waiting right outside your door.

For many years we kids on the east side of Newberry Lane were obsessed with playing stickball in the street. First and third base were right smack in the middle of a couple front yards, but the parents let it slide. We would start a game right after breakfast, and it would often last right through until dark. If you were called for lunch you yelled out "invisible man on second" and wolfed down a sandwich in record time…often getting back in time to score that run!

Elaine Hartpence lived on North Turn Lane, with her house immediately facing the opening at the end of Newberry. Legend said that if you could hit the ball over her house on the fly, it was an automatic grand slam home run. Never happened.

The ball-playing group included Henry Bach, Jeff Robidoux, Joe Raggi, and sometimes Chuck Brophy—an import from the other end of our street.

Other immediate neighborhood friends included Larry and Pat Case, and Carl Caldwell. Carl ran the audio visual team at Penn Valley, and he blocked me from joining because he said I was not serious enough.

PENNSBURY FOREVER

Our elementary school gang included Chuck, Bill McCarthy, and Harry Blackmon. We all lived in North Park and could meet up easily. Favorite activities included fishing in the little creek off Mill Creek Parkway, and ice skating in the winter on the pond behind Bill Winslow's barber shop.

Kids from Penn Valley were bused to Oxford Valley in Fairless Hills for just one year—sixth grade. That was a real turning point because that year I met friends who would become my closest life-long allies—Denny Milroy, Chick Kuprevich, Nelson Gray, Bob Raschke, and Dave Hetherington.

As we went on to junior high, a "wild bunch" family moved in right across the street from us on the corner of Newberry Lane. They filled their front yard with cars, and worked on them 18 hours a day. Though there was some grumbling, these motorheads were actually made to feel welcome, and for us kids they were instant heroes. They taught us all about cars and engines, and didn't treat us like little kids.

I stayed in the Pennsbury School system and graduated from the high school in 1968. I was so proud to be President of my class in 1967 and 1968. At graduation I led the crowd in the Pledge of Allegiance, and somehow left out the word "indivisible." Some of my classmates remind me of the gaffe to this day.

I'm sure I was considered a goody two shoes by some, but the fact is that I was always on the edge of some kind of trouble. Trouble was easy to find in Levittown in the 50's and 60's.

In second grade Chuck Brophy and I found a way to make switchblades from Popsicle sticks and rubber bands. We made them in bulk and sold them in school, hoping to get rich. Alas, there was not a high demand for fake switchblades in elementary school.

Years later I scored the real deal. Jordie Brown brought me a genuine switchblade from Mexico, and I carried it everywhere. Remember that the movie *West Side Story* was a major influence on kids our age at the time. One day my father noticed the bulge in my jeans pocket and asked me, "What's that?" I pretended not to hear, walked outside, and tossed the blade into our shed, but I knew I was busted. Dad confiscated my prized possession and told me he smashed it, but years later I found it in a box in the attic.

As we got a little older we pitched tents in our backyards and frequently slept out during the warm months. This opened up lots of opportunities for light misbehavior. We were never hungry because delicious all you could eat peaches were ripe for the taking in every backyard. If we were thirsty we would sometimes raid a neighbor's milk box where fresh milk was delivered in the early AM. I had one adventurous friend (who shall remain nameless) who would leave notes in the boxes saying "leaving two quarts of chocolate milk today." Nothing like a little adolescent larceny.

When we were 15 we were all itching to drive a car, and we discovered a way to jump the gun a bit. We focused on the two-car families, and we would go joy riding in the second car when the parents were out. I know this sounds unbelievably risky, but to my knowledge no one ever got caught, until an incident occurred that shook everyone. Three of my closest friends skipped school, took a ride in one of their fathers' prized Buick Electra, and drove the car right into a house in Holly Hill! They ran away, but were immediately picked up by the police, and the incident was all over page one of the *Courier Times* the next day.

Around the same time it seemed like everyone was experimenting with alcohol. We would combine our crimes by stealing someone's parents' car, then drive it across state lines into Trenton, where beer could be acquired more easily. Again, extreme risky behavior, but no one ever seemed to get caught. We would bring that beer right back across state lines to consume it, so at least we were closer to home when we got high.

Beer drinking became such a badge of honor that several of us formed a social club called the Burgundy Church Key Five (BCK5). Members had to spray paint a bottle opener with burgundy paint, then meet in the woods on Friday nights to consume a six-pack or two. The BCK5 has had a high mortality rate over the years, and today only Bob Raschke and I live to tell these tales. The departed include Denny Milroy, Chic Kuprevich, and Nelson Gray. Ex-officio members included Pat Hilgar, Dave Hetherington, Harry Blackmon and Bill McCarthy.

Those same guys, along with Gary Mahler, formed a street corner singing group called the Argons. We were inspired by older Pennsbury street singers like Jody Giambelluca and Doug Flor, who really understood music and harmonies, and later went on to become serious musicians. Along with Bobby Kondyra they wound up singing acapella in the first couple Rocky movies. Singing Doo Wop was cheap and portable—you could do it anywhere. Our favorite spot was the old Levittown train tunnel, because the acoustics made us sound almost good! We never played for much of an audience, though once a group of girls stood outside the music room in the high school listening while we practiced inside. They said they thought we were Jim Peto's group, which was actually a high compliment!

Senior year we took the drinking to a new level after someone discovered that a small back alley dive bar in Trenton called the Hi Hat would basically serve anyone with money. We were possibly the first white patrons of the bar ever, but were treated kindly by the mostly older African American neighborhood guys who were regulars. The only rule was that we were not allowed to use the pool table, because as the manager told us, "That can only lead to trouble." For a time, if you entered the

Hi Hat on a Saturday night, over half the patrons were Pennsbury seniors! Both guys and girls attended and it was a real social event. We became great friends with the manager. We would help him close up the bar at 2 a.m., then pile into his big Cadillac and go out to breakfast. Heady stuff for 17-year-olds.

My immediate friends had a beer-drinking house party just about every weekend, after we figured out that one set of parents went out partying every Saturday night, never returning before 3 a.m. As long as we cleaned up and bailed out by 2 a.m., we were golden! These gatherings led to some memorable capers. The most infamous was when two of our friends stumbled around after the party and wound up at the old Morrisville Airport. They thought it would be really funny to steal a plane, and they actually got one running! They taxied around the runway fine, but could not figure out how to actually go airborne. Thank God for small favors! Just another Saturday night.

There were always fights or the threat of a "rumble" in the air, especially at the Edgeley Fire Hall dances, and also the fire company dances on Newportville Road. Actual gang fights were rare; we usually had someone like Billy Noah or Bob Burke or Rich Richardson to stare down the other guys. One Friday night word spread of a fight with "West Trenton." A caravan of cars filled with Pennsbury kids drove from one location to the next, looking for those ne'er-do-wells from across the river. The opponents never actually appeared, but the cops caught onto the escapade, and cornered our caravan in the little shopping center in Yardley that houses Vince's Pizza. The cop cars sealed off both ends, and we were captive. I was with Denny Milroy and Chic Kuprevich in Denny's car, and we wound up stopped right in front of the restaurant. As the cops starting piling guys into squad cars, Milroy said wait a minute, we're not here for a fight, we're here for pizza. So the three of us walked in and ordered, and then left with our pizza, driving right past everyone being processed. For a long time after that people called us the "Getaway Boys." Some thought our strategy was wimpy; we thought it was just common sense.

Drugs had not yet become a significant part of the high school scene in 1968, but we did have one friend who was known for smoking a joint on the walk home from the school bus every day. This guy was ahead of his time, and it made us curious. After a deep discussion we bought a small amount of marijuana from him, then met at Nelson Gray's house on a Saturday afternoon to give it a go. We had no idea what we were doing, and eventually five of us huddled under a blanket and shared a little joint. We still laugh about that to this day. And that was the sum total of our drug experience during high school years! I do know that the scene changed pretty rapidly in subsequent years. When I was a senior at Penn State we were friends with a group of freshmen who had attended Pennsbury, and they told some hair-raising stories about drug use on the Pennsbury campus.

We did some outrageous things during our Pennsbury years, but in terms of risk and danger we were actually pretty tame compared to today's kids. Those were very different times, and by and large we had some fun and mostly got away with it. Today's kids should be so lucky.

CHAPTER 18

Eight Brown Siblings Graduated From Pennsbury

By Brian Brown, Class of 1984

I grew up in Falls Township with my parents, Edmund Sr. and Dorothy, and the amazing family they created over the course of 20 years. We had six sons and two daughters in the family. My father was a Falls Township police detective for 32 years and my mom worked as a lunch aide at Eleanor Roosevelt Elementary School for years.

My oldest brothers, Roy (1964) and Eddie (1965), graduated from the Pennsbury High School building located on Makefield Road. My brothers Danny (1970) and David (1975) were next in line to receive their diplomas. Then came Debbie (1976), Dotti (1980), Don (1983) and myself (1984). The five youngest siblings graduated from the Pennsbury High building on Hood Boulevard in Fairless Hills.

My brother Don played varsity football for Coach Chuck Kane's last two seasons and the late Jim Dundala's first season. Don was a three-year starter at running back and defensive back. Don was a member of the 1980 and 1981 Falcon football teams that won the last two Lower Bucks County League titles under Coach Kane.

Don was a captain of the Falcons in 1982. Among the honors Don earned in his

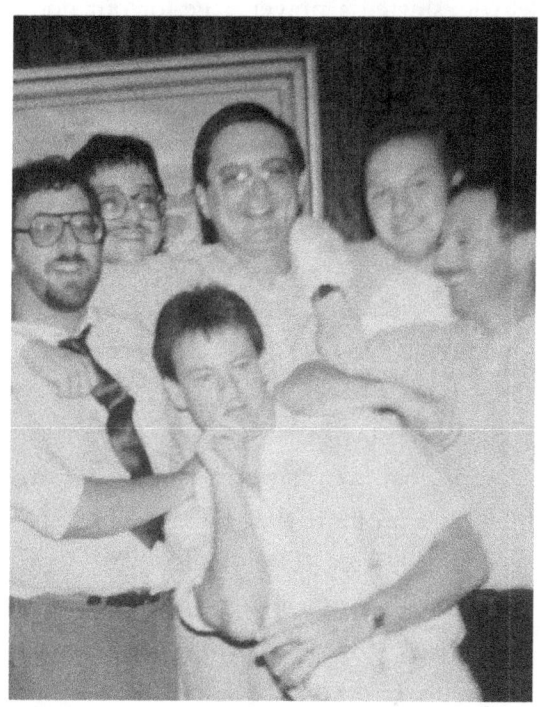

BIG FAMILY!—The Brown family included six sons David (front row), Danny, Brian, Roy, Don and Ed. They also had two daughters, Debbi and Dottie (not pictured).

three years with the Falcons were All-LBCL, All-Suburban One and All-Area honors. He also was selected team MVP in 1982. Don also was selected the male Falcon Award winner in 1982-83. In 2005, Don was inducted into the Pennsbury Athletic Hall Of Fame. Don also ran track, coached by legendary Guy Stewart. My brother Roy after graduation served in the Marines and my brother Eddie served in the Navy.

In terms of Pennsbury, I guess my most notable achievement would be helping to create a Facebook page that came to be a great meeting place for alumni of all ages. On December 11, 2020, my close friend and fellow 1984 PHS graduate, Darryl Moyle, started a prayer page for our good friend, Scott Stenerson. The page was set up so that friends and fellow classmates could leave prayers and messages for Scott, his wife Cindy and Scott's family. Scott had been battling several health issues.

As time went on, Darryl and I noticed that the page took on a life of its own. As more members joined the page, it truly became the PHS page. It has helped classmates connect and reconnect with each other.

Our goal is to have a positive environment and promote the good in Pennsbury. As our page grew, Darryl added two wonderful administrators, Carole Mendenhall (Class Of 1989) and Diane Fritsch Cochrane (retired PHS teacher). The four of us have become a tremendous team and family. The page has over 6,000 members, which has become what we call our Falcon Family. We enjoy each moment running the page for our family.

To describe what Pennsbury means to me cannot be done in one word. I have many wonderful and cherished memories from when I started in kindergarten through my senior year. I have made many friends over the years, many of whom I remain in touch with to this day. We will always share memories of different activities through the years: school dances, Saturday afternoon football games at Falcon Field, basketball games at the Falcons Nest, Senior Prom and graduation.

Being an Administrator for the PHS page has been wonderful for me personally. I have not only connected and reconnected with many of my classmates, I have made new friends with alumni from different graduating classes. I am very thankful for all the friends and classmates that made many great memories for me. I am thankful for the new friends that I've met through the PHS page. I feel blessed and I am thankful for the teachers that I had all through my time at Pennsbury. I will always be a Pennsbury Falcon and bleed Orange and Black.

Hail To The Falcons!!

CHAPTER 19

Do We Make Our Own Breaks in Life?

By Rich Dobos, Class of 1966

When asked to write about the past and life lessons learned, my first instinct was to say no! I am not the type to examine nor dwell on the past, but rather take my successes and failures, learn from them, and move on to the next phase of my life. That being said, I have contemplated the possibilities and decided to give writing a try.

Many people believe that life is a mixture of luck, timing, and circumstance. I agree to a certain extent. Some folks think our lives are predetermined, but the path we follow is of our own choosing.

Shakespeare once wrote: *"There are seas in the affairs of men, which taken at the flood, lead to fortune, and we must take the current when it serves…or lose our ventures."*

I believe both paths are correct in many ways. The following is something I have only told one person, a man whom I felt to be a mentor and friend. We are not as close today as we were many years ago, but we still have remained in contact.

In the book "Glory Days," I had related how lucky I was to find my way into the computer industry through a neighbor who pointed me in that direction. Maybe not so much luck but a "predetermined path" to follow towards a very good career. The reason I say predetermined is something many will not believe but try to have an open mind. Not too long before my decision to enter the field of computers I went to a movie at the long-gone Eric Theater in Fairless Hills. As always, I purchased my ticket and got in line to enter the theater. While standing there my attention was drawn to the back of the ticket. There was a logo (a large globe,) and the company name GLOBE TICKET COMPANY. This logo and name literally jumped out at me as big as life so I couldn't help but notice. I was about 17 years old at the time, I didn't understand, and it meant absolutely nothing to me until many years later.

Over the next couple of years, I went to school and found myself in a very new and growing industry. Computers were becoming a necessity in every business, and I was fortunate enough (or lucky, if you will) to be there from the beginning (great timing.) As in any profession you find an entry position, learn a little and move on to a more lucrative position. The field was growing so fast that jobs were open everywhere and the lack of experienced personnel to fill them made it such a sellers' market that "job hopping" became a way of life to many.

Experienced personnel were often recruited by "headhunters." There was no need to search want ads and apply for a job. After about five years in the business, I received a call from a headhunter I had used in the past who had a "GREAT OPPORTUNITY" for me with a company called "GLOBE TICKET COMPANY." I went on the interview, accepted the position, and began a career that would take me on a ride I couldn't believe possible for a kid from a blue-collar family in Fallsington. A career that had taken me from the onset of automated ticketing to the 1980 Winter Olympics in Lake Placid. The experiences I was fortunate to have, the amazing people I had met and the travels that I would never have experienced. Oh, the ticket. It wasn't until about the end of my first year at Globe that I found the ticket stub in a drawer and remembered why I had saved it for all these years. Luck, timing, circumstances or pre-determination? I believe we are all given opportunities and a path for success but must first recognize them and then act.

Life is constantly changing. My career at that time was very demanding and required me to be away from family, friends, and home about 75 percent of the time, meaning that I was away nearly three weeks of every month. Many people would say look at all of places you travel to and the people you meet from all walks of life -- athletes, business executives, etc. I worked in the "entertainment industry" with arenas and ball clubs. Everything was so exciting, but it all comes with a cost and over time you begin to question the value and the toll it takes on your personal life. You truly do "sell your soul."

My wife was a saint and NEVER questioned or nagged me to spend more time at home (didn't know if this was good or bad) but after over 50 years of marriage it seems to have been a good thing. We had a daughter with whom I was missing a great deal of her growing up, and friends, some of whom I have known since high school and before. It was time for a change!

I changed my job and found a position in IT Management at the corporate level. There were some long hours but very little travel. At some point I was sure I would miss the excitement of what I had left, but it was the right thing for me to do. It gave me time with family and friends that to this day I wouldn't change for all the money in the world.

I immediately found myself getting involved in youth softball with my daughter, coaching Little League and working with her and a pitching coach to learn fast-pitch softball. After Little League she wanted to move to a more competitive

ASA Travel softball. This went on for many years from the age of 12 to 18 and took us all around the country playing ball at the state and national level…here I go traveling again but this time it is with family and friends. This is the kind of change that makes it truly worthwhile. This was also a great learning experience for my daughter. She learned about competition, how to win and lose as life is truly about both, and how you deal with those experiences is how you grow. She was able to travel and meet people from all walks of life. She learned the true meaning of commitment and the need to finish what you start. Never quit!

This also brought me back to friends and relationships that I am fortunate to enjoy to this day. In "Glory Days" many of us talked about places where everyone gathered. One of the most important in my life was the Fairlanes Bowling Center which to my, and many others' dismay, is no longer standing. This establishment was just like the show "Cheers" on TV. Everyone truly knew your name. You could walk in anytime and always find someone you knew whether they were bowling, having a cup of coffee at the luncheonette or just hanging around, knowing something would happen to make the time enjoyable.

My closest friendships with Jon Stroop, Russ Snyder and Dan Forester remain strong to this day, and Fairlanes was at the center of it all. We all became bowlers and competed at a high level. We were very fortunate to have been in competition with many "Old-Time" greats. Bowlers such as Fred Lening, who was one of the first members of the PBA and managed Fairlanes; Jack Winters, who even today holds world records that are in the Guinness Book of World Records; Vince Mazzanti Sr., who was a National Masters Champion as well as winner of many tournaments.

These men were a strong influence on many of us. We often bowled with Vince's son, Vince Jr., (Neshaminy HOF) with whom Dan Forester and I were teammates in a very competitive scratch league (no handicap.) Bowlers came from Philadelphia, North and South Jersey just to compete in this league. The older men gave us the nickname of "The Kids" and we became real tough to beat. One year we actually won the league and didn't even have to show up the last two nights. After Fairlanes was taken down I virtually quit the game. Vince Jr. went on to become a professional, competing successfully at the highest levels. Dan Forester and Russ Snyder continue to bowl. As a matter of fact, Dan Forester became a member of the Bucks County Hall of Fame for his bowling achievements.

Then there were other sports that we managed to keep ourselves busy with such as softball, which we managed to play into our early 40's. Russ Snyder started playing much earlier than many of us and he opted for "Fast-Pitch" softball through the steel mill league where many of the guys who worked for US Steel were able to compete and enjoy time outside of the mill. He later moved on to the very competitive Penndel Softball League, where he played for many years. Russ would join Danny, Jon Stroop, and I as we got involved in slow-pitch softball along with several other friends such as Terry Komatic, Jim Peto, Jim and Bruce Forester, and Gary Mahler. We played and won in the strong Mercer County Softball League as well as several leagues here in Bucks County.

As we got "older" we needed to find something to keep us going, GOLF! This is a game that I believe is the most difficult at which to become consistently good. I do NOT believe anyone can truly master the game. There are pro golfers who are the greatest of golfers but even they have bad days!

Russ Snyder is the only one of us to have played golf at an early age. He grew up living by the Fairless Hills Golf Course and began playing as a kid. A story he relates to us is when he first asked his dad for golf clubs, his dad thought he was nuts and would never use them, but Russ showed him differently. Russ was one of the few guys of our day that played on the Pennsbury golf team and was very successful.

This early start has given him the ability to be one of the best from the area. Terry Nau relates a story of how he won the Fairless Hills golf championship in 1966 because Russ was too young. You had to be 18. Russ was allowed to play in the first flight and beat Terry's 36-hole score by four shots, but Terry, 19 years old, prevailed over Joe McManus Sr. in the championship round. Terry got drafted three weeks later! Terry still likes to bust Russ's chops occasionally. Russ did win the Fairless Hills Club Championship the next year after he turned 18. Behind Russ came two great young golfers, Tom and Wayne Bartolacci. Tom played golf at East Stroudsburg, then went on to become one of the best local professionals. Brother Wayne went to Ohio State on a golf scholarship and played for three years. Wayne might have been the best of all the golfers from Fairless Hills!

Russ, along with myself, Jon Stroop and Dan Forester, play a couple of times each week. We travel by car up to two hours one way to some of the nicest golf courses in Pennsylvania, New Jersey, Delaware, and Maryland, never playing the same course twice in a season. We also find ourselves on "Golf Trips" to places like Myrtle Beach, Florida and recently to Maui in Hawaii. At first the golf trips were just the guys, but our wives eventually joined us on vacations, and that is when we moved our travels to more exotic places. We plan to continue playing for many years to come.

Looking back at all the things I was able to accomplish and sports in which I had been fortunate enough to compete is truly amazing. I reflect on the bowling and softball leagues and how competitive they were only to realize that those opportunities are gone. How many truly competitive bowling leagues and tournaments for amateurs exist today, or men's softball leagues? The answer is NONE! When we were growing up, you would pick up a newspaper and look at the sports section there was a rundown of individual bowling league scores. You could find stories and the outcome of softball games from five or six leagues in PA and NJ. These wonderful pastimes are gone, and I feel so blessed to have been a part of it all.

In the beginning of this chapter, I mentioned my reluctance to write this story, but now I am so happy that I did. When I think about the experiences with my daughter, that many people never get the opportunity to enjoy, and the friends I have that continue to be such great part of my life. It truly makes me realize "What a Wonderful Life It Has Been!"

CHAPTER 20

Greenwood Sisters Loved Scouting

*By Arta Greenwood, Class of 1965
& Cathy Greenwood, Class of 1967*

Arta: Girl Scouts played a big role during our developmental years in Fairless Hills. We had experiences and made friends that remain in our hearts today. In my years at Oxford Valley Elementary, I was a member of Troop 214. We met weekly at the Northminster Presbyterian Church on Trenton Road. I remember the weekly meetings as having some common tasks that were done. We all brought our dues (we think it was 25 cents a week) and delivered it to one of the leaders. We sat in a

ROAD TRIP—*The Girls Scouts Troop 260 from Bucks County took a field trip to Washington, D.C. in March, 1963. Pictured are, front row, left to right: Arty Armagost, Barbara Packer, Penny Pentecost, Darlene Koontz, Barbara Packer, Pam Pottersnak, Linda Picciotti, Darcy Briegel, Donna Strouse, Sandra Wilkinson, Suzanne Poorman, Shirley Ogden, Cathy Greenwood, Priscilla Trease.
Back row: Mel Greenwood, John Armagost, Margaret Armagost, Margaret Williamson, Susan Guarino, Lynn Thomas, Linda Olinger, Vivian Gleason, Lindsay Hawkins, Harriet Armagost, Arta Greenwood, Diane Armagost, Elena Bujak, Phillis Olinger, Signe Thomas, Mrs. Strouse, George Strouse, William Briegel.*

circle and learned something from our leaders. We always ended the meeting with that special circle of friendship and the passing of the hand squeeze.

There was a song for every activity! There were special ceremonies that involved lighting candles, a wonderful bridge that we got to cross over, and camping trips at Camp Tohikanee as well as selling Girl Scout cookies for 35 cents a box.

Cathy joined Troop 260 in third grade, when Brownies crossed the bridge to Junior scouts. That troop met at the Fairless Hills Community Center, corner of Trenton Road and North Oxford Valley Blvd., (now the Falls Township Senior Center). I may have joined troop 260 to make it easier for our parents to transport us to meetings.

The age of the girls in Troop 260 varied, but Diane Armagost and I were "Senior Scouts" in the troop and remained in Girl Scouting through graduation from Pennsbury High School. I even earned the Curved Bar, the highest award in scouting. I credit the leaders of both troops for inspiring us to reach high goals.

Cathy: I don't remember much of my scouting years prior to joining Girl Scout Troop 260. I was in Brownies and it was a fun experience. But Troop 260 was different. Mr. and Mrs. John Armagost were the leaders. He was, at that time, the first male leader in Pennsylvania and only the second in the nation. In fact, the local Girl Scout council would only allow him to lead a troop if he had a female assistant. His wife, Margaret, assumed that role.

When our parents, Melvin and Ida Greenwood, learned of the unique leadership of the troop, our mom volunteered to be an assistant leader and our dad became active in the Troop Committee. Actually, we feel comfortable stating that GS Troop 260 had more parental involvement than any other Lower Bucks County troop. As we got to know them, we learned that the Armagost family was well respected as active church members and had been involved with the Boy Scouts for years.

Girl Scouts is celebrating its 110th year in 2022 and has adjusted to the needs and demands of girls throughout the decades. But the purpose has been consistent. Through this organization, girls of all ages are encouraged to empower themselves. Scouting promotes character, compassion, courage, confidence, cooperation and active citizenship. Leadership and entrepreneurship opportunities are intertwined in troop activities.

Our troop was active in the foundational tenets of community service, learning first aid, camping and learning a wide variety of practical skills and goal setting by earning many of the badges available in the GS handbook. Executive functioning skills were fostered, years before they were generally promoted to our gender. Scouting encouraged us to use processfully to manage ourselves and the resources available to reach goals that we personally set. These skills led to the success of many of our troop members later in life.

We mentioned that camping is an integral part of our scouting memories. We attended day camp at Whispering Trees, at the corner of Olds Boulevard and Route 1, across from the sample Fairless Hills houses. Memories of those days are scanty or replaced due to the many days and nights we got to spend at the joint GS and BS camp Mr. Armagost had leased. This camp area was on the land of Heston Farm, maybe in Langhorne. The Armagosts would travel there to buy fresh eggs.

In one of the numerous conversations with the farmer, our troop leader asked if he could have a piece of the wooded farmland to make a camp ground. It was agreed upon and for one dollar a year, the land was leased. At first, it was the boy's domain but when our troop entered the family, the camp's clientele expanded. No one is sure how the big circus tent was acquired, but it served as a great sleeping area for many nights. The woods were a wonderful place for endless exploration.

There was a crick (creek) that ran through the property and the mess (food preparation) area was located on the banks of that stream. On each camping adventure, one patrol (rotating groups of scouts) would be assigned the role of shopping, preparing and cleaning up from our meals.

Other patrols would have other duties. These opportunities to work closely with a variety of members encouraged camaraderie and problem solving. A Kaper chart was used to delegate each patrol's role in the camping adventure. For those who are unaware of this tool, Kaper charts are a classic GS tool used by leaders to preclude the unavoidable bickering by some that the job they were assigned was unfair. One of the fun tasks was being in charge of the campfire entertainment. This is when stories and skits were shared by leaders and scouts and we would end the night in a positive mood for a much needed good night of sleep.

One camping adventure took us to another farm on Durham Road in Newtown, but memories are unclear as to the exact location or name of the owners. But, the creation of a major theatrical production remains paramount in our recollections. This farm had an in-ground pool in the middle of a large field. In a burst of creativity, the girls attending this camp experience decided to stage the show "Peter Pan" using the pool as the center of the plot. Where else could Captain Hook menacingly capture Wendy and stalk Peter Pan when she came to find the lovely Wendy? Both of the writers of this chapter had starring roles; Cathy as Peter Pan and Arta as Wendy.

Time was spent practicing and parents of the campers were invited to enjoy the show on the final day of our campout. That weekend had been a rainy one but the skies cleared as people gathered around the pool as the production proceeded. During the "theatrical masterpiece" narrated by another troop member, giggles and laughs could be heard from the performers and guests alike. Wet swords brandished by Hook and Pan could not stand up to the inevitable duel.

Crew members riding on the floating pool mattress slipped off into the water while traversing the imaginary alligator infested lagoon. After significant applause, attendees began to leave. Unfortunately, the rain had made the field a muddy mess. Cars and trucks had sunk into the soaked earth and young adults, including our sister Beth, and adults tried to push the cars from the parking spaces. We still laugh at this original mud bath that so many took that day. Happy memories of the whole experience fill our hearts.

We often reminisce about two special "field" trips that our Girl Scout troop took during those years. We worked as a troop to earn funds for a week-long trip to visit Girl Scout Round Up in Button Bay, Vermont during July, 1962. We remember passing out flyers to each house in our neighborhoods for some company. One couple said they didn't want junk at their door but when the purpose of the job was explained, they handed us a ten dollar bill to help us reach our goal. We also set up a booth at the annual Fairless Hills carnival held at the shopping center. The booth was covered in bamboo fencing and had a "skill game" of rings to throw at a case of coke bottles with the goal of ringing one. We don't remember how much money we made but do remember the fun of making and manning the booth. The other trip occurred during March, 1963, when we stayed two nights at the Rockwood National Girl Scout Camp in Potomac, MD and visited the national Capital and other historical places around Washington.

Girl Scout Round Up was a celebration of scouting that brought together 7,500 scouts and 1,500 adults from around the nation. Only a few girls from each council in the United States were chosen through a comprehensive application process so our leaders suggested we go as a group. Eighteen members of our troop went to Button Bay during that July in 1962. We traveled to Vermont in a motor caravan, cars carrying people and pickup trucks carrying camping gear. At that time, there were not very many rest stops on the roads and it was common to stop along the highway and head for the woods.

Through that experience a few of the scouts learned that they had not paid enough attention to the lessons of how to identify poison ivy. Not a fun experience on a summer field trip! We had a "uniform" we wore when we traveled anywhere as a troop. It was green shorts, white blouse, white sailor cap and a red bandana. On the bandana were the troop identification, town, and other identifying Girl Scout insignia. We created our own "march." Counting to 20 out loud, taking a step with each count, and then doing our special dance step as we said "we are just a little bit crazy." It was easy to identify our group no matter where we traveled.

Those making the trip were: Diane Armagost, Harriet Armagost, Elena Bujack, Phyllis Flohr, Vivian Gleason, Arta Greenwood, Cathy Greenwood, Susan Guarino, Lindsay Hawkings, Peggy Louis, Shirley Ogden, Linda Olinger, Suzanne Poorman, Pam Pottersnack, Donna Strouse, Lyn Thomas, Priscilla Trease and Judy Wilson.

We camped in an apple orchard on the farm of Representative James Adams of Fairhaven, VT. Besides visiting the Girl Scout encampment, we visited Fort Ticonderoga where we learned about history, the Stowe chairlift where we learned about fear and a real dairy where some of us successfully milked our first cow. Adults accompanying us included our leaders and parents and our sister Beth.

Additionally we were lucky to have Mr. and Mrs. Strouse, Ms. Joan Fleish (our nurse) and young Artie Armagost attend. The most vivid memory we have of the whole trip is when it was discovered that one of our troop members was highly allergic to apples and began to have serious breathing problems so she was rushed to the hospital. It was tense times until we finally learned she was stable and would be returning home with her parents.

Working on badges was part of the fun of scouting for us. When it was decided that our troop would travel to Washington, DC in March, 1963, we spent several months working on the "My Government" and "Traveler" proficiency badges. Congressman Willard S. Curtin, who had spoken at one of our investiture dinners, greeted our group of 20 girls and eleven chaperones at the Capitol. He also gave us a tour of the buildings and then invited us to spend some time in a session of the House of Representatives. More than a few of us were hoping we would run into the current President, JFK and his family, as they strolled through DC. Our troop made as many of the stops around DC that we could fit in during those two days, from Arlington National Cemetery to the White House. It was so exciting to spend two nights at the Rockwood National Girl Scout Camp in Potomac, MD. The history of Girl Scouting was written on the posters and plaques that lined the walls throughout the building.

As we reflect on our years in girl scouting, we realize that the friendships made and lessons learned during those years served as a foundation for our later life choices. Both Arta and Cathy pursued lives in service of others, teaching in elementary, high school and college for rewarding lifetime careers. Fairless Hills and the wonderful families involved in our GS Troops combine to fill a treasure chest of wonderful memories for the Greenwood girls. Thank you to all of our GS friends who helped us with details, and refreshed our memories.

CHAPTER 21

A Girl Just Has to Have Fun in Life!

By Linda Golden Granett, Class of 1964

Life began for me in Ewing Township (next to Trenton). My parents, Robert and Lily Golden, decided to move across the Delaware River to Lower Makefield when I was 4 years old (my sisters Joan and Barbara were 14 and 12, respectively). The new family property had many, many trees, along with a creek that flowed across the front and then down the far side of the land. There was a pond in the corner where the creek turned. A canal bordered the back of the lot. It was paradise for a young girl and her friends.

My dad, who worked as a builder, constructed a 2-story, 3-bedroom house with a 2-car garage on our property. He

TIGHT GROUP—Linda Golden Granett, bottom right, has remained in close touch with many of the friends she has made over the years.

finished the basement with a rec room, laundry room and storage. We lived close to the canal and it was an easy walk for me when I went ice skating in the winter. Many times I would meet up with friends there. There were a lot of empty lots on Glen Valley Road back then and I loved to wander through the lots, make huts and tunnels and tried to copy the Little Rascals adventures. I never worried about getting "snatched." Another great pastime for me was climbing trees, which I loved and would do all over the area.

My two closest friends were Gail and Donna Ferguson. Gail was my age and Donna was two years younger. They lived on Crown Terrace (not too far from me). For some reason we always seemed to play outside in their yard. We'd make houses for Barbie dolls and other play things. At night we'd often play hide 'n seek.

When I was 7 my father had a pool put in the back yard. It was an in-ground pool and I had many pool parties with friends. I have a picture, which was probably taken at a birthday party for me, showing Billy Ingram in the pool. I didn't go to the public pools because of having a backyard pool, and I sometimes missed that socialization.

Other kids in the neighborhood included John and Bill Hoffman (on Evergreen Road), along with Linda Grey and Doug Sickles (on Crown Terrace). Halloween was a big deal because of all the kids!

The Morrisville Shopping Center wasn't that far away. I could ride my bike down there. There were more stores and better stores than what is there now. The main store was either a smaller Lit Brothers or Dunham's. They had a small post office on the second floor, and my mother would send me there to buy stamps. I also remember a toy store (where I'd get my Barbies) and a variety store (handy when it was time for Christmas shopping). I remember an Acme store, too.

Another childhood memory was going to my maternal grandparents' house in Ewing where they had a mini-farm, and I would often stay overnight. They had a vegetable garden, fruit trees, and a chicken coop. Grandpop was always good for buying ice cream cones. Grandmom was a great cook. Grandpop hated TV commercials and when one came on he'd get up and turn off the sound on the TV until the commercial was over. No TV remotes back then!

I attended Makefield Elementary from kindergarten through 6th grade. On the first day of kindergarten I met Lily Gocolinski and Miriam Eifert. Because they were cousins, they moved Miriam to another class. Lily and I had lunch together every day, and my lunch was always a ham sandwich and a bag of chips. I always put the chips on the sandwich before eating. Note: I don't do that anymore! Lily went to a different school for 6th grade. I'm still friends with both of them!

Seventh grade was the meeting up year for kids from various elementary schools.

PENNSBURY FOREVER

Because a public bus came down Yardley-Morrisville Road, my parents allowed me to go to Trenton on Saturdays for shopping, movies and maybe lunch. Often I would meet up with Ron Chanutin, who was there for synagogue. We would just hang out and walk around the stores. Other times I would meet Diana Warren there. She was on another bus route. We would go to the movies and try to meet boys.

My summers (when I was 13, 14 and 15) were spent with my paternal grandparents who lived in Tuckerton, N.J. There was a boatyard right across the street and my father bought a larger boat for himself and a little outboard for me. There were lots of kids around my age and we sure did have fun. Right down the street was something like a Dairy Queen which became a hangout for the kids and had a jukebox. And there was a little beach further down. I also had an aunt and uncle nearby who loved to play cards. I was always kept busy.

I stopped going to the Tuckerton shore because I turned 16 in June and my father bought me a red Porsche convertible. It had two small seats in the back which could accommodate smaller size people. I can't remember the year of the car but it was mid-1950s vintage. To say I had fun with that car is an understatement. Every weekend I took girlfriends with me to the shore. I pretty much always went to Seaside. That was my parents' choice of shores since I was a very young child. Back when I had the Porsche, if you passed by another sports car coming from the other direction, you waved. And if the other car was a Porsche, nine times out of 10 we stopped and talked. After having that car, I've owned two more Porsches, two 280ZX's, a TR3, a Volkswagen and an MG midget.

I also enjoyed driving to Pennsbury football games in the Porsche. I usually took Ron Chanutin with me. But to the HS dances, other dances and shopping adventures in New Hope, I always took my girlfriends! Some of those friends, that I haven't already mentioned, were Barbara Allen, Sterling Gardner and Diane Beecham. I still see Sterling around at events. Diane Beecham (who was my maid of honor when I got married) and I have reconnected. Diane happily lives in Florida with her husband.

I was so interested in music and dancing (from watching Dick Clark's American Bandstand on television) that I started dancing at a young age. My memory is foggy but I think I first started dancing in Yardley, possibly in the Community Center on Main Street. Probably in 7th or 8th grade I brought in a portable record player, and a stack of 45's, and played music and danced during lunchtime (in the hallway near the cafeteria). I'd also bring records with me that I no longer wanted and sold them there.

Before we were old enough to drive, our parents would drive us to dances in Trenton. The first dance I remember was at

Cathedral HS in Trenton which I believe was for girls only. We did a stomp there (before the Bristol stomp and it was a little different) and it was loud…really loud! Then a friend of Elaine Davis, Joan Mauro, took us to the dance because she was a year older and had her license. In addition to high school canteen, there were dances at St Joseph's the Worker, Hugh Carcella, Edgely Fire Co, and the Bristol Fire Company. There were also more dances in Trenton and Hamilton.

Elaine Davis and I decided we were going to lighten selective portions of our hair. This was done when my parents were in Florida, my grandparents were looking after me, and I was at Elaine's. We used straight peroxide and too much of it. We really looked bad. I remember the next day going into Trenton for something to fix it. We had to hide the 2-color hair with rollers and bandannas. I got this thing called a "color comb." It was a great idea and it "sort of" worked. Our hair was doable and so we went to a dance. It was okay until I did a slow dance with a boy and the color came off on his face. How embarrassing! The next day I went out with my hair in rollers (again) and a scarf over my head and bought real hair dye!

Another high school friend was Cindy Borden (class of '66). Cindy's mom was so sweet and very encouraging to me regarding any self-doubts I had. Cindy also had an aunt who lived in Princeton. That opened up a whole new world for me. The main thing I remember about her aunt is that we'd get in her car and she'd drive us around and she believed in driving slow… real slow!!! Everyone behind her was tooting their horns and she'd just ignore them. And we really ended up with a long line behind us! Another memory is that Cindy and I joined a group who were doing some kind of dancing outside in a big circle. I think they were doing a type of folk dancing and they were people of all ages. Only in Princeton (by a main road) would you find such a thing!

We would go roller skating at the rink on Lalor Street in Trenton. I know we got dropped off there (because we weren't driving yet) and I know sometimes we walked home which was pretty far. We were never scared to do things that could have ended badly! And especially when my parents weren't around and it was a case of "what they don't know…"

I became friends with June Davies, who lived in Yardley. She was a year younger and we both enjoyed cars…me with my Porsche and June had a VW. We had a lot of adventures together. Through June, I met Sterling Gardner. June's parents were great and had me over for dinner and included me in excursions. They owned a weekend home (in the Poconos, I believe) and I got to see "dirty dancing" just like in the movie.

Fast forward to graduation and attending Rider College (now Rider University). I attended Rider for three semesters and then married John (Jack) Granett (Pennsbury class of '65). We had two children (John and Julie) and moved around a lot (PA, NJ and Indiana). I worked for Mercer Medical Center, Starr Tours, Merrill Lynch, and then was self-employed. Jack and I lost our son at age 19 in an auto accident which contributed to our divorce. Jack is now deceased. My daughter Julie works in Lawrenceville, N.J. I live in Morrisville and am retired. I still do some dancing but at this point in life I am more interested in going to oldies shows. I continue to stay in contact with quite a few of the girls and we get together when we can. And I continue to stay in touch with those who are further away. Unfortunately, some have passed away. It amazes me that I met Lily and Miriam the first day of kindergarten and we're still friends!

CHAPTER 22

Moments to Remember...

By Karen Bopp, Class of 1969

Our family history began when my paternal great-grandparents emigrated from Germany to the Trenton, New Jersey area. Their grandson, my dad, Carl Bopp, was born in 1919. He grew up and attended Trenton schools.

My maternal great grandparents emigrated from present-day Ukraine and settled in Pennsylvania, in the little village of Oxford Valley, where they purchased land along Route 1, also known as Lincoln Highway. There they began farming on their seven-acre farm. My mom, Olga Chychota, their granddaughter, was born in Trenton in 1922, and lived there until the untimely death of her mother when

CUTE KIDS—Ken, Karen and Carl Bopp grew up in the village of Oxford Valley that predated Fairless Hills.

she was only seven years of age. At that time, she and her younger siblings, Stella and Raymond, were sent to live with their grandparents on their Route 1 farm. My mom and her sister and brother would begin attending Fallsington schools and eventually graduated from Fallsington High.

My dad had cousins living in the Fallsington/Oxford Valley area where he would often visit. They were Ed, Will, and Hannah Drews. When my dad came to visit during the winters, the cousins would go ice skating on a nearby swampy area that years later became part of the Fairless Hills Golf Course. Since my mom was a school friend of Hannah Drews, she would often join the Drews and go skating. Eventually, Olga would be introduced to cousin Carl, and over time they would begin dating. After their courtship, they married in August of 1941.

During WW II, my dad served in the Army Air Corps and was stationed in Walla Walla, Washington. During her first pregnancy my mom drove cross-country to join him. It was there where my oldest brother Carl (Pennsbury class of '61) was born. Dad was later transferred to Avon Park, Florida where he served until he was discharged from the Army.

Upon returning to Oxford Valley, my parents rented a portion of the farmhouse on Messer's Farm which was located off Oxford Valley Road on present-day Devon Road in Fairless Hills. While they were living at the farmhouse, my second brother Kenny (Pennsbury Class of '63) was born. The boys attended school in Fallsington, and later the newly-built Pennsbury schools in Fairless Hills. Six years after Kenny was born, I arrived in 1951 and our family was complete.

When I was 10 months old, we moved into a house that my dad and uncle built on a one-acre lot that was part of my great-grandparents' Route 1 property. The new house was located on Lincoln Highway. Following the sale of the Messer Farm, the old farmhouse where we had lived became headquarters for Danherst Corporation.

Along Route 1, in front of my mom's grandparents' house was a produce stand where they sold mainly apples, but also raspberries, currants and eggs. They also raised chickens on the farm. After we moved into our new house, our family was able to help with the planting of several new crops like corn, tomatoes, pumpkins, strawberries and cucumbers, which would also be sold at the stand. For many years, when my brothers and I were old enough, we would help out at the farm and the stand for extra spending money. If we got into trouble, we would be sent to pull extra rows of weeds as our punishment.

Even after the old farm was sold my parents continued to grow crops in our yard, and I would set up a table to sell the produce on our front lawn. Our backyard was often visited by a variety of wildlife thinking that the garden and crops were planted just for them.

Growing up we attended the non-denominational Oxford Valley Chapel. It was located on Route 1, on the opposite side of the highway from farmland that is now the Lincoln Plaza Shopping Center. This quaint little church was built in 1899 and originally had only 10 members. In 1945, Pastor Philip Weiss was asked to hold services on Thursday and Sunday evenings. He accepted the request and commuted from Trenton. Eventually he and his family moved into an apartment in an old farmhouse on Route 1 that later became Gallagher's Trailer Park.

In 1953 the Roosevelt Drive-In Theater was constructed in very close proximity to the Chapel. On summer nights, if there were evening services, you could see the movie playing from the church grounds, which probably made for some distracted congregants!

In the 1950's, as the population steadily grew, so did the little church family. By 1956 the tiny chapel was bursting at the seams. Danherst Corporation donated two acres of land on Bristol-Oxford Valley Road, near the Twin Oaks section of Levittown, allowing for the building of a new and larger church. Pastor Weiss resigned his job in Trenton and entered the ministry full time at the brand new "Oxford Valley Chapel." That church still holds services today at that same location. The old, vacated Chapel became the headquarters for the notorious Breed motorcycle gang.

Not far from the old Chapel stood Langhorne Speedway. On Sundays, crowds of spectators filled the bleachers to watch the races on what was known as the fastest mile-long dirt track in the country. Many famous drivers would come to participate in those races, and the sound of roaring engines could be heard for miles around. Once a year they would also hold weeklong motorcycle races on that dirt track that drew thousands of bikers from across the country. One year we even found some of the bikers sleeping on our front porch! Since the small Moon's Motel was next door to our house, and probably had no vacancy, some of the bikers ventured onto our porch to find their sleeping arrangements.

In the late 1940's, Morrisville Airport operated under the name of Aero Dusting Corporation and was run by brothers Norm and Bob Hortman. In addition to giving flight instruction and performing aircraft maintenance, they did crop-dusting for King's Farms and other farms in the area. They also assisted the Falls Township Fire Company with their annual children's Christmas party held at a local restaurant. Before the party one of the pilots would take Santa, who was a member of the fire department, up in a small plane to do a flyover to wave to all the children. After the plane landed, Santa would be taken by a fire truck to the party to hand out gifts to the waiting children. Bob eventually left the company and it was re-named Hortman Aviation. Norm, a senior TWA captain whom my dad knew well, would occasionally take my dad and I up for short flights in a small Piper Cub or a Cherokee. We had a bird's-eye view of the area and it was impressive seeing the large freighters docked at the Steel Mill looking so small. I missed those sightseeing adventures when the airport closed in 1970.

Aside from the temporary residents at Moon's Motel there were few houses or families near our house. Across Route 1 was the Stockert family with three Pennsbury graduates. Ernie was the oldest, then came Barbara, and Sandy was the youngest. There were also some families arriving with their mobile homes to the newly-formed Brian's Trailer Park. A little further up Route 1 (where the Falls Township Police Station is today) was the Reedman's car lot where all the new cars were dropped off to be serviced and readied for sale at their dealership further south on Route 1. One snowy day my dad discovered a lone car in our front yard. Since the tire tracks led back to Reedman's lot, dad walked across the street and asked, "Are you giving away cars today?" Needless to say, they were not and were shocked to see the car on our front lawn. Somehow it had slipped into gear and slid across Route 1. It was only prevented from hitting our house by a low stone wall in our yard, and luckily hadn't caused an accident on the Route 1.

Having no children my age near the house, I grew up playing baseball, football, and wrestling with my older brothers and their friends—if they would let me! I also learned how to shoot a BB gun, a .22 and a bow and arrow. I played with model airplanes and learned how to drive a tractor. I especially enjoyed playing engineer and running the Lionel "O" gauge model trains on the large elaborate train platform that was set up year-round in our basement.

When I started school, I met my first friend, Sharon Robinson, in kindergarten at the Fairless View Elementary School, and we still keep in touch to this day. Other classmates were John Wilson, Tom Painter, Alicia Byzek, Linda Byers, Charles Rolison, David Evans, Cindy Cutshall, Karin Lindblom and Mike Semeraro. Ms. Hislop (first-grade) and Ms. Campbell (third-grade) were two of my favorite teachers. Inspired by them, I majored in Elementary Education at Kutztown University. I wanted the future generation to enjoy learning as much as I did in their classrooms.

Our principal, Mrs. Buckley, was quite progressive and had us change classes in fourth through sixth grades. We had different teachers for English/Social Studies, Math and Science. She felt changing classes and teachers would help prepare us for the middle school format. We also studied French, which was unusual at the elementary level, then and now. Some other memorable teachers at Fairless View were Miss Hess, Mrs. Heatherington, Mr.

Houser, Mr. Westcott, Mrs. Skamser, Mr. Krespach and Mr. Bugay.

Since Route 1 was the dividing line for middle school attendants, I would now be assigned to attend Charles Boehm in Lower Makefield for four years. Almost all of my friends from elementary school would be going to William Penn in Fairless Hills, so now I had to make all new friends at my new school. Some of those new friends were Chris Kozak, Cherie Felser, Janet Young, Ginny Glatz, Kathy Luckie, and Dagmar Pospisil.

It was great when I was reunited with all of my Fairless View and Charles Boehm classmates at the High School for 11th and 12th grades. Some memorable teachers for me from Boehm and the high school were Mr. Ackerman, Mr. Ody, Mr. Gunderman, Mr. Kelly, Mrs. Nolan, Mr. Minsky, Miss Harrison, Mrs. Rago, and Mr. Picciotti. They helped pave the way for their students' future successes. When I was in high school my mom and I loved to attend the PHS football games. Because our team often had to travel long distances to play the more competitive teams, we would either drive to those games or ride the bus that was often provided. Mom and I were the sports' fans in the family!

A major event occurred close to home in the summer of 1967 when Graeber's Lumber Yard on Route 1 caught fire. We were awakened by all the sirens at two o'clock in the morning and we could see the towering flames and thick black smoke from the front lawn of our house. Since there were no fire hydrants nearby, about 15 fire trucks and tankers and 150 firefighters were called to battle the fire. The blaze caused more than $250,000 in damage and leveled the saw mill and storage area at the lumber yard. The raging fire also damaged six units of the adjacent Ace Motel. Both Graeber's and the motel were rebuilt after the fire.

My parents and I lived in our home on Route 1 until 1973. We then moved to a house off of Stony Hill Road, about three miles away where I still live today.

So many things have changed or disappeared that were part of our youth. I remember all the places we used to shop like Pomeroy's, Grant's, Woolworth's, Kresge's, Lit Brothers, Gimbels, and Strawbridge's. There was Big C, Two Guys, and Butch's Market that sold the green, yellow, blue, and pink baby chicks at Easter.

Most of the places where we ate or bought take-out food are also gone, like Burger Chef, Steer Inn, Roy Rogers, Rainforest Café, Seafood Shanty, and Chicken Delight.

My summer job was at the S&H Green Stamp Store where you traded in your books of collected stamps for merchandise. It was conveniently located a parking lot away from our side yard, making an easy walk to work for me.

I remember having a party line for our phone where we shared a phone number with another family. We had exchanges and not area codes. Our exchange was

Windsor, and a phone number would look like this, WI 6-6627.

Moving into early adulthood, I danced and partied with my friends at places like The Fairless Inn, The Thunderbird, Lambrou's, DeNucci's, Vernon's, The Woodbourne Tavern, and Big Daddy G's.

My parents were hard-working and devoted to their family. My brothers and I are so grateful for the guidance, support and sacrifices they made which allowed all of us to attend college and pursue our goals. (Carl and Kenny both attended Penn State and I attended Kutztown University.) Carl spent 38 years at Princeton University as an electronics specialist. Kenny, after serving in Vietnam, returned to college and received his teaching certificate and taught for over 25 years. After graduating, I found there was no longer a demand for full-time teachers in our local schools, so I did substitute teaching for several years at Pennsbury and Council Rock. Often when subbing at the middle or high school level a teacher would ask me for my "Hall Pass," thinking I was a student due to my height, or lack thereof, at an inch under five feet tall. I have continued working with children and presently work at before and after school programs.

Our dad worked at Charles Shick and Company in Trenton until his retirement. He always encouraged "his little girl" to learn about tools and cars and to become involved in many different types of projects. Likely, thanks to him, I was brave enough to enroll in a Shop Class Club in school. I was the only girl in that club.

Dad had a full and productive life. He died in 2010 at the age of 91.

Mom was an amazing seamstress who made most of my clothes from the time I was a baby through high school and she made costumes as well. For many years she was employed in the Custom Drapery Department at Sears. She also crocheted and liked to do many kinds of crafts. She had a bubbly personality and a fun-loving spirit. Earlier in 2022, she died less than two weeks after reaching her 100th birthday.

For many of us, it feels like time has gone too fast. We are often saying, "Remember the good ol' days." Although we have all chosen different paths to travel, the laughter and tears shared with our families and friends remain treasured memories. We have truly lived "Moments to Remember."

CHAPTER 23

Rob McBryar Learned Lessons on the Mat

By Aly McBryar, Class of 2003

Sports in Fairless Hills has always been a staple of the community, especially a way in which fathers and sons could bond and friendships among adults and kids could be made. Baseball, football, wrestling, whether formal or just pick up games in someone's yard or at the neighborhood school was the thing to do whenever there was free time.

"I played sports from the first time I could remember," my father, Rob McBryar (Class of '71), fondly remembered when I sat down to talk with him about his days at Pennsbury High School and growing up in Fairless Hills. "I always played baseball for FHAA (Danherst Corporation) and dad was the coach as well as the other neighborhood dads. They were tough guys to play for because they were all WW II veterans and worked at the mill so as a kid, I always thought they could spit nails and crack rivets."

Among children of that era, there was always a deep-seeded desire to succeed not just to make their parents proud, but because winning was very important to everyone.

As grade school turned into junior high and then high school, sports would consume more and more of Rob's time and energy, mainly football, wrestling and track.

"I was a discus thrower and threw shot put in 8th and 9th grade at William Penn

FAMILY AFFAIR—Aly McBryar's children, Jackson and Georgia, always feel good when grandpa Rob McBryar is around.

and Medill Bair," Rob said. "I also during those years played football for the great Al Matuza Jr."

As a new Duke graduate, Matuza signed on as an assistant coach on Chuck Kane's varsity football staff and worked with the junior high squad.

"Al brought a fresh look and a hard-nosed mentality," Rob said. "He was always expecting your best and definitely told you when you weren't quite up to snuff. Back then, coaching was different than it is nowadays. Back then if you did something and they said you were doing it wrong, they took you to the side and told you what you did wrong and they weren't happy."

Rob recalled that his coaches were never demeaning to players, but they didn't mince words and what they were saying certainly got across, loud and clear.

During a scrimmage, Rob's short football career came to an end when the 9th grade team was scrimmaging the JV team. On a trap play, "I broke through the line and nobody blocked me so I couldn't get down fast enough. Before I knew it, WHAM! I got run over by the pulling guard and broke my left ankle."

That day, as luck would have it, Rob's dad was there watching practice after his shift at the mill ended and saw the whole thing happen. One to neither mince words, nor sugar-coat anything, his dad walked out on the field and said, "Come on boy! Get up and let's go to the hospital," Rob recalled with a fond smile and shaking his head a bit. "I hobbled to the Jeep (with dad's help), went to Dr. Smith's office and then over to the hospital for it to be set."

His left ankle would never be the same, forcing Rob to switch sports and focus more on wrestling.

Although Rob started wrestling at William Penn in 8th grade, it wasn't until high school where he would find his niche, wrestling for JV and Varsity, lettering in both at the position of heavyweight. His crowning achievement was not just wrestling for the great John Kopack and Bill Pewterbaugh, but pinning his opponent to win a match for himself and the team.

Rob recalled that the dual-meet was at Pennsbury on Saturday, December 20, 1969. It was in the third period of the match and pressure was mounting on him to do something drastic to win against Frank Seier from Bethlehem Catholic.

"As clear as day I can remember Kopack standing on the mat with me nose-to-nose, pointing his finger at me and saying 'REGARDLESS OF WHAT HAPPENS, DON'T GET PINNED!' "

This was the final match of the dual-meet and Pennsbury would win, as long as Rob didn't get pinned. That was more than enough incentive to instill the fear and motivation that Rob needed to not let his coach and teammates down. Even so, during the first period, Rob slipped and fell, which resulted in his opponent scoring a two-point takedown.

"He rode me out the rest of the period

KEY MOMENT—*Rob McBryar gets advice from coach John Kopack prior to pinning his opponent in a 1969 dual-meet against Bethlehem Catholic.*

which gave me time to compose myself and strategize for the second and third periods," Rob said.

For the third period, the opponent was in the top position while Rob was on the bottom, giving Rob an advantage due to his upper body strength. With the words of Kopack repeatedly running through his head, a golden opportunity presented itself for Rob to win the match.

"He got too high over top of me and over my shoulder. I just reached back and grabbed him and threw him over me and that was it." Rob won the match with a pin and as he walked off the mat, Kopack put his arm around Rob's neck and hugged him. Next to winning the match, getting the love and admiration from Kopack was the best thing that could have happened.

As always in the crowd was Rob's dad cheering him on, which instilled the same fear and motivation to succeed.

"My whole family was watching from the bleachers and it sounded like the roof was going to blow off of the gymnasium. I think winning for my dad was the best part. It mattered to me that I won, but my winning and seeing my dad so proud of me was what I really cared about and what really mattered."

After Rob's triumphant win and stardom was publicized in the *Courier Times*, disaster struck on the wrestling mat one week later. At a meet in Boiling Springs, PA, a wrestler from Shamokin would deliver Rob an injury from which he would never fully recover. As Rob reenacts the moves of the match with his grandson Jackson on the living room floor, he describes the events vividly.

"I went into him collar and elbow and then I got underneath of him to lift him up. When I had him up I slipped on whatever was on the mat, either sweat or blood that wasn't cleaned up from the match before and we both fell on my right ankle."

After Rob heard a crack, he knew he was in trouble and the match was over, as well as his wrestling days for the next two weeks. Although he was dressed for the meet the following week vs. Truman High

School, he was sidelined and had to watch his teammate Mark Winder take his place.

"He wrestled pretty damned good that day, but he didn't win. He never got pinned, but he lost on points," Rob said. Two weeks after the initial injury, Rob was back in the wrestling room getting his ankle taped by Coach Pewterbaugh so he could practice and then compete in the match the following weekend.

The final dual-meet of the season against Council Rock would be Rob's last for Pennsbury. Rob would not be victorious, but he refused to go down without a fight and Kopack wouldn't have it any other way. Rob would wrestle Mike Evans who was in Rob's opinion probably the best in the area at that time.

"Mike had me at a huge disadvantage because I only had one good leg to wrestle on and he also had grown men from the mill to practice against, men who also worked with my dad."

Although friendly and not so friendly wagers happened at the mill on a regular basis, this one was different. The men Mike practiced against at the mill knew how big and strong he was and also that he outweighed Rob by about 30-35 pounds, so Mike was a shoo-in to win and perhaps even pin Rob. So, the men at the mill, including Rob's dad, set up a wager for this meet.

Rob was aware this was going on and felt the friendly but serious pressure from his dad.

"I can remember him saying to me, 'Hey boy, I have money riding on this so DON'T GET PINNED!' " Rob remembered thinking, "Thanks for the confidence, Dad!" He knew he may not win, but he could not get pinned. If he lost but avoided getting pinned, his dad would win the bet and he would gain not just the respect of his dad, but of those who did not think he had a chance of winning. In the end, Rob got everything he hoped for. Even though he did lose the match he sure didn't get pinned, his dad won the bet and he gained everyone's respect.

After recalling the stories with smiles and a glint in his eye, Rob took a minute to reflect on his time with John Kopack, a great coach and great man. "Kopack was a very dedicated coach and all he wanted out of you was the best that you could give. He was a little guy with a big heart," Rob said, tearing up. "I ran into Mr. Kopack years and years later and wouldn't you know it, he still remembered me. It made me feel good and I thanked him for everything he did for me. I miss that man." (Kopack lives in Florida nowadays.)

That would not be the end of the McBryar name in Pennsbury sports. Rob's oldest daughter Jennifer would play softball for Pancho Micir in 9th grade and also at the JV level for Joe Warne up to her junior year. Then it was my turn. A few years later in 1999, I would follow in Jennifer's footsteps and also play for the fun-loving Pancho Micir and his assistant coach, Cliff Stout, a Pennsbury English teacher who is now retired.

Mr. Micir was so much fun. He and Coach Stout were always so supportive and happy. It was such a great experience and such a happy time for me. I played junior varsity and then made the varsity team in my senior year. I didn't play much but my time with the Bristol Township Force travel team helped me earn nearly a full softball scholarship to Holy Family University. I majored in History and also focused on Political Science. I acquired a Master's Degree in Special Education and that led me to a full-time teaching job at Pennsbury in 2007.

I am the lead advisor for Pennsbury's Wall of Honor and work closely with alumni who have served in the military. This is my eighth year working on the Wall of Honor. Playing sports at Pennsbury was nice but my real and true love at my alma mater is working with veterans and fellow teachers to build up and improve our Wall of Honor exhibit on the West Campus.

My father, my mom, and my two children, Jackson and Georgia, are the most important things in my life. Fairless Hills is just an All-American blue-collar town and a great place to raise a family. It's a weird thing when you try to explain Fairless Hills to someone who was not born and raised here. It's something that's born not just into your body, but it is part of your soul and identity. Fairless Hills is definitely a place and a way of life which no matter if you leave, it always brings you back home.

CHAPTER 24

The Draft Shadowed Our Lives

By Bob Keiger, Class of 1965

At our senior party in early June of 1965, I was introduced to the Rolling Stones' iconic rock song "*Satisfaction*" by a couple classmates singing a cappella. Life was great—finished with high school, get a summer job and off to college with no daily supervision and a 2-S deferment—*registrant deferred because of activity in study*. I would study to become a chemical engineer in college at the University of Delaware. This is what life was all about, right?

September 1, 1965—The Vietnam War raged on and more and more American troops were conscripted—900 Americans in Vietnam in 1960 rising to 385,000 in 1966, eventually topping out at about 540,000 in 1968. And those draftees came disproportionately from young men who chose not to go to college and they were especially young black men. Colleges across the nation protested the war, draft cards were burned and chapters of Students for a Democratic Society popped up at many college campuses. ROTC was mandatory at the University of Delaware and even in this moderate sized conservative school the ROTC building was burned.

But I was still pretty safe from much of this for the next four years. I just had to go to class (mostly), study and have fun on weekends (football games in the fall wearing my London Fog raincoat that would fit two pint bottles of Bacardi in the pockets). I was on schedule to graduate in June 1969 when all of this Vietnam stuff would likely have resolved itself, find a job and then get on with life. Just the next phase in the continuing story of those "Glory Days" of growing up in Bucks County, PA. A really good plan but not exactly what unfolded.

In college you are on your own—pretty much responsible only to yourself and your moral compass. And unlike growing up in Levittown, I was exposed to a diversity of people and ideas for the first time, challenging what I knew as the "norm." I can recall many conversations not only in classes but also in the dorm lounge and the student center—listening, learning and trying to process all this new information and what I might believe. The Vietnam

War was leaving a lasting effect on American culture. I began to challenge the honor and morality of war and the efficacy of the US government and our elected officials.

And it just kept getting worse. Race riots in 1967 in Newark, NJ and Detroit, MI. MLK is assassinated in April 1968 and then Robert Kennedy killed two months later. What the hell is happening here?

I finished my undergrad degree (Math—what job was I thinking about?) in June 1969 and got married a couple weeks later. This was immediately followed by a stint in graduate school. On December 1, 1969 I sat glued to the TV to watch the first draft lottery—I drew No. 63 in the first "ping pong ball birth date drawing."

In May 1970, we all witnessed the Kent State massacre. I boycotted my finals, still have the arm band I wore in respect and memory and protest for that event. It was an emotional and intellectual tipping point. College kids shot on campus for protesting. Are we now finished?

As a result of my lottery "win," I was called into the U.S. Army on April 7, 1971. The war was winding down, conscriptions were decreasing but troops were still being sent to Vietnam. I rejected Officer Candidate School and was assigned to the infantry. I considered Canada but decided to wait until I received my final orders after training at Fort Dix, N.J. and Fort Polk, LA. While I was not a very good fit for military life, I did come to later realize that the discipline and order in the military was something from which I ultimately benefited.

The time in training also awakened me to racial conflicts and issues that were never a part of growing up in Lower Bucks County. Half the draftees in my unit were African Americans but they certainly were not half the national population. I do recall a life-changing incident from Fort Polk. We had a weekend pass and three of us went to Lake Charles, LA—me and two friends originally from Pakistan had been together since training at Fort Dix. We took a bus there and we sat toward the back of the bus at the direction of my friends. When we got to the lake there was clearly a white area and a black area. But here we three were—one white and two "medium brown"—their words—who together did not clearly fit in either group. So we hung out in the neutral DMZ between the two. This is who we are? And perhaps we might be sent to fight and maybe die in Vietnam—to preserve what?

At the conclusion of Advanced Infantry Training at Fort Polk I received my final orders. The time was here for the decision. I was a most fortunate draftee in as much as I was recruited out of training by The Old Guard (the ceremonial unit of the US Army at Fort Myer in Arlington, VA). I literally and figuratively dodged a bullet. But those 2.6 million soldiers who served in Vietnam were not as fortunate. I was very lucky and I knew it. I never had to make that fateful decision. But one interesting change did come out of this Vietnam mess in July 1971—if it weren't for the draft, 18-year-olds might not have been granted the right to vote. I left the Army with an Honorable Discharge on April 6, 1973. But one important aspect of that service lingers. Like many draftees at the time, I did not feel comfortable either revealing or talking much about my time in the Army. But over time I have become more proud of that military service.

So now what—I am 26, married (Bonnie Secor from Pennsbury, whom I first met in 7th grade at William Penn and later accepted her invitation to the PHS Turnabout Canteen in 1964), unemployed (never had a job except for the Army), angry about so many things and living in an apartment in Alexandria, VA. It was time to follow the advice of the The Silhouettes and "GET A JOB." I could prove the Pythagorean theorem, reduce a matrix to the identity matrix, explain Green's Theorem, solve a differential equation, take apart and reassemble an M-14 and an M-16 rifle and perform "Fix bayonets to the beat of a drum" so I did the only logical thing—I went to work for an insurance company, GEICO. So much for learned skills.

I was fortunate to survive a near bankruptcy of GEICO and then as it rebuilt, acquire several great mentors who had a significant influence on both my business career and my life. Everything changed in 1978 when our first son was born. And again in 1982 when our second son arrived. Both to a very different world and environment from which I grew up. Once again I found myself in a position with no contemporary skills to partner with Bonnie to now raise our sons in this very different world—we would certainly be guided by the life and experiences from our childhood. But you just can't go back to that place where you once lived because so much has changed since then that it's no longer the same place anymore. The challenge was now to not just bring it back the way it was but take the core values of that childhood and given the contemporary environment try to improve on it for my family.

Perhaps the world was indeed simpler then. This is what encouraged me to contribute to both "*Glory Days*" and "*Pennsbury Forever*." The stories from the first book remain great to share with those folks with whom I grew up. They elicit some good memories and perhaps some not so good. We own those stories and will always cherish them. But things have changed since then—really changed, and we must continue to adapt and move forward.

PART THREE
Extracurricular Activities

The PHS marching band has long been internationally recognized as one of the premier marching bands in the United States, and it has performed with distinction on five continents.
(Collage designed by Barry Miner)

CHAPTER 25

Musical Memories Never Fade

By Barry Miner, Class of 1964

Arlen Wolfe…a bit scary name for a teacher you haven't met, and the one designated to start "trying" to teach you (*you unwilling kid you!*) your first clarinet lesson at William Penn. After school no less, and baseball sign-up is just starting again, and the pool will be opening soon! This is when I really learned how to cuss (perfected later after almost thirty years in the Army!) However, the story does go on.

My *experiences* at Pennsbury are embedded in my soul, as *music* came to be, even though that "sounds" a tad dramatic, how else could I explain it? I never became a professional musician and did not major in it in college; quite the contrary. Remember now, there are seven decades of Pennsbury connections involved here: from Elementary through High School and then continuing with recurring linkups with classmates, friends, teachers that became friends, and with Veterans especially, and through the Pennsbury Wall of Honor Foundation efforts that keeps us tied to PHS Alumni Veterans, school administrators and so on…and I haven't lived in Pennsylvania since 1968!…my military career took me to other places around the world! I really think it is remarkable that so many of us who graduated from Pennsbury in the 60's are still connected and routinely stay in touch. But I digress.

I had taken some piano lessons, so I was not totally unfamiliar with reading the music and understanding the basics that Mr. Wolfe was pushing on me, poor man. As I mentioned in Chapter 39 of Terry Nau's Book *Glory Days,* my mom Mabel (who never took a piano lesson in her life, learned to play piano on her own, could play anything by ear, and was a self-taught musician) gently nudged me toward the joys of music. She led the children's choirs at church when we lived in Philly, and then at Fairless Hills Methodist she led the cherub choir and junior choir, and often played for the church on Sundays. Many of my PHS 1964 Classmates remember her fondly. She even got my dad to join the adult choir (*he really could sing*). And my brother Ron, who sort of led the way for me into the Army (reluctantly) had a great voice, auditioned with a recording company in Trenton, performed as a soloist at all Church and Community shows, was a DJ at 16 for a local radio station, but decided to elope two times while in High School, with two different gals. And, only after a 14-state missing persons search, the authorities found him and neighbor Jo Ann in Connecticut, working on a farm. My Dad and my uncle Bob had to go fetch them.

Soon thereafter my brother quit school, joined the Army, went to Korea, and served as a DJ on AFKN (Armed Forces Network Korea) out of Seoul. (By the way, both marriages were annulled), Ron led and still leads a sort of "off the grid life," but it has been a good one. Financially sound, a great family with kids and grandkids, a gold mine with his son Randy in Alaska, a huge house at historic Fort Seward, and an honorary PhD from The Colorado School of Mines after working there for 30 years running their labs and mining operations. Again, I digress, but so what.

So being a "band guy" did not endear you on the popularity scale at the time to fellow high schoolers, where at Pennsbury the public and "social" emphasis was on how well the football, baseball or basketball teams were doing. And rightly so. I still admire the Pennsbury emphasis on sports…and…I brag to my friends about how Pennsbury was really a trend setter with women's varsity athletics. There is no comparison sports-wise to what my current non-PHS lady friends had in high school against what my female PHS Classmates had: Field Hockey, Swimming, Basketball, Softball, Track. And during my high school years, Pennsbury Athletics across the board did very well.

And at just about every major sporting event…*there was music!*

During my days at Pennsbury, *the music in the air was everywhere and was excellent.* Think about this (and you may have heard some of this before, but it warrants repeating I think)—a high school jazz band (yes, a *high school* jazz band!) from Pennsbury is the first ever high school band (maybe the only one ever?) invited to play at the Newport Jazz Festival in Newport, Rhode Island! This was a big-time event with about every major professional jazz musician gathered there (Lionel Hampton, Gene Krupa, Pete Rugulo, Quincy Jones, Miles Davis, Herbie Hancock, Dave Brubeck, John Coltrane, BB King, and many others). (I was a junior at the time, so 1963). And then to appear on the Johnny Carson Show in New York! This is like being invited to the Super Bowl, TWICE! And there isn't even an opposing team! You are IT!

And, to top it all off, there was a standing ovation at Newport and a highly commendable follow-up article in Downbeat Magazine for the Carson show performance. I know I will inadvertently leave some names out, but we had a great Jazz

PINNACLE MOMENT—Newspaper clipping from Pennsbury Stage Band's appearance at the Newport Jazz Festival in 1963. (Bucks County Courier Times archives)

Band, with the likes of Joel White, Jim Graham, Skip Green, Dave Auge, Glen Seruby, Dick Bartels, (Bartels and Seruby were the best hide hitters in the County and always did a "battle of the drummers" at events!), Frank Zuback, Steve Speiser, Joe Stoddart, Johnny Byzek, Bruce Edge, Bill Condon, Bruce Fye. If, big IF, you are an aficionado of music during the 50's and 60's, you will understand the significance of some of the interconnections we young high schoolers were exposed to during these times. Big bands were declining in popularity during the 60's, but those that prevailed were immensely popular and active and the very ones we (the PHS Jazz Band) were invited to play with. Stan Kenton, we were the first act before him several times at St John Terrell's Music Circus in New Hope and once in Philly.

Kenton had an inspiring band director playing lead trumpet for him then, Maynard Ferguson (a HS dropout at 15), whose jazz orchestra we later played with at the Music Circus, and in New York (where we also appeared on TV several times, as well as on Philly TV shows).

I don't know if Don Smith, our PHS Music Director had great connections or whether it was our own reputation, but I recall sitting in the high school band room with a few others talking to Don Smith and listening to him getting down and jammin' on the tenor sax, and in walks Quincy Jones. Jones gave the three or four of us there his famous play-along jazz album (which I still have) and told us *"Whatever you choose to do in the future, whether it's music or not, commit to do it well, or don't do it at all."*

We also played in New York on a field trip with the Charlie Barnet band, which once had Doc Severinson as lead trumpet, later to meet us on the Carson Show! And our PHS concert band and marching band were equally renowned, though less televised! The Pennsylvania Regional and State Orchestra and Concert Band competitions were always fierce. To get to play in these, a student had to go through multiple auditions, and "not everyone got a trophy!" PHS won many band-on-band competitions throughout the east coast, and PHS students repetitively prevailed in lead band positions. The PHS marching band—a Rose Bowl band, Macy's Parade band, Mummers Parade band, etc.,—is still one of the finest in the Nation. Our bands were then (62'-64') led by Don Smith (followed by John Mack who came over from Wilson, and we also had Henry Mancia and Fred Bevan added to our list of fine music teachers).

Don Smith, a professional jazz musician himself, was an assistant band director at Penn State before PHS, so a lot of the PHS Marching band routines under his tenure paralleled that of the Nittany Lions Blue Band. Our pre-game opening was marching in formation to "Hail to the Falcons" while in several rows stretching across the field, then all rows at a certain point would about face in synch and end up returning to center field and balanced on either side of the 50-yard line, then we stop, turn to our fans, and then play our Alma Mater and the National Anthem. Mr. Smith had the fun idea to let our bass drummer fail to make the about face and continue marching, then by himself into the end zone, and once realizing he was alone, he would scurry back into formation with his arms waving in the air. Always got a laugh, especially since the bass drummer was sophomore Bob Henry, who looked like he was smaller than the bass drum to begin with! Quite a sight.

I do miss the "band" days and the camaraderie it allowed, and some of us "band aids" have stayed in touch. I also think the discipline required to perform well in public (not to mention the wool band uniform, passed down to each new generation since the 50's) in a way, helped prepare me for the Army and other careers in business. Just like so many other character building, teaching, and mentoring things we had at Pennsbury. (By the way, PHS still has "Alumni Band" get-togethers and a few of the old folks, and some youngsters still "jam" at annual events). You can do that with music! You won't see many HS football players or B-Ball players out there scrimmaging in their 70's! Just sayin'.

Fellow band members Terry Wallace (trumpet) and Ralph Rhodes (drums), among other Classmates, still help me with the Veteran's activities at PHS and with the PHS Wall of Honor Foundation. My good friend Johnny Byzek (sax) went to the Citadel after HS, and he passed away much too early. Bruce Fye (bass) (a renowned cardiologist at the Mayo Clinic) and Frank Zuback (bass) and I still communicate, as I did with Bill Condon (trombone), who became a veterinarian, and who unfortunately passed away in 2017. I finally convinced Paul Weinberg (clarinet) to come to one of our Class of '64 Reunions, and he did attend our 55th, but sadly passed away a year later in 2020. (Paul was a very well respected and admired doctor in Philadelphia). And even though I wasn't a sports player in HS, some of my best Classmate friends were sports icons, and I am convinced they always did and still know the value of music in their lives (Art Lendo, Tommy Mazenko (that guy can dance, clearly taught by his wife Cindy (Class of '65)), Ken Medlin, John Quattrocchi, to name a few).

After my military career, and while working for a major Defense Contractor, I had a little additional time to reengage with my PHS '64 Classmates. My secretary Norma (she was a retired Army Sgt) helped a lot. And between us, by the time the 50th rolled around, we had found current contact info on all but about 70 Classmates: not bad for a class of 560! And, we had a tremendous turnout for our 50th! I have continued working the lists all these years, and today I am down to about 30 "unknowns"; 130 who are deceased, and there are 94 Class of '64 veterans now added to the overall PHS Veterans list of 524, which I keep with Terry Nau. Just for your own consideration (possibly the initial makings of another book), let your imagination think how my detective work in finding Classmates "might" have turned up some extremely interesting stories about the lives and good and bad fortunes of those I talked to or researched. Let me just say we had some unique and TV series-type stories in the Class of 1964. No Steven King stories (well maybe one), but possibly some Columbo's. Keep guessing who, why, and what? I'll never tell.

While I tried to go to annual Class Reunions, being in the Army and overseas, it was hard to track me down. The first "big one" I attended was the 30th. I had just married Debra a few days before and we had flown in from Germany to attend. We won the prizes for "who has traveled the farthest to attend" and for "the most recently married." We laugh about the several gal Classmates sitting together at the next table to us (all divorcees it turned out) and within ear shot of me and Deb one said "Geez, couldn't he have waited a few more days!" It was funny. Mary Lazur, in her humorous, cute, and acerbic way, also said to me later, "If we all knew you were going to be a Colonel and travel to so many cool places, you would have gotten laid a lot more in HS!" Thanks Mary, tell me now 40+ years later! What was funnier was that Classmate Bob Ball won the prize for "most recent" parent since his wife had just had a baby a few days earlier. Sadly, Bob passed away in 2020. Mary passed away in 2018; never recovered well from a car accident. But, these things happen and we can't stop the advance of time or the aging that goes with it, but I do hate it when I see an older person and then realize we went to high school together! I really thought growing older would take longer.

Getting involved with Class Reunions, especially the 50th and then the 55th, kept me engaged with good people, wonderful Classmates, and I apologize in advance for leaving any names out [Trish Gordon, Marge (Robinson) Wysor, Caroline (Beers) Simmons, Hank Hoffmeister (Chair), Paula (Wallis) White, Lorraine (Zach) Tucker, Joyce (McCann) Devaney, Mary Ann (Peart) Wolf, Adrienne (Roller) Rolan, Rick Plank, David Fox, Mary Beth (Logan) Morris, John and Penny (Reynolds) Armagost, Margie Bott, Ray Parker, Jody (Crosby) Johnston, Sue (Garey) Whitney, Wayne Guenther, Tom Mazenko, Ken and Jean (Kettler) Medlin, Art Lendo, John Quattrocchi]. Spouses and significant others included. Overall, quite a productive family! Still friends, still caring, still in touch.

Getting back to music everywhere, one of the most important contributors to my musical love journey was Mrs. Caroline Keller, Director of the Choral Groups, Choir and Falconaires, and a simply wonderful, caring, inspirational teacher, and friend. She knew my mom well. She was also very persuasive. She collared me one day (about two months before graduation) and said "Barry, I have a special Choral piece we are doing for the graduation ceremony, and I thought it would be a good idea if you could write a score for the orchestra to accompany the choir. Could you?" Two words came to mind… the first one was "Holy" (go figure the rest of that phrase). Well, you didn't say "no" to Mrs. Keller…so I acquiesced and then spent every waking moment for about two months writing the orchestra score to go along with the choral arrangement. I will say, I simply do not know how I did it. But it worked and was a success; and you can see me in the Yearbook directing orchestra and choir at graduation. I almost thought then about taking up music in college… nah, too many other fun things to do, and I had my heart set on becoming a lawyer. (If you read my chapter in Glory Days, you will see my life took another turn, it was a right turn!). Serving America!

So, there isn't enough room on these few allocated pages to tell all the great stories and experiences, therefore I will conclude by sharing a personal challenge with the readers, and I wish I could say this challenge is something that I have been successful at achieving over the years. But not

PENNSBURY FOREVER

the case. And, I can't stop trying. Maybe it is the drive, ethics, and good mentoring I had growing up in Bucks County and attending Pennsbury, and sharing my life with good people there that prompted this challenge. So here it is: Actively and consciously try to do something good for someone every day. The caveat is, it cannot be a routine act (like opening the door for someone); you must think about it, then do it. Everyday! Meet the challenge and you are paying it forward!

And please remember the words of Jackson Pollock—*"Love is friendship set to music."*

CHAPTER 26

'Forgotten' Era in Pennsbury Sports History

By Kevin Lendo, Class of 1966

Pennsbury High School turned eight years old in 1956. Then, in the two years from 1956 to 1958, the growing school served notice to the rest of the Lower Bucks County League that the Falcons were a force to be dealt with on the athletic fields. Coach Al Matuza's football team tied Neshaminy in 1956. And in 1957, the Falcons beat Neshaminy 7-6 and clinched the LBCL title. That also ended the Redskins' four-year streak without a league loss. PHS would not beat Neshaminy for nine more years. Coach Erle Baugher's Falcons would later shut out the Redskins 60-0 in 1966.

OVERLOOKED—Reggie Turner, a three-sport star at Pennsbury in the mid-1950s, has not YET been elected to the Pennsbury Athletic Hall of Fame. (Levittown Times *photo*)

Coach Don Henry's Falcons won the school's first basketball championship at the end of the 1956-57 season. The following year, the Falcons finished a close second at 14-4. Coach Cy Bachman's 1956 baseball team tied for the LBCL title. But they lost out in a post-season tiebreaker playoff with Delhaas. The Falcons' baseball team came back stronger and won the LBCL title in 1957, only losing one game that year. The 1957 All-LBCL First Team (position players plus two pitchers) had an incredible EIGHT Falcons named to that squad! The *Courier Times* headline was "Pennsbury Dominates the Dream Squad." Unfortunately, there was no PIAA State Tournament in the 1950s. That denied the Falcons the chance to further solidify their place in athletic history.

PHS dominated in 1958, once again winning the LBCL Baseball crown. Five Falcons were named to the highly competitive 1958 All League Team. They were joined by two future Major Leaguers. Bristol's Pete Cimino (California Angels and Minnesota Twins) was one of the two pitchers named on the ten-player team. Morrisville's Dan Napoleon, who played for the New York Mets in the mid-1960s, was named as an outfielder. The 1958 Falcons again only lost one game.

Incredibly, senior year teams for the PHS class of 1958 only lost a total of 6 games combined in all three of the major sports. In the six major sports seasons from 1957 and 1958, Pennsbury won four titles and collected a pair of second-place finishes.

DOMINATION—Pennsbury High baseball players earned eight of 10 slots on the 1957 LBCL All-League team. (Levittown Times photo)

Who is Reggie Turner?

The classes of 1957 and 1958 have an incredible 16 people in the Pennsbury Athletic Hall of Fame. All are extremely deserving inductees. Reggie Turner is not one of the 16. So who is Reggie Turner? He was a starter in all three major sports. He was a starting running back on the football team. In basketball, he played two varsity seasons at point guard. His exceptional speed was a top asset in these two sports.

In the 1950s, baseball was still our national pastime. The prestigious Falcon Award was originally named the Babe Ruth Award until 1963. It was on the baseball diamond where Reggie excelled to the highest level. He made the Varsity as a sophomore and was the starting centerfielder. Opening day for his junior year came on April 5, 1956. That day, senior captain Chick Estadt was the starting pitcher and threw three hitless innings. Coach Bachman then called Reggie in from the centerfield to pitch the last four innings. Reggie struck out 11 of the next 12 batters to give the Falcons an Opening Day no-hitter. Reggie Turner went on to be named a First team All LBCL centerfielder as a junior.

The 1957 PHS baseball year saw the emergence of pitcher Chucker Watson. He went 7-0 and was named the top pitcher in the LBCL. On the days Chucker did not pitch, Reggie was on the mound. On May 24, 1957, for the final game of the season, Reggie was the starting pitcher for the clinching game over William Tennent, won by the resounding score of 25-5. It had been seven years since Pennsbury last won the LBCL baseball title. Reggie's senior pitching record was 5-1. He averaged almost 10 strikeouts a game. He batted .430 for the year and was a top ten hitter in the LBCL. He also hit three home runs. Reggie was named to the All-League First Team outfield again.

Ron Stowe, the leading hitter on the 1957 and 58 Championship teams, remembers Reggie as, "A good teammate and a great guy. He could do it all on the baseball field." Outfielder George Case, son of a former big league star, remembers Reggie as a "very quiet guy who was a gifted athlete."

Reggie Turner has fond memories of the 1957 baseball season. In an interview earlier in 2022, Reggie said, "One day Chucker Watson would be the starting pitcher and the next game I was on the mound. And that's how it went for the whole season." Reggie added, "We were mostly a veteran team but we did have a few newcomers that were important contributors." He recalls Coach Bachman as a strict disciplinarian on and off the field. "Coach Bachman regularly made us go to all our teachers and get a progress report that we were keeping up with our studies."

Where does the 1956 to 1958 era of baseball, basketball and football rank in school history? That is a good sports debate. Is the 1957 PHS Baseball Team the greatest sports team in Pennsbury History? Of the eight players selected to the All LBCL First Team, six are in the Pennsbury Athletic HOF (Des Gatti, Jim Lovett, Jim Ray, Chucker Watson, Woody Woodward, and Vern Von Sydow). And Reggie Turner has most impressive HOF credentials. I can only imagine how the Falcons would have fared in a State Tournament with pitching aces Chucker Watson and Reggie Turner.

Reggie Turner was on three different LBCL winning title teams, in three different sports. Where does Reggie rank among the greatest all-around athletes in Pennsbury history? That's another great debate topic. I never saw Reggie play, but at 5-9, 155 pounds, I might say he is, pound for pound, the best.

POSTSCRIPT: Based on my research, as of the current date of this writing, the 1957 and 1958 Baseball Championships are not currently listed at Pennsbury. However, Head Baseball Coach Joe Pesci is reviewing the matter and will look into getting an appropriate banner display for the PHS Sports Complex.

CHAPTER 27

Football Program Grew Into Pennsylvania Power

*(EDITOR'S NOTE: According to the website **pennsburyfootball.org**, the program's origin can be traced back to Fallsington School in 1930. That original Falls Township facility—which still stands today—contained Fallsington and Yardley students in Grades 1 through 10. Grades 11 and 12 were sent to neighboring districts: Bristol, Langhorne and Morrisville. Nevertheless, Fallsington fielded a varsity football team in 1930 that competed in at least two official games, losing to Newtown and Langhorne. A year later, head coach James P. Doheny led Fallsington, now serving all 12 grades, to a 5-1 record with 4 shutouts. The school became known as Pennsbury in 1949 and its football program would be rated No. 1 in the state in 1974.)*

By Terry Nau, Class of 1965

Chuck Kane has been associated with Pennsbury football since a few months after he graduated from West Chester State Teachers College in 1959. After coaching hundreds of student-athletes during his 22-year career at Pennsbury, Kane still loves to talk football and especially relishes the chance to see "his boys." The most recent occasion came on March 5, 2022—one day after the coach's 85th birthday—when a couple dozen alumni gridders surrounded their legendary coach and thanked him for all the lessons he taught them as teenagers.

Since Fallsington (nee Pennsbury) High launched its varsity program in 1930, there have been three unbeaten teams and two of them had Chuck Kane as head coach, stalking the sidelines in his familiar white shirt and long tie.

Asked how Pennsbury advanced from a fledgling program in the 1950s to one of the state's elite teams in 25 years, Kane came up with this answer:

"In the 1950s, there were three coaches (George) Jarmoska, (Jim) Egli and Al Matuza Sr. who were instrumental in building the program. I coached under Al Matuza beginning in 1959. It was a real learning experience for me, coming out of West Chester, where I played for Glenn Killinger, who was an All-American at Penn State. Coach Matuza had played in the NFL with the Chicago Bears. He shared his knowledge with the coaching staff. He allowed me to 'run the line.'"

A bit of a history buff, Kane pointed out that Pennsbury had played home games at the old Fallsington Field, Morrisville High and even Neshaminy in the early 1950s.

"But then the new high school (now Pennwood) was completed (in 1951) and football games began to be held on the field behind the school. They would set up wooden bleachers. Pennsbury did get more spectators at this location than at the Fallsington field," Kane said.

Pennsbury put together its first truly great football season in 1957 when Matuza's club finished with an 8-1 record and shared the Lower Bucks County League championship with Neshaminy. Among the key players for the Falcons were Frank Strang, Vern Von Sydow, Jay Leader, Bill Sunailitis, and Dennis Woolley.

Patricia Gordon, Class of 1964, remembered another side of Coach Matuza, who taught social studies and history at Pennsbury.

"Coach Matuza touched, affected and changed so many students' lives—not just on the football field," Gordon wrote on a Facebook tribute in 2022. "He was also a feminist before we knew what a feminist was. Will never forget his booming voice—'You go, girl!' He was a true gift."

Von Sydow would go on to play football at the Naval Academy, starting at guard for two seasons. The Levittown product, now 81, has spent his life after the Navy working with at-risk students in the San Diego area. Vern is proud to say he was teammates with two Heisman Trophy winners—Joe Bellino and Roger Staubach. Von Sydow served three tours of duty during the Vietnam War as a helicopter rescue pilot, piloting the craft as his crew fished pilots out of the Pacific Ocean after they had been shot down during bombing runs over North Vietnam.

When Von Sydow, Class of 1958, was elected to the Pennsbury Hall of Fame, he sent this message: "Football taught me that hard work and determination are keys to success in life."

Chuck Kane knew something about hard work. He would witness daily the growth of Pennsbury's school system and its sports teams as enrollment figures expanded throughout the 1960s. The first of the Baby Boomers generation were teenagers as the new decade began. By 1965, Pennsbury would graduate 725 students. The number surpassed 1,000 students in 1968. The old high school on Makefield Road would be replaced in 1966 by a new facility on Hood Boulevard in Fairless Hills. Falcon Field at Charles Boehm gave way to a full-sized stadium at the new school.

"Lower Bucks football became stronger every year because of all the families from around the state that moved in for jobs at the new steel mill," Kane admitted. "Some of the parents pushed us to play teams from 'upstate.' That was one of the reasons we eventually joined the Big Eight conference."

The rivalry between Pennsbury and Neshaminy would rage for most of the next 60 years. Crowds of close to 10,000 fans were estimated for several mid-1960s encounters as the Falcons finally overtook the Redskins' dynasty to build one of their own. In 1972, an estimated 12,000 spectators jammed Falcon Field to watch Kane's club edge Neshaminy to complete the first unbeaten season in modern school history (post-1950).

Neshaminy still ran a single-wing offense well into the 1960s under the coaching staff headed first by Harry Franks and then John Petercuskie. The Langhorne school, like Pennsbury, benefited from the rapid growth of Levittown. One of the greatest of county players, Harry Schuh, grew up in Feasterville and dominated local sports as a football star and champion wrestler. The 6-foot-3, 260-pound Schuh, third pick in the 1965 college draft, would play 10 seasons in the AFL and NFL.

Even in those formative early years of football in Lower Bucks, talented players began attracting notice of college scouts. Morrisville High's Dick Hart turned down Notre Dame to play baseball. But a few years in the minors impressed upon Hart the need in 1966 to switch sports. Hart became a starting guard for the Philadelphia Eagles in 1967 and played five NFL seasons. The number of NFL veterans from Lower Bucks would grow over the years. Pennsbury sent defensive back Troy Vincent off to Wisconsin and then the NFL, where he played several seasons with the Eagles. Troy became prominent in the players' union and is now Executive Vice President of Operations for the NFL.

As grade school students in the late 1950s, we youngsters looked up to high school athletes. In Fairless Hills, Frank Strang, Roger Sanders, Joe Griesbaum and Jay Leader seemed larger than life. Tom Broadwater and the Bray brothers from Fallsington blazed their own paths. Everyone knew who Von Sydow because of his German name. We recognized Levittown's Joe Yatsko from wrestling, another strong program that produced a state runnerup in Ed Abrahims, Class of 1957.

Neshaminy seemed to rule the Lower Bucks football scene every season (except 1957) but Pennsbury was never far behind. The Falcons, under new coach Erle Baugher, lost one-point decisions in 1963 and 1964, then fell by 7-0 in 1965 before finally taking over in 1966 with a resounding 60-0 victory over the Redskins. Pennsbury would rule the LBCL for most of the next decade. Special mention must be made for the terrific 1968 team that went 10-1, losing on the road to unbeaten Easton by a 13-12 score in what was billed as "Game of the Day" in the entire state. The Falcons had stepped out of Neshaminy's shadow into their own spotlight.

PENNSBURY FOREVER

1957 PENNSBURY FALCONS

First row: J. Andruskevich, W. Roberts, R. Mahler, R. Leaner, W. Nichols, R. Sanders, J. Starling, W. Fitzgerald, R. Baker. *Second row:* Coach Haney, W. Webb, A. Wall, J. Dougherty, W. Watkins, G. Wilkins, R. Stowe, T. James, A. Snyder, P. Ramsey, Coach Keller. *Third row:* Coach Matuza, W. Kramer, J. Horne, J. Miles, D. Dow, K. Kunn, J. Ward, J. Meszaros, W. Peterson, F. Moyes. *Fourth row:* R. Woodward, D. Dolinsky, F. Strang, V. VonSychow, J. Leader, W. Sunalitus, D. Woolley, J. Dobos, R. Baumer, and J. Mobley.

MR. KELLER

MR. HANEY

FOOTBALL

Under the capable guidance of head coach, Mr. Al Matuza and his assistants, Mr. Al Keller and Mr. Gordon Haney, the "Falcons" scalped six league opponents to deadlock with Neshaminy for the Lower Bucks County League title. This past season's team was the most powerful team Pennsbury had

MR. MATUZA

ever fielded. In compiling the finest record in Pennsbury's history, eight wins and one loss, the "Falcons" displayed the fine spirit typical of all our teams. The increased interest of the student body was also apparent, and our boys responded to this new support by taking the championship.

The "Orange and Black," after two wins over non-league opponents, opened league play by downing Council Rock 27-6, North Penn 8-0 and Ewing 6-0. The next league contest was a thrilling one in which we beat Neshaminy for the first time in several years, 7-6. After winning over Bristol 33-0, we suffered our only loss at the hands of Wm. Tennent 8-12. We then went on to win three in a row to tie with Neshaminy.

102

157

Pennsbury's football program peaked from 1972-74. Chuck Kane took over for Baugher in 1970 and produced unbeaten teams in 1972 and 1974. His 1973 team went 9-1-1 and could very easily have gone unbeaten, too. Even the 1971 team, which went 9-2, lost its two games by scores of 7-0 to Bethlehem Liberty and 21-17 to Neshaminy, which finished unbeaten for the first time in seven years.

Bob Crouch, who quarterbacked the 1973 Falcons after backing up Gary Kutzmeda in 1972, recalls the early 1970s with great enthusiasm.

"Before the first day of practice in 1972, Coach Kane told us, 'I'd like to go undefeated this year.' That was our goal. We had that in mind every day we practiced, from late summer on. We had a lot of great players returning, including Gary Kutzmeda, running back Dale Delise, and some good linemen—Gary Metroka, Mike Paige, Kirk Harmon and Mike McGrath. The linebackers were really good—Ron Dundala and John Lerch."

Neshaminy, coming off an unbeaten season, opened 1972 with a tough loss to Catholic League power Bishop Egan. That seemed to fire up the Redskins and they dominated opponents every week while Pennsbury played a couple tight games along the way.

"The *Courier Times* had a weekly poll and they had Neshaminy and Pennsbury tied for first place in November," Crouch remembered. "Neshaminy kept running up scores and I guess that's why they were tied with an unbeaten team in the newspaper rankings."

Pennsbury won the showdown over Neshaminy, 23-21, before an estimated 12,000 fans at Falcon Field to complete the first perfect football season in school history.

Crouch took over as quarterback in 1973.

"We were favored to do it again,' he said, "but we were overconfident in the first game and lost to Woodrow Wilson, 21-20. Because we had finished unbeaten the year before, a local radio station (WTTM) decided to broadcast all of the Pennsbury football games in 1973 and they even had a reporter on the sidelines, interviewing players DURING the game. Coach Kane fixed that soon enough but the damage was done. After that, Coach let nothing go. Our cheerleaders couldn't even decorate the locker room!"

Pennsbury took its anger out on Bethlehem Freedom 40-0 the next week. The tie came in a rainstorm against Bethlehem Liberty. A scoreless tie. After that, Pennsbury shut out its final five opponents, including Neshaminy 13-0 in the finale.

And then came the pinnacle 1974 season for Pennsbury football. With Joe Crossin taking over at QB, the Falcons threw the ball for over 1,500 yards (500 more than in 1972). The average margin of victory was 37-7. United Press International ranked Pennsbury No. 1 in the state.

"I believe the 1974 team was the best of the three," Crouch said in March 2022, "but they were all great teams. The 1974 team had Billy Austin, a running back who was also a sprinter in track. If Billy got outside, he was gone. Joe Crossin was probably the best passing quarterback Pennsbury has ever had. Bud Reichard was a great defensive end. Marty Sierocinski, who was a big tackle, went on to play at Penn State."

The Falcons fell back to 7-3-1 in 1975 and would remain a winning program over the next 40 years, fueled by a succession of coaches who often came up through the system. Al Matuza Jr., Jim Dundala and Galen Snyder were among the former players who carried on the Pennsbury tradition of hard-nosed football begun way back on the sandlot field next to Fallsington School.

Galen Snyder, who would play on the third unbeaten Pennsbury squad in 1985 under Coach Jim Dundala, recalls his first exposure to Pennsbury football while growing up in Fairless Hills during the late 1970s.

"At halftime, we kids would leave the stadium and play pickup games on the adjacent fields," Snyder remembered early in 2022 after he returned as head coach of Pennsbury following a five-year hiatus. "The kids would break up into small groups and throw the ball or run around. Sometimes we wouldn't stay for the second half."

Snyder's teams compiled a 116-48 record, winning two District 1 titles in the process and ranking among the state's most elite programs from 2002-16. Over the years, he has become familiar with the program's history.

"Looking back, I think you have to remember those early coaches who got the program rolling in the 1950s," Snyder said. "George Jarmoska coached and then became athletic director. Al Matuza Sr. was a very important person in the history of the program. He put it on a good course and then when Erle Baugher took over (in 1962), he took it to another level. Pennsbury was getting bigger and bigger as a school. That helped football a lot. Coach Baugher has the best winning percentage ever among Pennsbury coaches (based on a record of 62-14-4 from 1962-69). I think his contributions may have been overlooked."

When Erle Baugher passed away in 1984 at age 64, *Courier Times* sports editor Dick Dougherty wrote a wonderful remembrance, quoting Chuck Kane at length.

"Erle always stressed professionalism in coaching," Kane told Dougherty. "He introduced me to a lot of popular coaches in the area as far as college and also professional coaches at clinics. He made me into a professional coach. Up until that time, I was coaching as a part-time thing."

Baugher had coached at Ambler High in suburban Philadelphia for 13 seasons, compiling a 97-24-6 record. He was a perfect fit for Pennsbury at a time when student enrollment was exploding. The new coach made sure that all the junior high and middle school football teams in the Pennsbury district taught the same football schemes, from seventh grade on.

"Erle always thought football, even in the offseason," Kane added. "We studied films from other schools and colleges and observed college practices in the spring. From that information we could sit down with our coaches and try to improve our program. Up until that time, I never had that kind of experience."

From 1963 on, Baugher's rosters were as deep and talented as Neshaminy's but it took the pain of three narrow losses before the Falcons pounded Neshaminy 60-0 in 1966 to claim the first of four straight LBCL titles.

"I thought we should have beat them in 1963," said Bob Burkhart, an All-LBCL fullback and league scoring champion for the 1964 Falcons. "We were beating the Neshaminy teams in junior high and I just figured we would beat them when we got to senior high. I have a newspaper clipping from the 21-20 game that said we had won the hearts of the fans. We gained way more yardage than Neshaminy did. But somehow they won and then they beat us 14-13 in 1964."

Pennsbury had begun to expand its football schedule during the Baugher years, taking on teams from Allentown, Bethlehem, Easton, Chambersburg and Altoona. More and more players kept coming up through the youth football programs. There was a lot to work with for Baugher and Kane and the entire coaching staff.

Baugher's best season came in 1968 when the Falcons won 10 of 11 games, their only loss the aforementioned 13-12 crusher at Easton before an estimated crowd of 12,000 fans. According to research by Kevin Lendo, Class of 1966, Easton was ranked No. 2 in the state and No. 8 in the country. The *Allentown Morning Call* labeled this showdown the "High School Game of the Century." Hyperbole, perhaps, but not to the players and coaches involved.

The *Morning Call* described the game this way: "The game pitted massive Pennsbury offensive and defensive lines and power running game against deep and speedy offensive and defensive backfields for Easton."

When Easton Stadium was torn down many years later, the 1968 win over Pennsbury was named the greatest game in the history of the facility.

Pennsbury's best player that year was Billy Evans, an amiable kid from Yardley who measured 5-foot-11 and 215 pounds during his high school days. What made Billy great was his speed for a big man. He led Lower Bucks in scoring and rushing yards. Billy bypassed college and signed with the Canadian Football League when he was 19 but a knee injury took away the speed and his career ended quietly. Defensive lineman

Frank Dykes led the defense. Dykes made second-team all-state and went to Penn State on a football scholarship.

Kane retired as head coach after the 1981 season, turning the reins over to one of his former players, Jim Dundala, whose program produced a third and final unbeaten season in 1985. (See next chapter's story written by Marc Freeman.)

Al Matuza Jr. took over as head coach in 1988. By now, Pennsbury was competing in the Suburban League. The 1990 Falcons ruled the Patriot Division with an overall record of 8-2-1. And they won another Suburban division title in 1993 under Matuza's replacement, Larry Greene.

Galen Snyder became head coach in 2002, intent on restoring Pennsbury to its elite status around the state. And it didn't take long. The 2006 Falcons won the school's first District One championship with a 13-2 record. Running back Jackson Fagan rushed for an incredible 2,241 yards and 27 touchdowns. He was named second-team all-state. Linebacker C.J. Marck earned first-team all-state honors and was named the state's top defensive player by one publication.

The 2009 team claimed the Suburban National Division title with a 9-2 record. They would win it again in 2014 with another 13-2 campaign. Snyder stepped aside following the 2015 season to spend more time with his family. But when the

TAKING OVER—Galen Snyder played on the 1985 unbeaten Pennsbury squad and returned as head coach in 2002

program floundered during the pandemic years, Galen returned to Pennsbury in 2022 to take on a rebuilding job.

The program has come a long way in 75 years. Boys growing up in Fallsington during the 1950s would meet on the weekends and play tackle football on the old gridiron next to Fallsington School. They might see the high school team play if they were lucky. Mostly, the kids played football on sandlot fields. Some even had grass. Pennsbury benefited from youth football leagues sponsored by Falls Rec, AmVets and Pop Warner in the 1950s and 1960s.

By the 1970s, large crowds of football fans flocked to Pennsbury every Saturday to see the program performing at its zenith.

"Saturday was for football back then," said Cliff Stout, a defensive lineman for Pennsbury in 1972-73. "Tickets had to be purchased during the week, on Tuesday and Wednesday. I think it had something to do with the steel mill community. People worked hard all week and Saturday was when you went to the football game. As a little kid, I remember seeing cars come down our street (in Fairless Hills) after games, with black-and-orange pom-poms waving. My friends would ask me what was going on and I would say the Pennsbury game must be over."

Pennsbury went 9-2 in 1971 in Chuck Kane's second year as head coach.

"That team lost by inches to an unbeaten Neshaminy team that people were saying was the best team ever," Stout recalled. "If Pennsbury had won that game, they would have finished 10-1. And then the next three years, they did go 11-0, 9-1-1 and 11-0 for the greatest three-year run in school history."

The Falcons went a combined 31-1-1 during those golden seasons.

"I think the coaching staff had a lot to do with it," Stout admitted. "Our coaches were young, in their 30s, and they had all played college football."

Those coaches included Chuck Kane, Bob Buckanavage, Ron Davidson, Al Matuza Jr., Jim Dundala, Max Micsion, Joe Lelinski, Bud Baldwin and Joe Lowe. Matuza, Dundala and Lowe were star players at Pennsbury.

When the 1972 team was honored in 2017 by the school and alumni football players, the "Falcon Football Legacy Reunion Committee" produced a 24-page program for the event. The pamphlet covered Chuck Kane's early years, from 1970-75. Rosters and statistics for every season were provided inside the brochure.

"We started an alumni players club a few years back," Stout said. "Billy Evans was a big part of that. Billy was a great guy…we lost him too soon. I really think those years in the early 1970s were a continuation of what Coach Erle Baugher's teams did in the 1960s."

The program had come a long way over 75 years. Just look at the team photos through the years. Rosters got bigger. So did the players and the coaching staffs. Even the schedules expanded. From 10-game schedules in the 1960s, Pennsbury would play 15 games in the 2006 and 2014 championship seasons, boosted by a state playoff system that would have been fun to see in the early 1970s.

Players from those mid-1960s teams share a common bond that links them to players of the following decades. They all ran on to a gridiron called Falcon Field to hear the roar of hometown fans exhorting them on. And now they meet in their golden years to hoist a beer in honor of Pennsbury Football. They are maintaining a tradition of tough football players and hard-working teams that most definitely resemble the communities they represent.

CHAPTER 28

We Are The Falcons...

By Dave Morris, Class of 1966

Yes, we were Falcons during our "Glory Days." And that meaningful phrase was the beginning to the chant heard every Saturday in the Fall as the varsity football team marched from the locker room at Charles Boehm Junior High up to the old stadium to do battle.

We are the Falcons
Mighty, mighty Falcons
Everywhere we go
People want to know
Who we are;
So, we tell them
We are the Falcons ...

To our eyes, Pennsbury produced some of the best teams in Bucks County and beyond. We had the best school, many of the finest athletic facilities, any number of quality athletes, terrific student body support, strong community backing and supportive cheerleaders. One could not argue with that. The mid-sixties were a great time to wear the Orange and Black.

In 1961 and again in '62, Charles

DAVE MORRIS
...fond memories

H. Boehm Junior High produced back-to-back undefeated football teams. The '62 team, under the skillful coaching of Bruce McFarland, earned the pet title of

The Raggedy Ass Cadets. We heard Coach McFarland bark that label almost every day, and we wore that badge with pride. Barry Taylor (No. 11) was the QB. Jeff Dahlman (No. 22) was the left halfback, Bob Rowe (No. 33) was the fullback and I (No. 44) ran from the right halfback position. Numerous others such as Al Dunning, Jeff Westerman, Dave Purcell and Bill Dansbury anchored the line. And there were many others who deserve recognition. As these two Boehm squads merged on the Falcon varsity with a very good Medill Bair squad, we knew we had a few excellent years ahead of us. And we did. However, we were not alone at the top. There was still our number one nemesis, the Redskins of Neshaminy.

Neshaminy had dominated the area football scene going back to the days of having Harry Schuh as fullback. In 1963 we sort of caught everyone by surprise when we really outplayed them at their field but lost, 21-20. We had the talent; they had the coach. John Petercuskie, by all accounts, was the king of area high school coaches. He later went on to coach a couple of Division One college teams and then with the Cleveland Browns from 1978-1984.

In '63 he pulled out the win against us with a well-conceived trick play called "LEO." That stood for Left End Over. That left end moved over to the right end making the position of left tackle eligible to catch a pass. Neshaminy had substituted a running back named Tommy Dee, a sprinter on their track team, into the game at that position. We missed that move and treated the tackle as just that, a tackle. He, on the other hand, didn't miss his assignment and scored untouched. It was rumored that they had a surprise play for us and that was it. LEO was the difference in the game. All the stats, except the final score, favored Pennsbury.

In 1964 we played them at our stadium. Arguably, we may have had the best Pennsbury team to date and certainly, in my mind, the best in Eastern Pennsylvania. We were led by captains Ken Homa, Doug Powell, Bob Burkhart and Joe Fioravanti. Both teams entered the contest undefeated. It was called the game of the year and Falcon Field was nearly converted into a bowl when numerous steel stands were added to accommodate the crowd, reportedly over 11,000 fans. It was labeled as the top game in the state that day.

The contest was tight all the way through. In '63 and '64, we never kicked extra points; we always ran for the point and, at the time, PAT's were only good for one point, even if you ran it in. When we didn't convert; we lost in '63 by the slimmest of margins and again in '64 by the score of 14-13. Now, in defense of the coaches and play-calling, we had good backs and a great line on both sides of the ball. A great coach, Chuck Kane, saw to that. Our line was big and well-schooled. Running for just two yards seemed almost automatic. Unfortunately, this time we did not convert. Neshaminy's defense rose to the occasion.

Later during the following week, I managed to convince our coaching staff that my buddy, Gary Krapf, and I, had been practicing kicking PAT's together for a couple of years. The following week we played Delhaas. After the first two PAT's, via the traditional run game, coach allowed us to "see what you can do." Gary converted 6 of 7. On our first attempt, the snap was over my head and his. Had it not been, I am sure he would have been 7 for 7. I often wonder, had we kicked extra points in '63 and earlier in '64 would we have had a different ending against the 'Skins? Could be. In '65, Bill Cooper began to kick extra points and did so very well for the season.

Also, as I recall, there was another somewhat unconventional and memorable moment to the '64 season. Earlier in the year, the William Tennent coach had made a big fuss complaining that his school should not have to play the likes of Pennsbury and Neshaminy, whose enrollments were growing every year. We were too big and too good for his likes. He was probably right. His comments must have rubbed Coach Erle Baugher the wrong way. It was a home game for us and the coach dressed every man that wanted to dress; almost 150 went out for pre-game warmups ahead of our competitor, and that was never our practice. We lined up four rows for calisthenics 100 yards long. When Tennent came out, they had nowhere to go. They stood in the end zone until we were asked to move. The game was won before the kickoff. I believe the final score was something like 40-6.

During the season of 1965, my senior year, we began with a road trip to play the legendary Altoona High School. We practiced under the lights the night before the game in a stadium loaded with hundreds of locals there to check us out. On game day, our bus got a police escort to the field. It was gonna be big. On their first possession they surprised us with a halfback pass for the initial score of the game. The perfectly-executed play ignited the crowd and took some wind from our sails. We struggled in that first half. We finally got back to playing Pennsbury football and ended up scoring 26 points in the second half but, we did not convert on two extra points as we did not kick again. We lost, 28-26.

The long bus ride home was rather quiet. The next six or seven games saw us cruise past our competition, as well we should have. Unfortunately, we were beaten again in Langhorne 7-0 in front of another 10,000 fans. That game remained tied late into the 4th period when their Gerry Barr broke loose for a 48-yard touchdown run. The game happened to be shown live on WFIL-TV and a replay of the run showed that Jimmy Neeld had pushed the ball-carrier out of bounds at the one. I'll say it— we were victims of home cooking. But they won the game and I will always believe we had the better talent for the second straight year.

On a personal note, sometime around 1998 the company with whom I worked here in North Carolina hired a new marketing manager. The upper management team was called into a meeting to meet this new member. As he was introduced, and later spoke, I looked hard at his face. I somehow felt that I had seen it once before. He had grey hair but I was sure that it had been red at one time. I began to put it all together after I imagined what he would look like wearing a helmet with a face mask. When he was done, I began to ask a few questions: "Are you from Pennsylvania?" "Yes." "Bucks County?" "Yes." Did you play quarterback for Woodrow Wilson High School?" "Yes." "We used to kick your ass," I added. "I played for Pennsbury." It was Rick Lewis, an outstanding defensive back at Georgia Tech and then for a short stint with the Pittsburgh Steelers. We had a good laugh. He and I have remained friends. Small world. It was good to have a second Bucks County boy here in this small southern town.

I am fortunate to have lived in Lower Bucks as a young man, with all that it and Pennsbury High School had to offer, and I am proud to continue to call myself a Falcon. I often spoke (bragged is more accurate) of our Pennsbury teams to my sons as they too played sports. A few years ago, one of the local schools got a great deal of press as they prepared to play for the North Carolina 2A state championship. My older son challenged me by asking if my Pennsbury team could beat them. I said yes, but it would be a close game; after all, we were all now in our seventies!

CHAPTER 29

What Coach Jimmy 'D' Meant to Me

By Marc Freeman, Class of 1986

Between 1983 and 1985, I played football at Pennsbury High School. I was a defensive end. Former Pennsbury great Jim Dundala, Class of 1969, had taken over as head coach when Chuck Kane retired from coaching after the 1981 season. Many players called Mr. Dundala "coach" but others, myself included, referred to him as Jimmy "D." It was a fitting name for him because he was defensive-minded and clearly understood that while offense is important, defense wins football games.

I first met Jimmy D around 1982 when I was a student at Medill Bair High School,

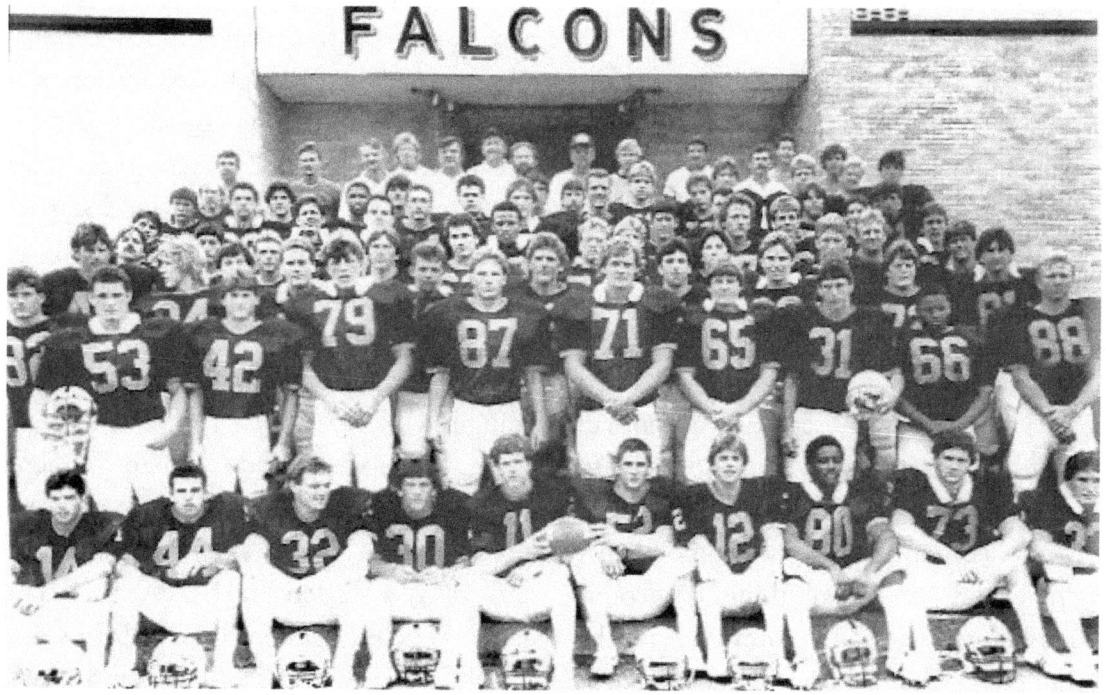

UNBEATEN CHAMPIONS!—The 1985 Pennsbury Falcons compiled a 10-0 record and remain the last undefeated varsity football team in school history. (Photo courtesy of pennsburyfootball.org)

and his brother, Ron, was the head coach of the junior varsity football team. Jimmy D came to speak to us because we were part of a pipeline that would eventually play for him. During the meeting, we were instructed to complete an index card with our name, height, weight, and shoe size. I thought it was unusual that they would want our shoe size, but I think they used it to predict how much weight we might put on.

After the meeting, I had a brief conversation with Jimmy D, and to my surprise, he knew me. He knew the position I played and was familiar with my athletic abilities. He thought I had a bright football career ahead of me. I didn't realize it at the time, but eventually, Jimmy D would play a pivotal role in my life.

Pennsbury Football

During my sophomore year, I learned about the term "Pennsbury Football," which Jimmy D talked about a lot. Although he never officially defined the term, based on his comments, he viewed it as a tough, hard-nosed style of football that respects opponents but also seeks to crush them.

Practices during my sophomore year were brutal, unlike anything I encountered before. It was like Jimmy D, and the other coaches on staff pushed us one inch from the point of death. I wasn't used to the amount of time we spent preparing for an opposing team and the endless intense drills. For example, in tenth grade, I held the bag for our starting linebacker, a fella by the name of Chip Chimera. For five whole minutes, he delivered blow after blow during that drill. He was unmerciful to the point I thought he would kill me. The message he sent that day was clear: this is Pennsbury Football. We are relentless, and we go hard every play, even in practice. We will not stop, and we will not quit. The butt-kicking I received that day was my introduction to Pennsbury football at the varsity level.

Jimmy D stressed the importance of going all out on the football field and created a culture where players were encouraged to go to college. He never said all his players must go to college, but it was obvious that he thought higher education was a good thing. Standing on the sidelines, I learned that some upperclassmen were going to universities near and far. I started hearing about Widener, William and Mary, Notre Dame, and other colleges. Thus, the question among football players was not are you going to college, but where are you going to college?

In 1983, we played William Tennent High School for the Suburban One League championship. I was still in tenth grade and wasn't a starter, but I dressed for that game. William Tennent beat us by a score of 19-6. After the game, I saw and heard my teammates crying. It was a terrible blow to see people I looked up to so broken.

In 1984, Jimmy D tapped me to be the starting defensive end for the Falcons. During that year, I learned more about his philosophy and approach to football.

- He taught us that it was good to be aggressive on the football field, but it wasn't good to be out of control.
- He taught us how to "get after people," but at the same time, he taught us how to be disciplined.
- He told us to "do whatever it takes to win," which refers to the planning, preparation, and dedication needed to succeed on the gridiron.

It was an incredible way to think about and approach the game of football. Later I applied some of his principles to other areas of my life. We were aggressive on both sides of the ball. For example, we had a running back named Scott Labreque who had the speed to run around people, but he certainly had the ability to run over them. He was strong, smart, and tough as nails. We also had a tight end named Andy Anderson. He was full of fire, intense, a fierce competitor, and I think he enjoyed flattening cornerbacks after he caught a pass.

Football is a violent sport, and under Jimmy D's guidance we were always prepared for combat. We didn't just want to win when we stepped on the field on Saturdays. We wanted to dominate, destroy people and break their spirits. I can't speak to the mindset of the offensive players, but on defense, we were always out for blood. If a quarterback or some other player tried to scamper down the sideline, we felt like we had every right; indeed, we felt obligated to knock him into next week (I am laughing as I type this. Ah, the memories). We were very good at hurting people, and when we did, we could hear the roar of the crowd. I think they were as bloodthirsty as was we were.

We went 8-2 my junior year and beat Neshaminy for the Suburban One League Championship. Shortly after the season ended, on a Friday afternoon, Jimmy D came to my classroom and asked me to step into the hallway. He was smiling from ear to ear and told me that I had made first-team All-Lower Bucks County. Ten of our players were selected, more than any other team. The Courier Times ran a photo of that group with Coach D. Looking at it now, we were so young! Jimmy D was smiling like a proud dad. In many ways, he was like a father figure to me and so many other players.

The rest of my junior year was uneventful. I continued to work out, take vitamins and prepare for my final year on the gridiron. I couldn't wait to hit the football field. I was young, strong, and healthy. My plans for my senior year were dashed, however. During a routine play in practice, I twisted my knee and heard a distinct crackle-TOCK sound. I thought I was a big football player, but my eyes instantly filled with tears, not because of the pain but because I knew it was a serious injury. Then something incredible happened. In an instant, in the twinkling of an eye, Jimmy D was standing over me. He was the first person I saw. As I lay on my back, I looked up at him through my tears and heard him utter the words I will never forget, "Oh, no. I hate this shit!" He knew I was hurt.

The MRI confirmed my worst nightmare. I tore my ACL. Surgery was an option, but cutting my knee open would mean my season was over. Instead, the doctors at Temple Sports Medicine in Fort Washington, PA, determined that I might be able to strengthen my knee, brace it, and then have limited time. Once a week, I made the journey out to Fort Washington for rehab, which included knee exercises on a piece of equipment called the "Orthotron." To this day, I never experienced pain that intense. However, I made sufficient progress, began to practice with my teammates, and eventually began to play in games.

Jimmy D made sure I received the best medical care available. The doctor who tended to me was the team physician for the Philadelphia 76ers, Dr. Michael Clancy.

My senior year, we went 10-0 and beat Neshaminy for the championship on the last game of the year! I started that game, played with a torn ligament and a heavy brace, and won the game's outstanding defensive player award. I broke up a screen pass on a critical 4th-down play and sealed the game for us. I have relived that play in my mind countless times. All the pain, suffering, blood, sweat, and tears—it was worth it.

I had knee surgery in January of 1986, and around that time, Jimmy D arranged for the head coach of East Stroudsburg University to come and speak to some of the football players. We met in a small room in the library. On the one hand, I was depressed because I was on crutches when I met the head football coach. But on the other hand, I was happy to see him, as I wanted to learn more about ESU's football program.

In the summer of 1986, I completed a remedial college prep program and was admitted to East Stroudsburg University. Although I never played football there, I did graduate. After college, I began working in an urban high school, first as a substitute teacher until I secured a position as a Student Assistance Counselor. My job was to help students overcome social, emotional, and educational hurdles. Over the next 30 years, I continued to take classes part-time at night and eventually earned two master's degrees and a Ph.D. in education. But it all started with Jimmy D. Not only did he teach me about football, but he helped me get into college. Where would I be if I didn't attend and graduate from ESU?

Jimmy D's Legacy

Jimmy D meant to the world to me. He made me feel like I was his favorite player, but later I learned that he made many of us feel that way. He inspired a generation of young men, and I don't think it's any coincidence that many of us went into the field of education. My former teammates are teachers, principals, college professors, coaches, etc. Several educators came out of the Dundala camp.

As fate would have it, one of our starting linebackers, Galen Snyder, is now the head coach of the Pennsbury Falcons football team. It's his second stint in that role. Like Jimmy D, he teaches social studies, so I guess you could say he is literally and figuratively standing in his shoes.

Jimmy D taught me lessons on and off the football field. He inspired me to do my best and taught me to never quit. While he had a certain toughness about him, he was always happy, always smiling. I like to think his efficacious spirit lives on in the many players whose lives he touched and me.

My only lament is that I did not get a chance to interact with him much before he died at age 54 in 2006. Regardless, I remember the lessons "Jimmy D" taught me on and off the football field. I will never forget him.

DR. MARC FREEMAN
...looking back in time

CHAPTER 30

Chuck Kane's Message Was All-Inclusive

By Brien Martin, Class of 1981

A story about Coach Chuck Kane and his effect on one person's life ...proof that good people find ways to inspire kids, perhaps in ways they didn't even know...

"You're a member of this team."

Six little words. Hundreds of players heard them over the course of Coach's career. But when he said them to me...the super-geeky kid with the prep school haircut, whose parents made him wear dress pants to school...Chuck Kane literally changed my life.

I never repeated them to anyone, and certainly not to the players. I always said I kept stats for the football team. Never said I was "on" the football team.

When we won the championship in 1980, I was on Cloud Nine. Some of the guys on the team had been my friends since kindergarten...and my good friend, Lou Menendez, was the QB of that team.

It wasn't until the post-season banquet that those six words really hit home. I got a

*BRIEN MARTIN
...keeper of the stats*

varsity letter...and the team picture plaque with our 1980 results. As a senior, I got the traditional beer stein with my name and "position"—Statistician. But when they handed out the championship medallions...I got the greatest surprise of my life. I got one, just like everyone else.

When Coach called my name, I went up towards him and said, "You mean I get one, too?" And that's when he repeated, *"You're a member of this team."*

My dad was there...a three-sport letterman for Bristol back in the 40s...of all the swag I walked away with, I'll never forget that the one thing he wanted to see, to look at, to hold…was that medallion.

Ever since that day, I've remembered that night and those words…though I never played a down, I was considered part of a team. Folks don't know what that means to the un-athletic, dorky kid who didn't fit in most places. To this day, no matter how tough things get, I remind myself of how it feels to be included.

Coach didn't have to consider me anything but the kid who dropped off the stats every Monday morning. But he did. And with just those six little words…that clearly mean so much if you play the game…he changed one more kid's life for the better, as well.

Players often speak of the coaches in their lives who made a difference. I understand that in ways maybe even the players don't realize. For kids who just want to belong somewhere, even if they never tell another soul, men like Chuck Kane come into your life and make you believe in yourself. Even if your only job is to know that Glenn Obert ran for 117 yards…or that we had 35 first downs…or knew that Mike Augustin's school-record field goal came from 54 yards out.

I get why the players played their guts out for him. Because those six little words really do mean so much to so many.

CHAPTER 31

Falcons' Basketball Program Always Competitive

By Kevin Lendo, Class of 1966

In the early "Glory Days" of Lower Bucks County League basketball, Pennsbury was one of the youngest members. It was also the fastest growing district with the development of the steel mill in Morrisville and the coming of I-95 through the area.

There were two great teams in the late 1950's. The Don Henry-coached 1956-57 team won the first LBCL title in Pennsbury history. Some of the early stars of Pennsbury basketball were: Des Gatti, Chucker Watson, Woody Woodward, Reggie Turner and Jim Lovett. All were multi-sport varsity athletes, as was common in that era. After that championship season, Don Henry moved on to administration and became principal of Pennsbury in 1964.

The 1957-58 season was the first year for Joe Gavin, who would coach from 1957 to 1971. The team started that year playing in the small old PHS Gym that could seat 475 fans. In February of that year, they moved into the Charles Boehm Jr. High Gym that could seat 3,200. Gavin would also coach the Falcons when they moved into the current PHS gym in Fairless Hills.

In 1957-58, the team compiled a 14-4 record and finished in second place in the very competitive LBCL.

FALCONS' FIVE – Chuck Gardner, center in back row, was Pennsbury's first basketball superstar. He is flanked by Joe Lowe and Rick Kelleher. Front row: Mike Kondrya, Tim Foster.

PENNSBURY FOREVER

1960-1963

As Pennsbury basketball entered the Sixties, a standout player for the Falcons in 1960-61 was center Ben Quattrocchi. He had to play against much taller opponents. Especially troublesome was Delhaas, with 6-foot-7 John Hellings, who later would lead Penn to an Ivy League title to cap his collegiate career.

At 6-foot-1 and 210 pounds, Ben was undersized for a center. He relied on his strength and athleticism to slow down taller centers. There was one very heated contest that year at Boehm against Morrisville. PHS won the hard-fought game, 65-53. At the final buzzer, a Morrisville player punched the Falcons point guard. People from the stands came onto the court and became involved. It took some time to restore order.

Quattrocchi became one of the top ten scorers in the LBCL. He averaged 16 points a game and made the All-League team. He got a scholarship to a small college in Kentucky. While there, Ben's interest turned to boxing. He trained as a heavyweight for the Golden Gloves in Kentucky. Also at the Louisville Boxing Club complex was a young light heavyweight named Cassius Clay who later changed his name to Muhammad Ali.

In 1961-62, the first superstar basketball player in Pennsbury history emerged. During his junior year, Chuck Gardner moved up from the Junior Varsity. He grew three inches from 6-foot-4 to 6-foot-7 by his senior year, which was a breakout season. Gardner scored a then-school record 40 points in a game at Bristol. That record stood for an amazing 46 years at Pennsbury. Gardner is believed to be the first Falcon to ever dunk in a game. Chuck's final game was on February 21, 1962 at first-place Neshaminy, The Falcons routed the Redskins 85-59 and cost them a share of the LBCL Title. Chuck scored 32 points that night to win the LBCL scoring title, averaging 23.7 points a game. The team finished the season at 12-10. After his senior year at the University of Colorado, Gardner (now listed at 6-foot-8) was selected in the NBA Draft. He decided to sign with Denver of the old ABA. He played one season in Denver. He was later inducted into the University of Colorado Hall of Fame and eventually into Pennsbury's Hall of Fame.

The 1962-63 season saw one of the great nights in Lower Bucks County basketball history. The athletic department decided to take full advantage of the incredible Boehm Gymnasium. The idea of a high school doubleheader was planned. Pennsbury would be the home team in the second game of the doubleheader and host Council Rock. For the first game, non-league rivals Woodrow Wilson and Bishop Egan would play. Wilson was the defending LBCL champion and possessor of a 16-game winning streak. Egan was a member of the powerful Philadelphia Catholic League. Wilson had the returning Player of the Year in flashy Mel

"Mousey" Durant. He could handle the ball like no one outside of Philadelphia. They also had the twin 6-foot-5 towers of Dick Davidson and Gary Steele. Steele would go on to become the first African-American varsity football player at West Point. (Steele's daughter, Sage Steele, can be seen regularly on ESPN Sports Center).

Wilson beat Egan in game one, 59-46. The Falcons won game two over Council Rock, 72-60. Pennsbury had a set rotation that season. The iron man six were seniors Rick Kelleher, Harry Hamilton, Ed Keith, Ken Mortenson, Bob Fisher plus junior Art Lendo. All six were capable of having big scoring nights. Council Rock was led by future Baltimore Orioles pitcher Billy Dillman. The 2,900 fans who turned out on February 9, 1963 established an all-time record for regular season high school basketball in Bucks County.

The 1962-63 team also set a one-game record for points versus a strong Bristol team. With 3 minutes to go, the Falcons had 96 points and the Boehm crowd chanted for the magic century mark. The starters were replaced. Sonny Vucin added two points to make the final total of 98 points. Coach Gavin said he did not want to run up the score on Bristol. Kelleher and Keith combined for 60 points that night. Kelleher was named to the Bucks/ Mercer Counties All-Area Team by the *Trentonian*. He played at Villanova.

1963-1966

The 1963-64 season was highlighted by a championship win over Ewing (N.J.) High in the Newtown Chamber of Commerce Christmas Tournament. Seniors Tom Mazenko, Jack Dale, and Bill Houser helped secure the trophy. The tournament experience was further enhanced by a banquet given for the four teams at the Washington Crossing Inn. The guest speaker was Princeton University All-American senior and future U.S. senator, Bill Bradley. He was just three years older than the Pennsbury seniors.

There was an early-season LBCL matchup at Wilson that year. This

TEAM DEFENSE—Pennsbury's Art Lendo, Rick Kelleher and Harry Hamilton defend a William Tennent shooter during 1963-64 season.

important January game was highlighted by who refereed the game. Art McNally was the Supervisor of NFL referees at the time. He became the first NFL referee selected for the NFL Hall of Fame in February 2022. The other referee that night was Jack Madden, who refereed in several NBA Finals games during his 25-year NBA career.

The Falcons trailed by 10 points but rallied late and tied it up at the end of regulation. They lost in double overtime, 49-48. Once again, the Falcons had a 6-foot-1 center named Quattrocchi. In 1963-64, it was John Quattrocchi who had to battle much taller opponent centers. Junior Bob Matuza and senior Art Lendo were named to the All-League Team. They were the second and fourth leading scorers in the LBCL. The pair averaged almost 40 points a game.

The 1964-65 Falcons had a formidable front court led by senior Bob Matuza, junior center Dick Olson, and sophomore forward Bill Katz. During Matuza's final game, a 78-71 home loss to Morrisville, he scored a career-high 33 points. That propelled him to the LBCL scoring title at 19.5 points a game. He was voted Player of the Year. The team record was 10-10 for the year. Matuza is part of the greatest Pennsbury sports family. Father Al Matuza Sr. was a former PHS Head Football Coach. He played for the Chicago Bears. Brothers Al Jr. and Lenny both excelled in basketball and football. All four are in the Pennsbury Sports Hall of Fame. Bob played in college at Bloomsburg. That season also featured the first live radio broadcast by WBCB of a Falcons basketball game. Currently WBCB live streams many Falcons home games

The 1965-66 season started with a tough loss, 65-63, to Abington. Senior Dick Olson, who was an All-League selection as a junior, had 32 points in the loss. PHS hosted the Lower Bucks Chamber of Commerce Christmas Tournament at Boehm. The Falcon starters in the championship game versus Bishop Egan were Rich Hamilton, Bill Katz, Mike Hoffman, Kevin Lendo, and Steve McCusker. PHS rallied from 10 points down to defeat Bishop Egan 66-63 for the trophy. Dick Olson came off the bench in the second quarter to be high scorer with 25 points. The early record was a promising 4-1. But during practice a short time later, Olson suffered a season-ending injury. He was the leading scorer in the county at that time. The Falcons finished 10-10. The 1965-66 season was noteworthy as it was the last season the Falcons used the Boehm Gym as their home court. All future games would take place at the new high school in Fairless Hills.

1967-1972

1966-67 was the third year as a starter for Bill Katz. The Falcons had a big early-season game at Woodrow Wilson. PHS jumped out to a lead but the score got closer in the fourth quarter. Late in the game, a Wilson player who was driving ahead to the basket was fouled by Katz. The referees had a huddle which was joined by Wilson coach Massari. It was then decided that Katz would be removed from the game for a hard foul. Wilson won by two points. It was another close loss to Wilson.

That year the team had a 14-6 record and just missed the LBCL Title. The champion was determined by a playoff between the First and Second Half winners in a game at Boehm. Bristol beat Neshaminy. The Redskins, however, got the lone PIAA State Tournament Class A invite because they won the First Half, even though Pennsbury had a better record for the year. Katz was a unanimous All-League Team selection and the leading scorer in the league. With 972 points for his career, he just came up short of becoming the first Pennsbury 1,000-point scorer. Teams of that era played far fewer games than they do today. Bill played freshman ball at Penn and then transferred to Rider. In his first game at Rider, Katz scored 27 points in a win over St. Joe's. It was the first time Rider beat a Big 5 School. Katz finished at Rider with 1,194 points. Bill was later a Vice Principal at PHS for nine years and then Principal for 16 years.

That 1966-67 season also marked the debut for the sophomore duo of Tony Reed and Ron Givens. They would be key Falcon players in the late 60's. There was a historic game in February of 1968.

Pennsbury finally beat Woodrow Wilson, ending an 8-year drought. The thrilling 39-38 victory at the first place Rams was spearheaded by leading scorers Tony Reed and Kurt Traub.

In 1968-69, veterans Givens and Reed would lead the Falcons to a 15-4 record. The key big men were Tom Cress and Len Matuza. PHS was 12-3 in the LBCL but came in second to Woodrow Wilson, who had 6-foot-7 Earl Williams at center. He would become the first high school player from Bucks County to play in the NBA.

1969-70 was a rebuilding year and the Falcons finished in last place. One highlight early in the season was Bill Harrison scoring 36 points versus Morrisville. Gavin's last year as coach was in 1970. Seniors Tony Fortson, Kevin Cassidy and Kevin Kelleher guided the Falcons to a 16-6 record. Kelleher played at West Chester and was later inducted into the PHS Hall of Fame. Next, Ed Cochrane arrived from Western Pennsylvania to be the new head coach. Cochrane had a great 15-year run as coach, gaining an elusive LBCL title in 1973 with high-scoring Steve Nielsen and Pennsbury's first 1,000-point scorer, Wayne Emme. Nielsen would go on to be a successful Head Baseball Coach at Pennsbury after pitching for Penn State. Pennsbury would win four league titles under Cochrane.

PENNSBURY FOREVER

Summary

Back in the Glory Days of the LBCL, Pennsbury had some really tough competition. Neshaminy was always battling for the league title. And Morrisville was a big rival in the early 60's. On more than one occasion, some Morrisville fanatics dumped blue and yellow paint on the William Penn statue outside Pennsbury High's campus before big games. Woodrow Wilson and Delhaas were always at the top of the league. Those two schools would combine in the 1980's to form Truman High School.

Bristol brought a supportive fan base. Its teams consistently produced All-League players. The best being Pete Cimino in 1960. He brought national attention to Bucks County. That year, he set a then-national record for scoring 114 points in a bizarre game versus Palisades High School. He attempted 79 FG's and took 29 foul shots. In the second half, no other Bristol player was allowed to shoot. This is quite a contrast to Coach Gavin not wanting to run up the score versus Bristol in 1963.

There were some significant differences in early LBCL basketball that affected individual and team statistics. There was no three-point field goal. That came into high school in 1987. Teams played far fewer games. In the Sixties, 20 games would be common. Today, some teams play 30 games. Only the league champion would be invited to the PIAA State Tournament. Today multiple teams play post-season basketball. However, the local media coverage of high school games back in the Sixties was extensive. At certain Pennsbury games, there could be writers from the *Courier Times*, *Trentonian* and *Trenton Times* newspapers. Currently, it is hard to even find the final score of games in what remains of our local newspapers.

The Falcons had multiple LBCL scoring champions and many All-League players during the Sixties. Chuck Gardner won the scoring title in 1962. Bob Matuza finished second in 1963 and led the LBCL in 1964. Bill Katz was a runner-up in 1966 before he finished at the top of the scoring list in 1967. Dick Olson was leading the league before his season-ending surgery in 1966. There were no league titles. There were, however, two prestigious Christmas tournament championships.

The Charles Boehm Gymnasium has always been a special place. In those early days, ten NBA Hall of Fame basketball players, including 7-foot-1 Wilt Chamberlain, played there in a time when pro basketball was still trying to grow its product. Before every home basketball game at Boehm, the Falcon players headed into the locker room and gathered in the team cage. We lined up in the tunnel, and awaited the final buzzer of the JV game. When the court was cleared, we ran out of the tunnel onto the court in front of our supportive fans. Being able to lead the Falcons onto the court was an experience that I will always cherish

OFF TO THE NBA—Lavoy Allen, a 6-foot-9 center, graduated from Pennsbury in 2007, starred at Temple, then played two years with the 76ers and four more with Indiana.

Epilogue

There have been numerous Pennsbury players from the modern era who have gone on to excel at the next level. A few are: Gary Jones (LaSalle), Mike Jones (Rutgers), Kurt Bergmann (Randolph-Macon), and Jason Vegotsky (Bucknell). Torrian Jones was a two-time Captain at Notre Dame, 2003-04. And in 2019, 6-foot-4 Gary Francis set a new single game scoring record of 47 points in an overtime game in February.

Pennsbury had three remarkable achievements in the PIAA State Tournament. The 1980 team was the first to advance past the early rounds of post season play. Rick Block, at 6-foot-5, was the key man at the center position. Guard Jack Pepper established a career scoring mark that year of 1,505 points. His son, Dalton, now holds the career mark at 2,207 points.

In 2015, under Coach Bill Coleman, the Falcons made it to the PIAA State quarterfinals. The opponent was Roman Catholic High School, champion of the Philadelphia Catholic League. The game had a controversial start. It began with Roman shooting two technical foul shots and possession of the ball. It was determined that Pennsbury brought the wrong color jerseys, a rules violation. That penalty proved decisive as Cameron Jones' last-second shot went in and out and Roman won, 58-57. Roman won the state title two games later. The Falcons finished the year at 25-7 in the now Suburban One League (SOL).

Coach Frank Sciolla's Falcons won seven SOL Titles in 15 years. During that period, Dalton Pepper scored 41 points and broke Chuck Gardner's single-game scoring record that stood for 46 years. Dalton was named the PA Player of the Year in 2009 by the Associated Press. Pennsbury lost in the state quarterfinals to Penn Wood 54-50. Penn Wood won the state title two games later. Pepper played in the NCAA Final Four with West Virginia. He transferred to Temple where he was their leading scorer in his senior year. He currently plays professionally in Italy. Coach Sciolla also had 6-foot-9 Lavoy Allen who starred at Temple. Lavoy is one of only three Bucks County players who have played in the NBA. He played two seasons with the Philadelphia 76ers and four years with the Indiana Pacers. Coach Sciolla had an incredible four-year run, 2005-2009, when the Falcons never lost a league game.

NOTE: For this chapter, I interviewed numerous Pennsbury Alumni as well as current and former PHS coaches. I also researched extensively through *newspaper-archives.com*, *classmates.com* and *The Pennsman* yearbooks which are all housed in the PHS Library.

CHAPTER 32

Soccer Is a Life-Long Passion

By Bill Emanuel, Class of 1968

Soccer started for me as 9-year-old southern boy who had just moved to Trenton after my parents' divorce. My first venture into this game that I had never heard of was attempting to play with the Harrington brothers, Jackie and Michael, in an alley no wider than 10 feet while using a tennis ball and rocks as the goal.

I remember being pushed, kicked, and elbowed to the point of tears. Being the runt of the neighborhood they definitely took advantage of me. Once Mr. Harrington took me and his sons to soccer try-outs. I was horrible but ended being placed on a team with his sons. Looking back it was his influence that got me on the team.

SOCCER TEAMMATES—At the 50th reunion of Pennsbury High's Class of 1968, soccer players Bill Emanuel, Bob Tjader, Simon Dratfield and Scott Springfield posed for a photo.

I was excited as this was my first foray into competitive sports.

Our family had no extra money as my mom was starting out on her own trying to raise two kids. So my shoes were "hand me downs." I will never forget the big wooden toe. I got to play 5 or 10 minutes every game and was told where and how to play on the field. I was definitely a fish out of water compared to the other kids who came from a hot-bed foreign influence as soccer was in their parents' blood and passed down to the next generation. Being of Greek descent, the sport was never mentioned in our house. Despite my lack of cultural heritage in the sport, I played for several years in the West End League and also for my junior high team on the west side of Trenton.

One day my brother came home from school with an injured eye. He had been cut with a knife by another child. Shortly after that my mom said we are moving to Yardley. This was 1963 and I was 13. My brother and I were plucked out of school without any goodbyes and towards the end of soccer season. I was very upset. We moved to Manor Lane off River Road. I was the new kid on the block and the oldest in the neighborhood. Nobody played soccer. I was enrolled in the 9th grade at Charles H. Boehm Junior High. All I wanted to do was to play soccer. I inquired where and how to play on the school team and was told to see Mr. Kennedy after school at the practice fields.

I introduced myself and explained that I came from Trenton and wanted to play on the team. He told me the season was almost over and I could only practice but not play. I remember watching practice and thinking I could help this team. But not this year. At least I knew I could play in the recreational leagues in Trenton during the winter.

Fast forward to my sophomore year. I tried out for the team and was chosen to play on the junior varsity. Mr. (Ben) Kennedy was the varsity coach and Mr. (Joe) Walls was the JV coach. Mr. Kennedy was not your stereotypical soccer coach. He dressed more like a baseball coach with his shorts, socks, hat and shoes. Guess what? He was an assistant baseball coach on Vic Napolitano's staff. He was a nice guy and seemed to know the game. Mr. Walls, however, did dress like a soccer player and would engage in the game at practice. Later I learned that Mr. Walls played semi-pro on the German Hungarian team out of Philadelphia. I felt like an outsider as most of the guys knew each other and played together in the past. I played mostly at the right wing position. I had a strong kick and could send the ball into the middle of the goal area. I could dribble well and had a good understanding of the game.

I will never forget the practice that Mr. Walls pulled me over on the side of the field and started one-on-one drills with me. He made me run around him in a circle and pass him the ball while he stood in the middle of the circle. It was a drill I had never seen and he had never done that with anyone else before. I was kind of perplexed and wondered, "What's up with this?" The next game he started me as the "center forward." That was a big deal. Center forwards were your goal scorers. That started a new path for me.

Mr. Walls saw something in me that I didn't and he brought out the confidence I never had before. I started scoring more goals; the JV team was winning more than the varsity. With only three games left in the season I was moved up to varsity along with Bob Tjader, who was a fantastic player. I remember being subbed in as a sophomore and I think the upper classmen didn't like it. I felt like a ghost on the field. Very different than playing with the JV team where everyone was engaged together. The season ended with the JV doing well and the varsity not so much. But one thing for sure was that Neshaminy was the team to beat.

Coach Walls used to tell me to "always stay with the goalie when he has the ball. Make him nervous, put pressure on him."

One very memorable game we were playing Neshaminy at their home field. It was a scoreless game with about one minute left. Someone kicked the ball into the goalie and he was bouncing the ball out to kick it and I was right on him. Suddenly he bounced the ball and it hit a clump of grass and bounced away. I pounced on the ball and kicked it in for a goal. The ref blew the whistle and we won the game, 1-0!

That was such a great feeling and a happy ride home on the bus even though the varsity got beat. We didn't care. It was all about us. At the end of the season I got my JV letter. Bob and I weren't eligible for a varsity letter as we didn't play enough games. I was looking forward to the winter leagues in Trenton.

In my opinion my junior year was disappointing. I think Mr. Kennedy had high expectations for me and I fell short, only scoring two goals. I found it difficult to work with the seniors. It was very different than JV. I remember Mr. Kennedy coming to me after the season and telling me if I didn't improve he was going to move me to another position. Once again I played in the winter leagues in Trenton. This time I convinced Bob Tjader to come join my team and he did. That was a plus to keep playing with him.

After school let out for summer break my brother and I always had to go to Georgia to visit our dad as part of the divorce agreement. I hated it because I could never hang out with my friends from high school during the summer. Soccer was becoming a big part of my life. Coming from a divorced family and not having my dad around, it was hard to fit in. Everyone I knew had a mom and dad. So I craved that male attention that I got from my soccer coaches. Mr. Kennedy and Mr. Walls had always been there for me. My dad would encourage me by sending me articles on

Pele who at the time was the world's greatest soccer player and highest-paid athlete in the world. Pele was my idol.

In the summer of 1967, professional soccer came to America. Atlanta had a team and I was excited to see pro players from all over the world play. The Atlanta team was playing the Santos of Brazil, Pele's team. I could not believe I was going to be watching my idol play. Pele's team beat Atlanta and I was fortunate to snag an autograph from Pele as I rushed on to the field after the game. I still have that autograph in my possession today.

During the summer of '67, my dad was friends with some Greek guys who played pickup soccer on Sunday mornings. They invited me to play. My dad would drive me and drop me off. Here I was this kid 16 years old playing soccer with these men who were semi-pro players from Germany, Italy, England, Scotland, Greece and Africa. They let me play but I was like a "nuisance"—they would dribble around me, steal the ball from me and out-ran me constantly. It just really humiliated me. But on the positive side a couple players took me under their wings and showed me how to anticipate the ball and how to not get easily faked out. They took the time to school me. I looked forward to Sunday mornings. It was like going to my own soccer camp. Also during the summer I had a part-time job at my dad's apartment complex doing yard work. Our boss, the resident manager, was also an Atlanta police officer. He was a big guy. Everyone called him "Tiny." My dad and Tiny were good friends and my dad told Tiny about my love for soccer. One day while on a lunch break at the apartments, Tiny wanted to show me something. Tiny worked out with weights and had a weight room set up in the basement of an apartment. He set me up a routine to build up my legs and calves. Every lunch I would work out my legs with weights. I would wear ankle weights every day. My thighs and calves were getting big.

Early August approached and soccer practice was starting. Senior year. The old group was gone. The junior varsity players had grown up. Things were different. My skills were better, my legs were stronger, my shots were harder. We had a good team. Bob Tjader was center halfback, Simon Dratfield played center defense. Dave Barto performed on the wing. He could run like the cartoon character, Roadrunner. Bernie Huber was our goalie and he was really good.

We had two scrimmage games prior to the season opener. We beat both Peddie School and Trenton High. The Trenton game was memorable as I was playing against guys I teamed up with in the winter leagues.

First game of the season, we played Lower Moreland. I scored three goals in the first half and three more in the second half. They were not a very good team. I remember Mr. Kennedy pulled me out of the game and said "you've had enough" with a smile on his face. We won 9-0. Unheard of and the newspapers only reported the game as 6-0 and I got credit for only 3 goals. Still, I knew those six goals in one game was probably a school record. But it was never brought up.

Our next game was New Hope-Solebury, a new team in the league. It was an away game. They were a very good team and they beat us on a late goal, 1-0. We played a couple more games and won both. We were in second place behind unbeaten New Hope-Solebury. I had a good feeling about this team. Then disaster struck. Our goalie, Bernie Hubert, got caught smoking cigarettes on the bus. Ben Kennedy kicked him off the team. I couldn't believe it. I pleaded with Mr. Kennedy to give him a second chance but he stuck to his convictions. I respected him for that. Hard lesson to learn but part of life. Mr. Kennedy was just trying to make the team better. He recruited Scott Springfield, a baseball player with no experience playing soccer. I thought, "What he is doing, putting in this guy that played zero soccer?" Scott took to the game quickly with our help as a team. Scott went on to play college soccer. He and I still meet up when he visits Atlanta twice a year. We always talk about Mr. Kennedy and Scott getting his chance to play soccer.

Mr. Kennedy took an interest in me and would guide me, give me advice. He would drive me home after games as he

BEN KENNEDY
...a caring coach

lived nearby in Yardley. We would talk soccer. If I had a bad game, he would help me understand my mistakes and how to do better.

Mr. Walls also showed interest in my life. We connected because we both had that love of soccer. He would play Sundays in Philly and I would play in Trenton. I cherished our Monday morning talks before school started on the outcome of our Sunday games. He played no favorites as I had him for math and he failed me!

Another person who had an influence and took interest in me was Mr. Donaldson. He had played soccer at Temple University. But when I was looking for colleges to apply for that had a soccer program he steered me through the maze of applications and put in a recommendation for me. He also took me to a college soccer game in Philadelphia one Saturday. I had never been or seen a college game so that was awesome. He was a very down-to-earth person.

The season progressed. We had our ups and downs since Bernie was gone. We were a contender but one thing for sure, win or lose, I was scoring. I never paid any attention to the number of goals scored. I just wanted to win. But the newspapers did. I remember our rematch with New Hope at home. They were in first place with only one loss. We played them hard once again and ended in a scoreless tie. The newspapers made a big deal that the top two scorers in the league were shut out, me and their star player. Evidently he and I were leading the league.

I remember after every game the following morning in school. The morning news was broadcast throughout the class rooms and my name would be announced for scoring goals. My classmates in home room would cheer. I have to admit I was embarrassed.

As the season ended we placed third. My senior year was fun. I was looking forward to the Trenton winter leagues. The word got around that I had a very successful season and was moved up to the forward line on my Trenton team and did well for them.

One day while sitting class I got a call from the office. A person from the *Bucks County Courier Times* was there to take my picture. I had no clue what it was for. One night my neighbor called my mom and told her my picture was in the paper. They gave us the article in which I was chosen to the Lower Bucks County Soccer All-Star team along with Bob Tjader and Simon Dratfield. We were selected on the first team. Jimmy Baxter made second team. Coach Kennedy said I would have been unanimous but the Neshaminy coach didn't vote for me. He said it was politics. LOL. That didn't matter to me. I was just honored to be selected. When Mr. Kennedy presented me with my Varsity letter in my senior year I remember he said to me, "I wish I had more to give you."

Other accolades continued to my surprise with being named to second team All-Area All Stars which included all the Trenton teams. But the greatest award was when I won the Lower Bucks County Scoring Championship with 13 goals in 12 games, not including the 3 goals from the Lower Moreland game. I will never forget how the article began: "Last year, Bill Emanuel scored only 2 goals. You can say he improved." It was an honor to represent my high school in this manner. A secondary sport that took a back seat to football. No fans and no parents. I am very grateful to my friend Terri Miller Detrick who was a cheerleader and was able to round up the ladies to cheer for us at one of our games. That was cool. She also nominated me to the Pennsbury Athletic Hall of Fame. If chosen, that would be the pinnacle of my soccer career to be honored for my high school achievements. Dreams do exist.

My soccer career continued with playing on the inaugural team at Georgia State University, as well as many 1st division amateur teams in Atlanta, forming and playing on my ship's team in the Navy throughout the Caribbean and Europe, being invited to try out for the Olympics and having played on an over-55 amateur All-Star Team from Atlanta that won the National Championship in 2005. I finally hung up my cleats at age 60.

My Pennsbury years were my launching point into this sport that I love so much and is in my blood today. Without the mentoring, compassion and confidence of Ben Kennedy, Joe Walls and Bill Donaldson I really believe my path would have been much different. These three male influences were always on my mind.

My biggest regret was living so far from home. Communications were hard. No cell phones, no Facebook in those days. The recent passing of Joe Walls just hurt my heart. I still keep up with current Pennsbury soccer team, thanks to social media and live streaming. I try to participate in fund raisers and sponsor kids who need help. I've been blessed and I love giving back.

On a recent trip back home to Yardley I was able to watch a game and meet the new coaches. Sitting in the stands watching the game was hard. One parent who I met said, "I bet you want to be out there." He was absolutely correct.

CHAPTER 33

Coach Kopack Combined Sports and Art

By Alan Berkes, Class of 1979

This story is about the influence of long-time Pennsbury wrestling coach John Kopack on my life. But not in wrestling. In art. John Kopack was the only person I knew who was an athlete and an artist.

The two things I did most growing up in Levittown: play sports and draw. I loved to draw cars and in second grade, we drew so much, we were banned from drawing in class. But sports was always on my mind, so I drew football helmets and painted electric football players on different teams.

Most of the days, however, I played every sandlot sport you can imagine. Football, basketball, street hockey, soccer, kickball, ga-ga,

TEAM CAPTAINS – Alan Berkes, John DeMaria, Dennis McQuaid with head coach John Kopack.

softball, you name it. Little League baseball was my only organized sport, though, until 7th grade. That's when my gym teacher, Les Brassington, also the tennis coach, recruited me to wrestle. He saw how much of an athlete I was in gym and my first year wrestling I was only one of two 7th graders to make the 8th grade wrestling team, beating and pissing off an 8th grader in the process.

Then, at night, in between weightlifting (curls for the girls) I was drawing wrestlers and football players. The 8th grade wrestling season, I went 10-1, winning the end of year tournament, and even though I still played soccer and baseball, wrestling was now "my" sport. In 9th grade, I would meet John Kopack, head wrestling coach at Pennsbury High School since 1964, for the first time. This was November, 1975.hen that wrestling season started, sophomores practiced before seniors and juniors to get them used to leaving Medill Bair and Charles Boehm to head to the high school. They invited a few freshmen to sophomore practices before our practices started. I had finished soccer season and was in great shape for wrestling. The HS coaches took notice and what I didn't realize was that it was the first year the PIAA was going to allow freshmen to wrestle varsity. The coaches were scouting.

Coaches John Kopack, Joe Keifer and Chub Schickley were all in the wrestling room, where I shined, beating any sophomore near my weight. That lasted a few weeks and then our 9th grade practices started. My 9th grade coach pulled me aside after one practice and said, Coach Kopack wanted to speak to me about moving up to Varsity. I didn't want to leave my 9th grade friends but he encouraged me to talk to John and I met him before the next varsity match. John said he had a spot at 112, my weight class, and he wanted me to move up to varsity. I really wasn't sure, I'd only been wrestling two years … was I good enough? Coach Kopack said to stay here, watch the match tonight, and think about my decision.

Pennsbury wrestling matches were fun. The lights were out and a single spotlight on the mat made every wrestler look huge. I'd been to many matches over the years, the dark upper bleachers was where I had my first real kiss in 7th grade, with an unnamed 8th grader…

But, seeing the competition in that light scared me. I told my 9th grade coach the next day I wasn't going to do it, but he changed my mind. Coach Kopack was also pretty persuasive, saying they wouldn't ask me if they didn't think I couldn't win at that level.

That year I also was taking art seriously. My first design award boosted my confidence two years before and I was able to take art classes at Bair. Besides drawing, I was designing graphics, doing leathercraft and starting to paint. None of my sports friends were interested in art, so it was a unique part of my identity. And not that many people were wrestling fans, so I was even more unique in my eyes. My family didn't really draw, or play sports. I was a one-off, left-handed, athletic artist.

My parents didn't really figure in my decision to wrestle varsity. My dad was a politician and rarely home. My mom was supportive of whatever I wanted to do. They would soon divorce and with my brother and sisters out of the house, it was just me and my mom. I felt honored to be asked to step up and be the first freshman to ever wrestle varsity at Pennsbury. Beating older wrestlers was something I was used to doing. So, I said yes.

But, there was a catch. One I didn't know about until the day came for me to wrestle-off for the 112-pound spot. Coach Kopack told me I needed to win my wrestle-off because the Athletic Director, Bob Buckanavage, made a rule that freshman could ONLY wrestle Varsity. Not JV, so they wouldn't deplete the 9th grade teams. That was ridiculous. There were plenty of wrestlers at Bair and Boehm. That rule would prove costly for me.

When I learned that, right before my wrestle-off, I got nervous. What if I lost? Would I sit the bench? The best freshman in school not wrestling? The pressure got to me and my wrestle-off was too close for comfort, winning by one point, almost failing to make the team. Coach Kopack was relieved, but he looked disappointed. I would learn later that was his look.

My first matches were at a tough Christmas Tournament in Boiling Springs, PA, where wrestling is religion. I got hammered. Our three best seniors made the finals, but it was a bloodbath for the rest of us. Easily the best competition I'd seen yet and I was terrified.

The next match was my first home meet and the intro to the Pennsbury wrestling crowd. Needless to say, I was scared shitless. Luckily, my opponent was too and I hung on for dear life for a close win. Coach Kopack was ecstatic! See, I told you! You can win at this level! Exhaustion was all I felt. But, the first freshman to ever wrestle varsity at Pennsbury won his first home match. Awesome. Then I lost 11 matches in a row. Not so awesome.

During this incredibly difficult time, I turned to art to take my mind off getting the crap beat out of me, night after night. It also helped me think about something else other than eating. It wasn't easy keeping my weight down when depressed. Drawing was my main medium by now, colored pencil and graphite portraits.

John Kopack was the graphics art teacher at Pennsbury and he owned a silk screen shop in Trevose. I would ultimately work for him at that shop, honing my design skills as I job hunted in NYC, chasing my dream to be an Art Director at a big, *Mad Men*-style Advertising Agency. I also needed the money to take the train to New York. After graduating with a BA in Advertising Design from Syracuse, I was trudging my portfolio in to the city during the week, and working for John on weekends.

Our journey from my freshman year to John helping me look for work in advertising post-college was a rocky one. I never lived up to my potential as a wrestler. And I'll never forget the look on his face, that disappointed look, when I lost in the first round of Sectionals my senior year, one of many matches I should've won over the years, but didn't. My high school wrestling career was over. In the locker room, I broke down. Four years of frustration, pressure and disappointment came flooding out in what seemed like an hours-long cry. My senior year was a disaster. Starting with a rough break-up with a two-year girlfriend and ending with an embarrassing first-round loss in sectionals. That look on John's face…

As always, though, art was my sanctuary and point of pride. During the year, my portraits became popular. I drew collages for John and basketball Coach Ed Cochrane. I painted Sports Night and Prom murals and Falcon heads on the gym wall and floor. For college, I was headed to Syracuse, taking an early acceptance to their Professional Art Program, so in reality, I couldn't wait to put high school in the rearview mirror. I even planned to walk on to the Syracuse wrestling team, knowing that I could be better and wanting to prove it.

During our Senior Awards night at Pennsbury, the end of the school year, the moment came when I realized how much John really cared about me. With my dad pretty much busy with politics, I hadn't had a present male father figure and certainly, I was a disappointment to John. But during that night, in the cafeteria of all places, John presented me with the Falcon Sportsmanship Award for Outstanding Male Athlete. I didn't feel deserving, but when he gave me the award he said that he hoped his son would grow up to be like me. Maybe wins and losses didn't matter as much as I thought. I was a team Captain for two years and a leader in the wrestling room, where I was unbeatable. And more importantly, I was going to college to be an art major, something that made John proud.

The other award I received that night was the Gold Pin in Art. Although, my other artist friends, I thought were outstanding and inspiring, I was really proud to have gotten top honors in sports and art. I'd be curious if that was ever repeated at Pennsbury. John gave me a huge hug that night, and I was grateful for his love and sincerity.

When I got to Syracuse, though, I quickly learned that trying to be really good at both art and sports at the college level would be like oil and water. Long classes and long practices just didn't mix. I stayed on the wrestling team most of my time at Syracuse, in a practice dummy role. Even wrestled a few varsity matches my freshman year, uggghh, with the same results.

In the summers John gave me hours at the silkscreen shop. I even was a printmaking major for a semester when I wasn't accepted into Graphic Design. Right then and there, my ability to overcome adversity, learned through wrestling, shaped my life as I refused to accept not being accepted and worked my ass off to reapply, then succeed in multiple majors, ultimately choosing Advertising Design. The summer after graduation I was determined to get a job in NYC, the mecca of advertising.

John came through for me again, giving me weekends at the shop so I could job hunt during the week. I even took a night class at the School of Visual Arts to beef up my portfolio. It took six months to land a job, but I secured my own office at a global Ad Agency working on major international brands and having the time of my life. If it weren't for John giving me the hours I needed to make money to pay for the train into the city, it may never have happened.

My first several years working in NYC, I lived at home in Levittown and commuted on the train. The time on the train was spent thinking and jotting down ideas for my assignments. It was similar to my nights sketching ideas, and coming up with designs for John. I had created a system of generating ideas that lasts until this day.

But the story doesn't end there. In the "what goes around comes around" category, assistant coach Joe Keifer asked me to coach some of the youth teams in the Pennsbury Wrestling Club on weekends. My time spent in the Syracuse Wrestling room, with state and nationally ranked wrestlers, qualified me to coach kids, something I've done now for 38 years. And I was determined to avoid my experience, and put kids in a position to succeed. In a weird way, losing as much as I did helped me coach kids who needed more help. We didn't lose a match in the four years I coached, partly because I could make those kids on the fence believe in themselves.

That youth wrestling program fed John's successor, Joe Keifer, for years and included two PIAA State Champions, Joe's son Kip and Chuckie Conner, who still runs a youth wrestling program locally. Joe's wrestling teams dominated the Section for years. For me, it started years of coaching youth sports, my son and daughter in soccer and my son in baseball, basketball, flag football and of course, wrestling.

But the inspiration learned from John, that I can combine sports and art, working in advertising ultimately led me down that path. Along the way, I won a Sports Emmy for the launch campaign of the NFL on FOX, started an ad agency called The Ballpark, and shot commercials with some of the most famous athletes in the world like Wayne Gretzky, Peyton Manning and Ken Griffey, just to name a few. Now I am currently in charge of the brand for a youth sports company. The day I started making a living by advertising sports was the day work stopped being work.

Sadly though, I have lost touch with John. He was in North Carolina with his wife and kids and is in Florida now, I believe. But, I still have that Falcon Award and Gold Pin and have re-connected with many friends and Pennsbury grads through Facebook. I won't forget his disappointed face, which was his proud face, and happy face all in one.

CHAPTER 34

Falcons Still Building Program Legacy

By Joe Pesci, Class of 2000

Baseball has been my identity for as long as I can remember. It's who I am. But I guess you can say that about so many coaches and the sports they coach. To me baseball is not something I do, it is everything I do (outside of family and work). Most of my ventures are taken with the baseball community in mind. The coaches in this community have built this district and its baseball program. Without the community, without the coaches, and without its alumni, this school and this program would not be where it is today.

As a lifelong member of this baseball

STATE CHAMPIONS—Pennsbury High players celebrate 1-0 victory over Dallastown in 2017 that brought the school its first and only (so far) state baseball championship.

community, I played meaningful ball for 20 years through Levittown Continental Little league, Levittown Babe Ruth, Falls Legion, and Pennsbury High School, before going on to play in college. I have coached high school baseball for 17 years, four at the junior varsity level and then 13 more as the current varsity coach at Pennsbury. I have coached my sons' youth teams for seven years now. I have run a summer camp business for 12 years and have owned a sports training business for the past five. All of these things are part of my baseball life, my identity.

My fondest memories growing up are around sports, baseball in particular. I can still remember specific plays and games. I remember being cut from the William Penn team in 7th grade, making it in 8th grade and never playing. Again making it in 9th grade and barely playing, just to start on varsity in 10th, 11th, and 12th grades for the Falcons.

Being lucky enough to play in college was an amazing opportunity, but I also remember the days, weeks, months after my final college at bat. They were listless, without meaning. Baseball has been my identity, my life, and with the exception of my time at college, so has Pennsbury.

I was thankful to have the opportunity to play both baseball and basketball in high school for high-level coaches. I wish I would've played three sports, but I digress. I played for Steve Nielsen and Frank Sciolla. Nielsen, the Head Baseball Coach at the time, was also my JV Basketball Coach. I was fascinated with his knowledge of the game of baseball and his intensity and passion for the game. I was prepared for college baseball because of his methods. On the other side, Frank Sciolla was just hired as Head Basketball Coach a few years prior to me starting high school. As a student in his mythology class and a basketball player, I was inspired to become a teacher and a coach because of Frank Sciolla. His charisma, energy, and desire to develop and provide the best experience for kids made me want to do the same. Even though I barely saw the floor, it was arguably the best sports experience of my life. I knew I needed to have the same impact on kids.

So when I left college in May of 2005, I called the Pennsbury Human Resources department at least twice per week throughout that summer asking if there were open positions. Finally, a position opened up for both a special education teaching position and the JV baseball coach. Pennsbury baseball alum Bill Ritchey had been my JV baseball coach and a Physical Education teacher at PHS. He was taking a new Athletic Director's position in Jenkintown, leaving the JV Baseball coaching position vacant. It was a perfect situation for me and I relished the chance to stay involved in baseball and give back to Pennsbury.

I cut my teeth as the JV coach for four years. I had the opportunity to learn from Steve Nielsen, Mike Barnes and Jesse Toner, all Pennsbury alumni, who were handling the varsity team. I learned from those coaches, but also from the players. I knew I wanted to continue to coach at higher levels.

Shortly after the start of school in 2009, Nielsen walked into my classroom on the second floor of PHS East and told me he was resigning. To say I was taken aback was an understatement. You could see that it was hard for him to step away, but Steve knew it was time.

At my interview in December of 2009, I was asked why I wanted to be the coach of Pennsbury Baseball. To me it was about having a stake in the game. My entire life has been centered on the Pennsbury community. I'm not sure what it was that made them believe in me, but I made my goal explicit: bring Pennsbury Baseball back to the forefront. The drought between titles was long enough. It was time to stop being a bridesmaid. With the changing climate of youth sports, especially with travel baseball, hitting/pitching instructors, etc., it was going to take time. Growing the program back from the Tee-ball ranks and up was going to take a shift culture to bring it back to a place where the legacy of coaches and baseball alumni could be proud. What I realized over the course of my career was that it wasn't the wins or the titles that would bring us back. It was the people.

Letter from "Nap"

Four months later, it's the start of my first season and I have an envelope in my school mailbox. "Joe," handwritten on Pennsbury Baseball stationary, "Congratulations on getting the baseball job. Good luck this season. If I can be of any help, please call me. My best to your Dad." Signed simply, but meaningfully, "Nap." Nobody sends handwritten letters anymore. But I got one, from the legend. I immediately filled up with pride.

Pennsbury Baseball Coaching History

In Pennsbury High School's 74-year history, there have been just five head baseball coaches. Inaugural Coach William Ingraham had a successful 5-1 season in 1949. In 1950, mathematics teacher Wilmer "Cy" Bachman took over the program and won the Lower Bucks County League Championship in his first season. In 1956, Pennsbury was in a three-way tie with Delhaas and Neshaminy, and was declared "co-champions" only to lose a controversial playoff game to Delhaas. The sting didn't last long as Bachman led the Falcons to Lower Bucks League titles in 1957 and 1958. Bachman led Pennsbury for 15 seasons before ending his tenure in 1964. Some information is difficult to find. I scoured the yearbooks, researched news archives, but I am still missing some results from Bachman's career.

In 1965, Bachman passed the torch to Victor Napolitano. Vic became a Health and Physical Education teacher at Pennsbury in

1956, teaching and filling multiple coaching roles over a 36-year career. Coach "Nap," as he was called, led the Falcons for 29 seasons, winning 13 league titles, three district titles, and making the State Final Four on two occasions. His dynasty was impressive. League titles were earned in '72, '73, '75, '76, '77, '79, '80, '85, '86, '89, '90, '91, and '93. Napolitano's teams were the class of Lower Bucks County, District 1, and the state. One of the biggest "what ifs" of his career may have been his 1972 team that went 17-0, but never got to participate in a district or state playoff since district and state playoffs did not start until 1977. Napolitano ended his career in 1993 with his 13th League Championship, third District Championship, and second state Final Four appearance. He amassed 403 wins to just 156 losses in his 29-year head coaching career.

Napolitano was inducted into the Pennsbury Athletic Hall of Fame in 2001 and into the Temple Hall of Fame in 2009 for his contributions to its Soccer National Championship in 1951 as the goalkeeper. He captained the baseball team, and played on the basketball team. Napolitano graduated from Temple in 1952 before going on to play three years in the St. Louis Cardinals organization before taking the teaching position at Pennsbury. He was also inducted into the Bucks County Chapter of the PA Sports Hall of Fame in 2010. This is when I first met him, as we honored Coach Nap with a ceremony on our field for his induction. It was such an honor to finally meet him. I never heard a bad story about the man. He was so happy to be back on that field. His field. Coach "Nap" passed away in 2012 at the age of 83.

When Napolitano decided it was time after the 1993 season, ready and willing was Steve Nielsen. Nielsen, a physical education teacher at Pennsbury and assistant coach for Napolitano, took over the helm in 1994. A 1973 graduate and Pennsbury Athletics Hall of Famer, Nielsen was a standout baseball and basketball player at Pennsbury. He was a "Big Orange" Award winner for the basketball team, but earned a scholarship to play baseball at Penn State University. Nielsen went on to be drafted by the Cleveland Indians in the 8th round of the 1976 draft and the Texas Rangers in the 11th in 1977. He played professionally for five seasons in the minor leagues, reaching AAA with the Rangers before transitioning to a coaching position within the same system. Nielsen coached professionally until about 1985 when he returned to Pennsbury as an assistant under Napolitano. Nielsen was a part of five league titles and two district titles. When Napolitano retired in 1993, Nielsen took over and won the Suburban One League Championship in 1994, his first season. Nielsen hired a long-time friend and Pennsbury alum, Mike Barnes, as his assistant. Barnes also played professionally in the Pirates organization. Nielsen served at the helm of the program for 16 seasons.

The league was always strong with great teams from Council Rock, Neshaminy, and Truman. We also played teams from North Penn, Pennridge, Central Bucks. Pennsbury had multiple winning seasons and trips to the district playoffs in those 16 years under Nielsen. His dedication to the team and the school showed with his contributions to the facilities. Nielsen gained sponsors and raised funds to make the baseball field the premier field in the area. It featured double-turfed batting cages, a 30-foot scoreboard and a sprinkler system. He put the time and energy into that field to make it a place that the program could be proud of. I learned so much in my time as a player and a coach under Nielsen. My playing resume and my knowledge of the game pales in comparison. This man played and coached at the AAA level in pro baseball. I was a sponge around him and I will be forever grateful for my time coaching with him.

My career officially started in 2010. It probably should've ended quickly. The first three years were difficult. 2010 we finished 8-11. 2011 we are 9-10. Progress. 2012, 6-14. Oh boy, this isn't as easy as I hoped. In 2013 we finished 12-7 and missed the playoffs by one game. In 2014, we finished the regular season 12-8, beating Neshaminy in the last game of the year to send us to the playoffs. We made a first-round exit, but it's the first playoff game of my career. Progress.

2015 was special. We finished the regular season at 16-4, 12-2 in the league and won the program's first Suburban One League Championship in 19 years. The drought was over! We went to districts and ended up winning the first round, losing the second round, and playing our way back into fifth place, sending our team to states for the first time in 23 years.

We won a first-round game and faced North Penn in the second round. Unfortunately we lost to North Penn 3-2, leaving the potential winning run on second in the bottom of the 7th inning. North Penn went on to win the state championship. We finished the year at 20-6 and Pennsbury Baseball was back on the map. It was an amazing feeling being there, but still left a sour taste knowing we were right there and lost to the eventual state champion. 2016 was another successful year. We finished the regular season at 14-6, losing the final game when we had a chance to clinch a share of the SOL Crown. We won our first-round district game, but lost in the second round to Boyertown, 3-2. Boyertown went on to win the state championship. We had our chance and squandered it.

There was never a season like 2017. We knew from the first day of practice that this team was different. Efficient is probably the best word to describe them. We weren't a great hitting team, but we were fast, we could defend, we could pitch, but most importantly we were never out of it. The season didn't start off great with an 11-1 loss to CB South. At one point in the season we had a 9-6 record after coming off a loss to Souderton. We played at the Trenton Thunder's stadium two days later vs. Holy Ghost Prep and no-hit them. This was the start of "the run." We finished out the regular season with a six-game winning streak to capture our second SOL title in three seasons. We had a first-round bye, and faced Downingtown East in round two. Losing 4-0 in the bottom of the 7th we rattled off five runs, capped off by a walk-off single by Ryan McCarty to send us to the quarterfinals. That was the moment the team knew this was going to be magical. A 2-0 win over Neshaminy in the semifinals and a 5-3 win over North Penn in the District Championship brought the District title back to Pennsbury for the first time in 25 years!

Dominant pitching and timely hitting was the name of the game for our state run. Round one was an 11-inning battle capped by a walk-off sacrifice fly, again by Ryan McCarty. We gave up a run in the second inning of that game and it would be the last run our team allowed the rest of the tournament. A 3-0 win over Perkiomen Valley in the quarterfinals and a 12-0 win over Liberty in the semifinals on graduation day sent us to Pennsbury's first-ever State Finals appearance. The state championship game against District 3 champion Dallastown was an ordeal. A delay from the previous state game and a three-hour rain delay had us start our game around 8 p.m. Again, dominant pitching by both Ryan McCarty and Billy Bethel led us into the bottom of the seventh inning locked in a scoreless tie. With two outs and Justin Massielo on second base, Nick Price sent a 1-2 pitch to left field, Massielo came around to score. Cue the dogpile. We won the first State Title in Pennsbury Baseball history and the first for any team in Lower Bucks County. The 2017 champs are the most decorated baseball team in school history: League, District, and State Champs.

In 2019, we won our third league title in five years, we were the No. 1 seed in districts, but lost in the second round. In 2020, COVID shut down the entire season. The 2021 season came and went. The 2022 season, shows great promise. We are mid-season as this is being written, "but we're good on paper…

Standing on the Shoulders of Giants

It's often hard to find success in coaching. It doesn't always come with wins, losses, or titles. It's similar to the idea that money doesn't buy happiness. While winning the State Championship was validation, there was no relief. Pennsbury's very successful basketball coach, Frank Sciolla, has become one of my greatest mentors and friends. After winning the state title he said to me that my coaching career just became harder. That this would be the most difficult year of my career, because I set the standard now. Anything less would be deemed a failure in my own eyes. First of all, "thanks a lot," but he was right. More than he probably realized at the time. My wife Tammy, a Pennsbury graduate and teacher, asked me if I felt successful. When I answered no, she was at a loss. I was, too.

I'll take it back to my job interview. Pennsbury baseball was on the map, but it still didn't feel complete. I realized after the state title that the missing piece was Napolitano. In 2019, with the help of the school board, Athletic Director Lou Sudholz, Hall of Fame President Michael Augustin, and former Pennsbury Administrator Jack Massielo, grandfather of SS Justin, we were able to finally honor Victor Napolitano the way he deserved.

On April 6, 2019 in front of Napolitano's wife Ginnie, his family, friends, former players, and colleagues, the Pennsbury Baseball Field was dedicated as Vic Napolitano Field. Honoring him for his dedication and sacrifice as a coach and an educator in Pennsbury was imperative. The stories I heard from coaches and former players who were now parents of current players set Napolitano apart. When I began the process in 2012, there was an administrator that once asked me, "Do your players even know who Napolitano is?" And to me that was the problem. They needed to know. You can't know where you're going without knowing where you came from. Isaac Newton said, "If I have seen further, it is by standing on the shoulders of giants." For me Napolitano and Nielsen were those

FAMILY AFFAIR—Dennis, Joe and Mac Pesci are all involved with the Pennsbury baseball program.

giants. Without those men, the success of our current program does not exist. Every player that comes through this program as long as I coach, will know where we came from. That letter from Coach Nap hangs on the wall in my office. It is a constant reminder of who I'm coaching for. It's for Ingraham, Bachman, Napolitano, Nielsen, and all the assistant coaches.

Steve Nielsen was a 1972 graduate. He played for, then coached under Napolitano and became the head coach. I was a 2000 graduate. I played for, then coached under Nielsen, and became the head coach. I was able to get Nielsen to come back and coach with me for one season. From 2011-2016, I was able to bring Jesse Toner, a 1972 graduate, back to coach. He is another Pennsbury Hall of Famer. He has coached with Napolitano, Nielsen, and with me. Jesse's son Dan is the current Neshaminy head coach. We played against each other in high school and college. We coached together, against each other, together again, and now against each other again. I currently have an assistant coach on my staff, Brandon Garrett, who played for me from 2010-2013. Garrett has coached with me now in different capacities since 2017. Nick Price, the hero of 2017, played for me from 2014-2017, came back to coach our 9th grade team for a few years before pursuing a college career. I have some former players coaching at Neshaminy and Council Rock North. It kills me to see them in different colors, but I'm proud to see them earn their stripes.

My dad, Dennis Pesci, played for Napolitano in 1966. He played with Jim Bergmann, a 1967 graduate. I went through elementary, middle, and graduated in 2000 from PHS with Kurt Bergman, Jim's son. We were teammates on CYO teams and PHS Basketball. Kurt was our 9th grade coach for a few years, too. We both have two sons and all four of them are friends. My youngest, Mac, and Kurt's oldest, JD, are the closest of friends, teammates in football, basketball, and baseball, and are class of 2031 in Pennsbury.

My dad is now one of my assistant coaches. I told him in 2017 that he could coach with me when he retired. I didn't think he would retire the following year, but I kept my word! He has been on my staff since 2018. And yes, he still tries to parent me in front of the players. It's the only time I get away with yelling at my dad. The players call him "Coach Dad Pesci," coined by 2020 graduate Sam Ruta.

That 2017 run was magical for our team, our community, our family. My wife brought my boys to every game. Even

NICE TOUCH—Pennsbury High re-named its baseball field in honor of long-time coach Vic Napolitano in 2019.

my older son Dean, who pretends to like sports for me, was interested in the games and would take pictures and videos on his tablet. My younger son Mac wears jersey No. 19 because his favorite baseball player was Justin Massielo. That team made Mac fall in love with baseball, but helped him learn to hate Neshaminy. Mac now serves as our bat boy.

Unknowingly, the goal all along was to connect Pennsbury's storied past with the current team and future Falcons. At the dedication ceremony, I was able to stand next to my dad and my two sons on the foul line for the National Anthem. The place where Napolitano coached and Nielsen coached. The place where the great teams played. The place where my dad played. The place where I played. The place where I hope my sons can play.

When you're a young coach, you don't necessarily understand who you are or who you are supposed to be or what you are supposed to do. It took me quite some time to realize, I'll never figure that out. One thing I did come to understand. It was never about the wins, the banners, the trophies, or the rings. Coaching Pennsbury Baseball has and always will be about the people.

CHAPTER 35

Making Memories Is the Key

By Hollie Ritter Woodard, Class of 1993

When students walk into Pennsbury High School's gymnasium, if they listen closely they can hear the cheers of championship seasons past as they look to the walls in remembrance of those who played and won before them.

Most noticeable is the success of the Women's Softball team. Memorialized with large black and orange championship banners, Pennsbury Women's Softball proudly boasts five state championships. Impressively, responsible for each state championship, spanning three decades (84, 93, 01, 05, and 07), is the leadership of head coach Frank McSherry, who possesses the superpower of motivation. With three simple words, he connects with each player, regardless of their position or role on the team, by giving them one simple yet inspirational direction: "Make some memories."

Hidden within the hope of nostalgia is the brilliant simplicity of this directive. He doesn't demand that his players hit for a certain average, or score a certain amount

FOREVER A FALCON—Hollie Ritter served as the starting catcher on Pennsbury's softball teams for four seasons, culminating in a 1993 state championship.

of runs in a game, or even beat our town rival to bring home yet another league championship. Instead, he simply tells them to make memories. As such, each girl is left with her own interpretation of what those memories should be. For some, it's the memory of dancing to Motown music with Coach McSherry and the team on the bus after a big win. For others it's being picked up by upperclassmen who help you sneak out of your house to paint "The Rock" under the cover of darkness, and for others it's vulnerably revealing your most inner secrets to your teammates in the back of the bus, fully aware that you put yourself at risk to being humiliated, but you do it anyway because you innately know that in doing so you will earn your teammates' respect, trust, and friendship.

No matter who you were, freshman or senior, starter or reserve, McSherry's words had a way of motivating you to dig down deeper, play harder, and to give just a little more than you thought you could because memories were at stake…not just for you, but for your teammates who would be the supporting characters in the memories you worked so hard to create.

For me, the challenge of making memories spoke deeply to my soul. Profoundly aware that my youth had a shelf life, I worked to make each play, game, and season better than the next until I obtained the ultimate memory.

It was my last at-bat, and it would serve as the final contribution I would make to Pennsbury Softball and end my career that proudly stretched four years, as I had the privilege of serving as the starting Pennsbury catcher between 1990 and 1993.

It probably should have been a nostalgic moment, where I contemplated the impact of the numerous life-long friendships, memories, and life lessons, but I didn't.

I probably should have paused just for a moment and acknowledged that my at-bat would end the legacy of my family's contribution to Pennsbury athletics that began when my mom, Sandy Bender ('69—gymnastics and cheerleading) earned that first varsity letter as a sophomore gymnast. A legacy that stretched over two decades and included my dad, Jeff Ritter (class of '69—football), Jeff Ritter Jr. (class of '89—football and baseball), and Mike Ritter (class of '92—football and volleyball) resulting in an accumulation of 21 varsity letters, but I didn't.

Instead, I was hyper-focused on the task at hand—which was to find a way to help my team erase a 2-1 deficit in the bottom of the seventh and win a PIAA Softball State Championship. There were runners on first and second, with one out. I had been 2-for-2 on the day and as the number four hitter on the team, I was excited to have the opportunity to hit a line drive up the middle and score these runners to win the game, but that's not what happened.

Instead, McSherry did the unexpected. When I approached the batter's box, I did my ceremonial two fake swings followed by the tapping of my cleats with the bat head, before staring down at coach who would give me a sign which was almost always a series of fake signs that would end in a closed fist that signaled "you got this," relaying the confidence that I had earned over a career that saw me lead my team and county in hitting, resulting in a Division One college softball scholarship.

This time there wasn't a choreographed mirage of fake signs or the fist of confidence. He was quiet and motionless. He simply looked at me, and without anyone noticing, he subtly gave me the sign to bunt for a base hit. Without hesitation or question, I turned from him and stepped into the front of the batter's box, and on the first pitch I laid down the most perfect beautiful bunt for a base hit I had ever placed in my varsity career. I can say this with confidence because it was the first time I had ever been asked to bunt for a base hit…ever! After striking my bat, the ball fell two feet from home and spun in the dirt. With a body built for defense, the gamble was not in my ability to get the bunt down, but rather to get to first before the ball. I ran as fast as I could, staring at the bag in fearful anticipation that I would lose this race, but I won it.

No play was made. Intimidated by my previous at bats, the corners were so far back, that they never had a chance to field it, and shocked by my coach's call, the catcher never made the play.

Coach McSherry's gamble paid off, as my at-bat advanced the runners into scoring position, and the next batter tied the game when Joanne Gunkle belted a fly to left to score Kara Morgan with the tying run. That was followed by Beth Dance, who hit the game-winning single between third and short to score my fellow senior, Michelle LaBonge, to win the game. As she crossed home to secure the win and our spot in Falcon history, my fellow teammates (Andrea Dow, Randi Larsen, Jen Bray, Sheila Ferry, and Jessie Flowers) and I met her there, and we experienced what can only be described as pure joy.

The following day, local media outlets boasted with pride of another state championship win for Pennsbury Softball and Head Coach Frank McSherry. However, they got the story wrong because their focus was on the win. The story that day was not about the win but rather about the memory. Charged with the task of making memories, my teammates and I did it.

Eight years later, my teammates and I gathered once again, dressed in orange and black to cheer on the next generation of Falcon softball players as they endeavored to win a third state championship. Before the game, McSherry allowed us to speak with the girls to share with them the enduring impact that winning that game would have on them. He presented us with a shirt that read "back for more," and it couldn't have been a more perfect gift. For anyone that didn't play for McSherry it would be difficult to understand why we took the day off, got babysitters, and made the drive out to watch a high school softball game, but once again it was never really about the softball. McSherry knew why we were there, following his directive once again, we were "back for more" memories.

It's now several decades later and the championship medal and newspaper articles have long ago been misplaced. Worn by age, my body no longer has the physical strength, flexibility, or balance that a catcher needs to command a field and catch a game. Hindered by responsibility and the type of self-preservation that comes from being an adult, I no longer have the courage to step into a batter's box and square up to a pitcher throwing 60 miles per hour in the hope of laying down a perfect bunt.

My ability to play the game has left me, but my ability to remember it has endured. I simply have to think about it, and without struggle I'm 17 again, stepping into that batter's box for the last time, laying down a perfect bunt, and celebrating the ultimate success with my teammates.

Within the brilliance of his directive, McSherry did more than coach me to a state championship, he challenged me and all of his athletes to make memories. Because of that and because of him, the game will always be with me…forever.

EPILOGUE

We Did Make Memories!

Thanks to a Facebook page started by Pennsbury alumni Brian Brown and Darryl Moyle last year to honor their dying friend, Scott Stenerson, this book project gained exposure among younger alumni who volunteered to write stories. Their presence solves the only shortcoming we had with our prior Pennsbury-related book, *Glory Days*, which was written almost entirely by those dreaded Baby Boomers who think the world reached its peak during the 1960s.

So I first want to thank Brian and Darryl for their support. Showing how strong the Pennsbury alumni group can be, that Facebook page, titled PHS, gained over 2,000 members in its first week and leveled off after 6,000 people signed up. From that group, we found younger (read middle-aged) writers for the book. That makes all the difference. Now we have the best of both worlds. The old folks could still tell stories while the next generation or two added their own perspective. Among those "younger" writers, I want to thank Marc Freeman, Brien Martin, Brian Brown, Alan Berkes, Hollie Ritter Woodard, and Aly McBryar for participating.

We were fortunate to gain the support of football coaches Chuck Kane and Galen Snyder. Baseball coach Joe Pesci did deep research and created his own historical chapter on the Pennsbury program, dating back to 1949.

At 90 years old, Ginnie Napolitano recalled how small the enrollment was at Pennsbury when she first arrived in 1956. Her memory for details remains amazing. Thank you, Ginnie!

Bill Katz laid the foundation for this book by describing the path he took from student to principal. Former English teacher Bill Donaldson recalled his arrival at Charles Boehm in 1959. Bill loved having the chance to reconnect with Pennsbury nearly 40 years after he retired from teaching and administrative work.

Some of the old folks can still write. Barry Miner weaved a wonderful story about the Pennsbury Band. If there is a more tradition-laden student activity at Pennsbury than the band, you have to tell me what it might be.

The Class of 1964 gave us five writers: Barry Miner, Ralph Rhodes, Patricia Gordon, Linda Golden Granett and John

Quattrocchi. I have learned in recent years how close the Class of 1964 has remained over the years. They are a model for all of us alumni to follow. (Of course, our Class of 1965 and Ron Myers are responsible for the quarterly reunions we have been holding at Puss 'N Boots Tavern for the last decade.)

I need to especially thank Kevin Lendo, Class of 1966, for his hard work on this project, writing three chapters while providing advice and information that only he would know. Kevin spent numerous hours in the Pennsbury library looking at old yearbooks and newspaper clippings. His story of the "forgotten era" in Pennsbury sports is a gift to those early Falcons of the 1950s.

Several writers shared painful memories, in hopes that today's young people can learn life isn't always wonderful. We make mistakes along the way, bad things inexplicably happen, we learn from them, and we move on. That is a message we all learn at some point in life.

Back in 1961, President John F. Kennedy (now there was a President!) spoke about the torch passing to a new generation of Americans. Well, the Boomers took that torch and carried it for 40 years. We're not sure if we made the world any better but that torch is still flickering. We handed it over a decade ago, and some day we hope today's Pennsbury students will team up to record the memories they are creating and put them into a book.

Just like Hollie Ritter wrote in her chapter, softball coach Frank McSherry always tells his players, "Go out and make some memories." Well, this book is about the memories we made at Pennsbury High and beyond. The high school remains an integral part of our lives, no matter what age we are.

—*Terry Nau*

www.ingramcontent.com/pod-product-compliance
Lightning Source LLC
Chambersburg PA
CBHW080501240426
43673CB00006B/254